LEADING CASES FOR AOR EXAMINATION

VOLUME 1

PRASOON KUMAR MISHRA

Made with ♥ on the Notion Press Platform
www.notionpress.com

I DEDICATE THIS BOOK TO ...

My Parents who are my real God, My brothers, Sisters & Relatives

Who are my Emotional Strength,

My wife who is my Soul mate And my dear Son.

Contents

Contents

Contents

Preface

Leading cases are those cases which involves the creation of new legal principle and is very important historical and legal point of view and guides the court below for adjudication of matters. It also guide the legal professional to broaden their thinking on the concerned cases.

For every advocates, studying Leading cases of Supreme Courts are very important because in every this type of cases some legal issues are raised and which also been discribed at the time of adjudication of any case. Looking into the importance of the Leading cases, Supreme Court of India has inserted this as one of the papers for "Advocate on record Examination" conducted by this apex court.

This book is the first volume of Leading cases which is prescribed under syllebus for AOR Examination. Myself tried to write notes on the Leading cases as per my own understanding and it is always advisable to read actual judgments in details for better understanding of the case. Hope the book will be useful for those advocates who are going to appear in AOR Examination. Suggestions from readers are welcome for making this book better in the next publication.

Prasoon Kumar Mishra

Delhi

Dated: 19 - 11- 2021

CHAPTER ONE

His Holiness Keshavananda Bharati Sripadagalavaru v. State of Kerala,[1973] Suppl. SCR 1 : (1973) 4 SCC 225

(Under this case Supreme Court of India outlined the "Basic Structure Doctrine" of the Constitution which forms and gives basic powers to the Indian Judiciary to review or to amend the provisions of the Constitution enacted by the Parliament of India which conflict with or seek to alter the basic structure of the Constitution. It overruled Golaknath vs State of Punjab case, which stated that parliment has no absolute / unlimited power to amend the constitution. It was held by the Apex Court by a majority of 7:6 that Parliament can amend any provision of the Constitution to fulfill its socio-economic obligations guaranteed to the citizens under the Preamble subject to the condition that such amendment won't change the "Basic Structure" of the Indian Constitution.)

FACTS OF THE CASE:

Before moving to the facts and Judgment of the case one must know the background of the case:

1. The Bihar Land Reforms Act, 1950 which was in Contravention of then Fundamental Right to Property (Article 31). It was hit by Article 13(3) as it was infringing Article 31 (Part III, Fundamental Rights). The Act was tested in High Court which held the demonstration to be Unconstitutional for being violative of Article 14 of the Constitution.

2. Consequently keeping in mind the end goal to ensure and Validate Zamindari Abolition laws, the Government made First Amendment of the

Constitution of India which rolled out a few improvements to the Fundamental Rights arrangements of the Constitution. Article 31-A and 31-B was likewise included. Ninth Schedule was embedded which ensures any Legislation embedded inside the Schedule, from Judicial Review.

3. Keshavananda Bharati was the chief of the Endeer Mutt which is a religious sect in Kasaragod District of Kerala. Keshavananda Bharati had certain pieces of land in the sect which were owned by him in his name. The State Government of Kerala introduced the Land Reforms Amendment Act, 1969. According to the Act, the Government was entitled to acquire some of the sect's land of which Keshavananda Bharati was the Chief.

4. On 21st March 1970, Keshavananda Bharati moved to the Supreme Court under Article 32 of the Indian Constitution for enforcement of his rights which guaranteed under Article 25 (Right to Practice and Propagate religion), Article 26 (Right to manage religious affairs), Article 14 (Right to Equality), Article 19(1)(f) (Freedom to acquire property), Article 31 (Compulsory Acquisition of Property). When the Petition was still under consideration by the Court, the Kerala Government introduced another Act i.e. Kerala Land Reforms (Amendment) Act, 1971.

5. After the landmark case of Golaknath vs State of Punjab, the Parliament passed a series of Amendments in order to overrule the judgement of the Golaknath case. In 1971, the 24th Amendment was passed. In 1972, 25th, 26th and 29th Amendments were passed subsequently. The following amendments were made after Golaknath's case which was challenged in the present case are:

24th Constitution Amendment:

1. The 24th Amendment was enacted as a reaction to Golaknath case, 1967. In the case of Golaknath, it was laid down in the judgment that every Amendment which is made under Article 368, will be taken as an exception under Article 13. Therefore, in order to neutralise this effect, the Parliament through an Amendment in Article 13 of the Constitution annexed Clause 4, so that no Amendment can have an effect under Article 13.
2. The Parliament in order to remove any kind of ambiguity added Clause 3 to Article 368 which reads as follows, "Nothing in Article 13 shall apply to any Amendment made under this Article."
3. In the case of Golaknath, the majority decided that Article 368 earlier contained the provision in which the procedure of Amendment was

given and not the power. So, in order to include the word "power" in the Article, Article 368 was amended and the word "Power" was added in the Marginal Note.

4. The Parliament tried to draw a distinction between the procedure in an amendment and an ordinary law through an amendment in Article 368(2). Earlier the President could exercise his power to refuse or withhold a bill for the amendment. After the 24th Amendment, the President did not have a choice to refuse or withhold a bill. This was done by the Parliament in order to protect the amendment from the exception that is mentioned under Article 13 of the Indian Constitution.

25th Constitution Amendment:

1. In the "Bank Nationalisation" case (1970, 3 SCR 530), the Supreme Court has held that the Constitution guarantees right to compensation, that is, the equivalent in money of the property compulsory acquired. Through this Amendment, the Parliament wanted to make it clear that they are not bound to adequately compensate the landlords in case their property is taken by the State Government. And in order to do so, the word "Compensation" was replaced with the word "Amount" under Article 31(2) & Article 31(2A) of the Constitution.
2. The link between Article 19(1)(f) and Article 31(2) was removed.
3. Under Article 31(c) of the Constitution, a new provision was added in order to remove all difficulties and to fulfill the objectives laid down under Article 39(b) and 39(c), it was decided that Articles 14, 19 & 31 will not be applied to any law. In order to make Article 39(b) and 39(c) effective, the Court was immunised from intervening in any law made by the Parliament.

26th Constitution Amendment: (Abolition of Privy Purse):

1. The payments of "Privy Purse" were made to the former Rulers under Constitutional provisions of Article 291 and Article 362. However, it was often questioned as a relic of the Colonial past.
2. Privy Purse conferred "special status" to ruling class, which continued the British practice of Ruler and ruled.
3. It went against the idea of equality enshrined in Preamble and Part III of the Constitution.

4. The concept of rulership, with "privy purse" and special privileges was incompatible with principles of democracy, equality and social justice and it was unrelated to any current functions and social purposes.

29th Amendment:

The 29th Amendment was passed in the Year 1972. It inserted the Kerala Land Reforms Act into the 9th Schedule. It meant that the matters related to the Kerala Land Reforms Act will be outside the scope of the Judiciary to try. All the amendments which were made by the Central Government in some or the other way, protected the amendments made by State Government from being tried in the Court of law. Provisions of the Kerala Land Reforms Act along with 24th, 25th and 29th Amendments were challenged in the Court of Law.

ISSUES BEFORE THE COURT:

1. Whether the 24th Constitutional (Amendment) Act, 1971 is Constitutionally valid or not ?
2. Whether the Constitutional (Amendment) Act, 1972 is Constitutionally valid or not ?
3. The extent to which the Parliament can exercise its power to amend the Constitution.

ARGUMENT OF PETITIONER:

It was contended by the Petitioner that the Parliament cannot amend the Constitution in a way they want to, as they have a limited power to do so. The Parliament cannot exercise its power to amend the Constitution by changing its basic structure as the same was pronounced by Justice Mudhokar in the case of Sajjan Singh vs State of Rajasthan. The Petitioner pleaded for the protection of his property under Article 19(1)(f) of the Indian Constitution.

It was argued by him that the 24th and 25th Constitutional Amendments violated the Fundamental Right which was provided under Article 19(1)(f) of the Indian Constitution. Fundamental Rights are rights available to citizens of India to ensure freedom and if any Constitutional amendment takes away such right then the freedom which is ensured under the Constitution to its citizens will be deemed to be taken away from them.

ARGUMENT OF RESPONDENT:

The Respondent was the State. The State contended that Supermacy of Parliament is the Basic Principle of the Indian Legal System and so the Parliament has the power to amend the Constitution unlimitedly. State also contended that in order to fulfill its socio-economic obligations, which have been guaranteed to the citizens of India under the Preamble, it is important that the Parliament exercises its power to amend the Constitution without any limitations.

JUDGEMENT:

It was held by the Apex Court by a majority of 7:6 that Parliament can amend any provision of the Constitution to fulfill its socio-economic obligations guaranteed to the citizens under the Preamble subject to the condition that such amendment won't change the "Basic Structure" of the Indian Constitution.

24th, 25th & 29th Amendment Acts held valid. Power to amend the Constitution is located in Article 368 and the word "Law" in Article 13(2) does not mean the Constitution. Constitution is the supreme law. Amendment of Constitution is an exercise of constituent power. Majority view in Golaknath case is wrong. There are no express limitations on power of amendment. There are no implied & inherent limitations on power of amendment. Neither Preamble nor Article 13(2) is limited on power of amendment. Power to amend the Constitution is unlimited and wide. In exercise of Constituent power Parliament can amend any provision of this Constitution. Power to amend can also be increased under Article 368. Amendments of Article 31(2B) is also valid. Article 31(2) & 19(1)(f) are mutually exclusive. Article 31C merely removes restriction of Part III from legislation giving effect to Directive Principles under Article 39(b) & (c).

The majority decision was delivered by S.M.Sikri CJI, K.S.Hegde, B.K.Mukherjea, J.M.Shelat, A.N.Grover, P. Jagmohan Reddy JJ, & Khanna J. Whereas, the minority opinions were written by A.N.Ray, D.G.Palekar, K.K.Mathew, M. H.Beg, S.N.Dwivedi & Y.V.Chandrachud JJ. The minority bench wrote different opinions but was still reluctant to give unfettered authority to the Parliament. The landmark case was decided on 24th April 1973.

The Court upheld the 24th Constitutional Amendment entirely but the 1st and the 2nd part of the 25th Constitutional Amendment Act was found to be intra vires and ultra vires respectively. It was observed by the Court in relation to the powers of the Parliament to amend the Constitution that it was a question that was left unanswered in the case of Golaknath.

The answer to the question was found in the present case and it was deducted by the Court that the Parliament has the power to amend the Constitution to the extent that such amendment does not change the Basic Structure of the Indian Constitution. It was laid down by the Court that the Doctrine of Basic Structure is to be followed by the Parliament while amending the provisions of the Constitution.

The Doctrine of Basic Structure:

According to the doctrine, the Parliament has an unlimited power to amend the Constitution subject to the sole condition that such amendments must not change the basic structure of the Constitution. The Parliament should not in any manner interfere with the basic features of the Constitution without which our Constitution will be left spiritless and lose its very essence. The basic Structure of the Constitution was not mentioned by the bench and was left to the interpretation of the courts. The Courts need to see and interpret if a particular amendment violates the basic structure of our Indian Constitution or not.

The Court found that as contended by the respondents actually there is a difference between "Ordinary Law" and "an amendment." Keshavananda Bharati's case to some extent overruled "Golaknath's" case. The Court, in this case, answered the question which was left unanswered in Golaknath's case in relation to the power of Parliament to amend provisions of the Constitution.

The Court found that the word "amend" which was included in Article 368 does not refer to amendments that can change the basic structure of the Constitution. If Parliament wants to amend a particular provision of the Constitution then such amendment would need to go through the test of basic structure.

It was also decided that since the Parliament has an unlimited power to amend the Constitution subject to the basic structure then Parliament can also amend Fundamental Rights as far as they are not included in the Basic Structure of the Constitution. 24th Amendment was upheld by the Bench whereas the 25th Amendment's 2nd part was struck down. The 25th Amendment's validation was subject to two conditions:

1. The Court agreed that the word "amount" and "compensation" is not equivalent to each other but still the "amount" which is provided by the Government to the landlords should not be unreasonable. The "amount" need to be equal to the market value but should be reasonable and

closely related to the present market value.

2. The 1st part of the 25th amendment was upheld but it was subject to the provision that the prohibition of judiciary's reach will be struck down.

CHAPTER TWO

Maneka Gandhi vs. Union of India. Citation: [1978] 2 SCR 621 : (1978) 1SCC 248

(In Maneka Gandhi case adopted the dissenting view of Justice Fazal Ali in A. K. Gopalan vs. State of Madras. Therefore, the Court held that the Procedure established by law should be reasonable, just and fair. It shall be free from any unreasonableness and arbitrariness. Phrase used in Article 21 is "procedure established by law" instead of "due process of law". However, the procedure must be free from arbitrariness and irrationality. Provisions of Article 14, 19 & 21 are to be read in synchronisation and they are not mutually exclusive. Section 10(3)(c) of the Passport Act, 1967 is not violative of neither Article 21 nor Article 19(1)(a) or 19(1)(g). Section 10(3)(c) and 10(5) is an administrative order, therefore, open to challenge on the grounds of mala fide, unreasonable, denial of natural justice and ultra vires. The rights discussed under 19(1)(a) and 19(1)(g) are not confined to the territorial limits of India.)

Date of Judgment: 25.01.1978.

Bench: M.H.Beg(CJI), Y.V.Chandrachud, P.N.Bhagwati, V.R.Krishna Iyer, N.L.Untwalia, S.Murtaza Fazal Ali & P.S.Kailasam, JJ.

FACTS OF THE CASE:

1. Maneka Gandhi (the Petitioner), the daughter-in-law of the former Prime Minister Indira Gandhi. She was holder of a passport issued to her on 1 June, 1976 under the Passport Act, 1967. On 4th July, 1977, the time around which she wanted to travel out of India for a speech

2. she received a letter dated 2nd July, 1977 from the Regional Passport Officer, Delhi, informing her that under Section 10(3)(c) of the Passport

Ac,1967, the Government of India has decided to impound her passport "in public interest". She was asked to surrender her passport within seven days from the receipt of the letter.

3. She wrote a letter to the Regional Passport Officer requesting him to furnish a copy of the statement of reasons for making the order as provided in Section 10(5) of the Act. But in its reply, the Ministry of External Affairs, Government of India stated that 'in the interest of the general public' it has decided not to furnish her copy of the statement of reasons for the making of the order.

4. Maneka Gandhi filed a Writ Petition under Article 32 of the Constitution of India challenging the action of the Government in impounding her passport and declining to give reasons for doing so and for enforcement of Fundamental Right mentioned under Article 14 against the arbitrary action of the authorities.

The Petition was further amended and enforcement of the following Articles:

Article 21 i.e. Protection of Life & Personal Liberty;

Article 19(1)(a) i.e. Right to freedom of Speech, and

Article 19(1)(g) i.e. Right to freedom of Movement.

Among the major reasons contended for the filing of such petition, the petitioner contended that the impugned order is void as it took away the petitioner's right to be given a fair hearing to present her defence.

LEGAL BACKGROUND OF THE CASE:

Satwant Singh Sawhney vs. D. Ramarathnam, Assistant Passport Officer-

In 1966, the Assistant Passport Officer, Government of India, Ministry of External Affairs, New Delhi wrote a letter to Satwant Singh Sawhney that Union of India, had decided to withdraw the passport facilities extended to the petitioner calling him to surrender the said two passports immediately to the Government.

The Petitioner filed a Writ Petition in Supreme Court, alleging that the said action of the Respondents (Government) infringed his Fundamental Rights under Article 21 and 14 of the Constitution. The Petition was allowed and the Supreme Court by majority settled twin positions:

(i). the expression "personal liberty" in Article 21 takes in it the right of locomotion and travel abroad and under Article 21 "no person can be deprived of his right to go abroad except according to procedure established by law" and "it is not disputed that no law was made by the State regulating or depriving persons of such right."

(ii). the discretion with the executive in the matter of issuing or refusing passport being un-channeled and arbitrary, it was plainly violative of Article 14 and the order refusing passport to the Petitioner (Satwant Singh Sawhney) is also invalid.

In the Petitioner's case, the Court held that the 'right of travel and to go outside the country is included in the right to personal liberty.' This decision was accepted by the Parliament and the infirmity pointed out by Supreme Court was set right by the enactment of the Passport Act, 1967.

A.K.Gopalan vs State of Madras- The legality and validity of A.K.Gopalan vs State of Madras was questioned in Satwant Singh Sawhney vs. D. Ramarathnam, Assistant Passport Officer. The main debate was around the scope of the word "procedure established by law" on the point that can such procedure be arbitrary or unreasonable or should it always be just, reasonable and fair.

The majority Bench however rejecting all the arguments of the petitioner held that the word "law" under Article 21 doesn't necessarily be in conformity with the principles of natural justice. But Justice Fazal Ali dissented with the majority by holding that the right to life under Article 21 does constitute Principles of Natural Justice and the Courts should check that any procedure established by law do not suffer with the problem of unreasonableness and arbitrariness. The spirit of Justice Fazal Ali's argument was that the procedure should be just, fair and reasonable.

The Court in Maneka Gandhi case adopted the dissenting view of Justice Fazal Ali in A. K. Gopalan vs. State of Madras. Therefore, the Court held that the Procedure established by law should be reasonable, just and fair. It shall be free from any unreasonableness and arbitrariness.

Judges in the case of Kharak Singh's case for the first time took the view that "personal liberty"

R. C. Cooper vs Union of India - That each freedom has different dimensions and there may be overlapping between different Fundamental Rights and therefore it is not a valid argument to say that the expression 'personal liberty' in Article 21 must be so interpreted as to avoid overlapping between that Article and Article 19(1). The expression 'personal liberty' in Article 21 is of the widest amplitude and it covers a variety of rights which go to constitute the personal liberty of man and some of them have been raised to the status of distinct Fundamental Rights and given additional protection under Article 19."

E. P. Royappa vs. State of Tamil Nadu & Another - This Court held that Article 14 strikes, at arbitrariness in State action and ensures fairness and equality of treatment. The principle of reasonableness, which legally as well as philosophically, is an essential element of equality or non-arbitrariness pervades Article 14 like a brooding omnipresence and the procedure contemplated by Article 21 must answer the best of reasonableness in order to be in conformity with Article 14. It must be "right and just and fair" and not arbitrary, fanciful or oppressive; otherwise, it would be no procedure at all and the requirement of Article 21 would not be satisfied. How far natural justice is fair essential element of procedure established by law.

LEGAL ISSUES BEFORE THE COURT:

1. Whether the right to go abroad is part of personal liberty ?
2. Whether the right under Article 19(1)(a) has any geographical limitation ?
3. Whether the Section 10(3)(c) of the Passport Act, 1967, is violative of Article 14, Article 19(1)(a) and Article 21 ?

SOME RELEVANT SECTIONS OF THE PASSPORT ACT :

Sub-section (1) of Section 10 of the Passport Act, 1967, empowers the Passport Authority to cancel the endorsement on a passport or travel document or to vary or cancel it on the conditions subject to which a passport or travel document has been issued.

Sub-section (3) provides that the Passport Authority may impound or cause to be impounded or revoke a passport or travel document on the grounds set out in Clause (a) to (h).

Clause (c) reads as follows: "If the Passport Authority deems it necessary so to do in the interest of the sovereignty and integrity of India, the security of India, friendly relations of India with the foreign country, or in the interests of the general public."

Sub-section (5) requires the Passport Authority impounding or revoking a passport to record in writing a brief statement of the reasons for making such order and furnish to the holder of the Passport or travel document on demand a copy of the same; in any case, the Passport Authority is of the opinion that it will not be in the interest of the sovereignty and integrity of India, the security of India, friendly relations of India with any foreign country or in the interest of the general public to furnish such a copy.

PETITIONER`S ARGUMENTS:

1. By the administrative order of impoundment of the Passport on 4th July, 1977, the respondent has infringed Petitioner's Fundamental Right to Freedom of Speech & Expression, Right to travel abroad, Right to life and personal liberty & Right to freedom of movement.
2. The provisions of Article 14, 19 & 21 are to be read in synchronisation and they are not mutually exclusive. These provisions in itself though not explicitly constitutes in itself principles of natural justice. A combined reading of the three provisions will give effect to the spirit of the Constitution and Constitution makers.
3. Even though India has not adopted American "due process of law" in its Constitution, the procedure established by law must be reasonable, fair & just free from any sort of arbitrariness.
4. Section 10(3)(c) is violative of Article 21 of the Constitution in the sense that it violates the right to life and personal liberty guaranteed under the said Constitutional provision. By the virtue of this provision, the petitioner was restrained from travelling abroad. This restrain on the petitioner was unconstitutional since it was generally accepted that right to travel abroad was within the right to life & personal liberty under Article 21.
5. Audi Altrem Partem i.e. opportunity of being heard is universally recognised as an essentially ingredient of principles of natural justice. These principles of natural justice find no explicit place in any constitutional provisions. However, the spirit of Fundamental Rights constitutes in itself the essence of these principles. Further, Article 32 provides an opportunity to the affected parties to directly approach Apex Court in case there is any violation of Part III provisions. This provision of Article 32 was coined as Heart & Soul of the Constitution is equivalent to Audi Altrem Partem. Therefore, it cannot be said that Principle of Natural Justice are separate and exclusive to the Constitution.

RESPONDENT`S ARGUMENTS:

1. The respondent contended before the Court that the Passport was impounded because the petitioner was required to appear before some committee's for enquiry. The Attorney General further promised the Court to do away with all the appearances in the said committee's as soon as possible.

2. The respondent reiterating the principle laid down in Gopalan case contended that the word "law" under Article 21 cannot be comprehended in the light of Fundamental Rules of Natural Justice.
3. The respondent further contended that the principles of natural justice are vague and full of ambiguities. Therefore, the Constitution should not read such vague and ambiguous provisions as a part of it.
4. The ambit of Article 21 is very wide and it generally contains the provisions of Articles 14 & 19. However, any law can only be termed unconstitutional to Article 21 when it directly infringes Article 14 & 19.
5. Article 21 in its language contains "procedure established by law" and such procedure need not pass the test of reasonability. Further the said provision need not necessarily be in conformity with the Articles 14 & 19.
6. The Constitution Makers while drafting this Constitution had debated at length on American "due process of law" and British "procedure established by law." The conspicuous absence of due process of law from the Constitutional provisions reflects the mind of framers of this Constitution. The mind and spirit of the framers must be protected and respected.

JUDGMENT:

That this judgment expanded the scope of Article 21 exponentially and this judgment truly and really made India a Welfare State as promised in the Preamble. The Seven Judge Bench gave a unanimous decision except some Judges concurring on some points.

There were seven separate opinions in which the majority opinion was written by Justice Bhagwati for himself, Untiwalia and Fazal Ali jj. While Chandrachud, iyer and Beg(CJI) wrote separate but concurring opinions.

THE MAJOR FINDUNG OF THE COURT:

1. The Court while delivering this landmark judgment changed the landscape of the Constitution by holding that though the phrase used in Article 21 is "procedure established by law" instead of "due process of law". However, the procedure must be free from arbitrariness and irrationality.
2. Even though the Constitution Makers must be respected, but they never intended to plant such a self—destructive bomb in the heart of the Constitution. They were never of the mind that the procedure need not

necessarily be reasonable, just and fair. They drafted the Constitution for the protection of the "people of India" and such interpretation of Article 21 will be counter-productive to the protection offered by the Constitution.

3. The Court overruled A.K.Gopalan case by stating that there is a unique relationship between the provisions of Article 14, 19, & 21 and every law must pass the tests of the said provisions. Earlier in A.K.Gopalan case, the majority held that these provisions in itself are mutually exclusive. Therefore, to correct its earlier mistake the Court held that these provisions are not mutually exclusive and dependent on each other.
4. The Court held that the scope of "personal liberty" is not be construed in narrow and stricter sense. The Court said that personal liberty has to be understood in the broader and liberal sense. Therefore, Article 21 was given an expansive interpretation. The Court obligated the future courts to expand the horizons of Article 21 to cover all the Fundamental Rights and avoid construing it in narrower sense.
5. The right to travel abroad as held in Satwant Singh Sawhney's case is within the scope of guarantees mentioned under Article 21.
6. Section 10(3)(c) of the Passport Act, 1967 is not violative of neither Article 21 nor Article 19(1)(a) or 19(1)(g). The Court further held that the said Passport Act, 1967 provision also not in contradiction of Article 14. Since the said provision provides for an opportunity to be heard. The Court rejected the contention of Petitioner that the phrase "in the interest of the general public" is not vague.
7. The Court held that Section 10(3)(c) and 10(5) is an administrative order, therefore, open to challenge on the grounds of mala fide, unreasonable, denial of natural justice and ultra vires.
8. The Court also suggested Government to ordinarily provide reasons in every case and should rarely use the prerogative of Section 10(5) of the Passport Act, 1967.
9. The rights discussed under 19(1)(a) and 19(1)(g) are not confined to the territorial limits of India.

CHAPTER THREE

Minerva Mills Ltd. & Ors. Vs. Union of India [1981] SCR (1) 206:(1980) 3 SCC 625:

Date of Judgement: 31.07.1980

(Minerva Mills case held that the harmony and balance between fundamental rights and directive principles is an essential feature of the Basic Structure of the Constitution. It also restored the "power of the Court" to "review" any "amendment to the Constitution". The Supreme Court held that the introduced Clause (5) of Article 368 transgresses the limitations on the amending power of Parliament and hence unconstitutional. Since Clause (4) and Clause (5) of Article 368 are interrelated, the Court declared Clause (4), too, as unconstitutional. Clause (5) of Article 368 removed all limitations on the amending power of the Parliament and Clause (4) deprived the Courts of their power to review any amendment to the Constitution.)

FACTS OF THE CASE:

1. Minerva Mills Ltd. was a textiles production company. In 1970, the Central Government appointed a committee under Section 15 of the Industries (Development Regulation) Act, 1951, to investigate the affairs of the Minerva Mills. The Government was of the opinion that there had been a substantial fall in the volume of production of the mill.

2. The Committee submitted its report to the Central Government in January 1971. On the basis of this report, the Government passed an order under Section 18A of the Industries (Development Regulation) Act, 1951, authorising the National Textile Corporation Ltd. to take over the management of the Minerva Mills. The order was based on the grounds that

the affairs of the Mill are being managed in a manner highly detrimental to the public interest.

3. Minerva Mills was nationalised and taken over by the Central Government under the provisions of the Sick Textile Understanding (Nationalisation) Act, 1974.

4. Minerva Mills and the other petitioners challenged the following by filing petitions under Article 32 of the Constitution in the Supreme Court:

CHALLANGES OF MINERVA MILLS & OTHERS BEFORE THE COURT:

1. The Constitutional validity of certain provisions of the Sick Textile Undertakings (Nationalisation) Act, 1974.
2. The Government Order that authorised the National Textile Corporation Ltd. to take over the management of the Minerva Mills.
3. The constitutionality of the Constitution (39th Amendment) Act which inserted the Nationalisation Act as Entry 105 in the Ninth Schedule of the Constitution.
4. The validity of the Article 31B of the Constitution.
5. Constitutionality of Sections 4 and 55 of the Constitution (42nd Amendment) Act, 1976.

QUESTIONS OF LAW BEFORE THE COURT:

1. Is the power of the Parliament to amend the Constitution limited by the Constitution?

2. Should there be a balance between Fundamental Rights and Directive Principles of State Policy?

RELEVANT SECTIONS INVOLVED:

Sections 4 and 55 of the Constitution (42nd Amendment) Act, 1976:

Section 4: Section 4 made an Amendment of Article 31C. It states, "Notwithstanding anything contained in Article 13, no law giving effect to the policy of the State towards securing all or any of the principles laid down in Part IV shall be deemed to be void on the ground that it is inconsistent with, or takes away or abridges any of the rights conferred by Article 14 or Article 19.....".

Section 55: Section 55 made an amendment to Article 368. It inserted Clause 4 and Clause 5 under Article 368.

Clause 4 reads., "No amendment of this Constitution (including the provisions of Part III) made or purporting to have been made under this Article [whether before or after the commencement of Section 55 of the

Constitution (42nd Amendment) Act, 1976] shall be called in question in any Court on any ground."

Clause 5 reads, "For the removal of doubts, it is hereby declared that there shall be no limitation whatever on the constituent power of Parliament to amend by way of addition, variation or repeal the provisions of this Constitution under this Article."

The challenge to the validity of Section 4 and 55 of the 42nd Amendment rests on the ratio of the majority of Keshavananda Bharati case which states that "Article 368 does not enable Parliament to alter the Basic Structure or framework of the Constitution". The question to determine on the basis of the majority view in Keshavananda Bharati case is:

"Whether the amendments introduced by Sections 4 and 55 of Constitution (42nd Amendment) Act, 1976 damage the basic structure of Constitution by destroying any of its basic features or essential elements."

PETITIONER`S ARGUMENTS:

1. Petitioners challenged the Constitutionality of Sections 4 and 55 of the Constitution(42nd Amendment) Act, 1976, on the grounds that "though by Article 368 of the Constitution Parliament is given the power to amend the Constitution, that power cannot be exercised so as to damage the Basic Features of the Constitution or so as to destroy its Basic Structure".

2. The Petitioners also challenged the constitutionality of the Constitution(39th Amendment) Act, which inserted the Sick Textile Undertakings (Nationalisation) Act, 1974, as Entry 105 in the Ninth Schedule to the Constitution.

3. They also challenged the primacy given to the Directive Principles of State Policy contained in Part IV over the Fundamental Rights conferred by Part III of the Constitution.

4. They argued that Section 55 of the Constitution(42nd Amendment) Act, 1976 deprived them of their right to seek legal remedies, as the concerned Section bars the "Judicial Review."

RESPONDENT`S ARGUMENTS:

1. The respondents argued that the issue formulated for consideration of the Court that is, "whether the provisions of the 42nd Amendment of the Constitution which deprived the Fundamental Rights of their supermacy and made them subordinate to the Directive Principles of State Policy are ultra vires the amending power of Parliament", is too wide and academic.

2. The Union of India argued that securing the implementation of Directive Principles by the elimination of obstructive legal procedures

cannot ever be said to destroy or damage the Basis Features of the Constitution. Further, laws made for securing the objectives of Part IV would necessarily be in the public interest.

3. The Directive Principles being themselves Fundamental in the governance of the country, no amendment to achieve the goals specified in the Directive Principles can ever alter the Basic Structure of the Constitution.

4. It further argued that a law which fulfils the Directive of Article 38 is incapable of abrogating Fundamental Freedoms for of damaging the Basic Structure of the Constitution in as much as that Structure itself is founded on the principles of justice, social, economic and political.

5. The deprivation of some of the Fundamental Rights for the purpose of bringing about a social order to achieve social, economic and political justice cannot possibly amount to a destruction of the Basic Structure of the Constitution.

JUDGMENT:

The Supreme Court held that the introduced Clause (5) of Article 368 transgresses the limitations on the amending power of Parliament and hence unconstitutional. Since Clause (4) and Clause (5) of Article 368 are interrelated, the Court declared Clause (4), too, as unconstitutional. Clause (5) of Article 368 removed all limitations on the amending power of the Parliament and Clause (4) deprived the Courts of their power to review any amendment to the Constitution.

Court opinioned that "if Courts are totally deprived of the power of review, the Fundamental Rights conferred upon the people will become a mere adornment because rights without remedies are as writ in water." Clause (4) of Article 368 totally deprives the citizens of a right guaranteed by Article 32. Directive Principles of State Policy are Fundamental in the governance of the country and Fundamental Rights occupy a unique place in the lives of civilised societies. Parts III and IV together constitute the core of the commitment to social revolution and they together are the conscience of the Constitution. The Indian Constitution is founded on the bedrock of the balance between Parts III and IV. Giving absolute primacy to one over the other will disturb the harmony of the Constitution. The Supreme Court held that the harmony and balance between Fundamental Rights and Directive Principles is an essential feature of the Basic Structure of the Constitution.

CHAPTER FOUR

Sharad Birdhi Chand Sarda v. State Of Maharashtra [1985] 1 SCR 88 : (1984)4 SCC

n 17 July, 1984

(Interferenc by the Supreme Court with the concurrent findings of fact of the courts below, normally not permissible-Special circumstance like errors of law, violation of well established principles of criminal jurisprudence etc. would be necessary for interference. Interferenc by the Supreme Court with the concurrent findings of fact of the courts below, normally not permissible-Special circumstance like errors of law, violation of well established principles of criminal jurisprudence etc. would be necessary for interference. Prosecution must prove every link of the chain and complete chain-Infirmity or lacuna in the prosecution cannot be cured by false defence or plea-A person cannot be convicted on pure moral conviction-False explanation can be used as additional link to fortify the prosecution case, subject to satisfaction of certain conditions. Doctrine of Proximity was also evovled in this case.)

BENCH:

FAZALALI, SYED MURTAZA

VARADARAJAN, A. (J)

MUKHARJI, SABYASACHI (J)

FACTS OF THE CASE:-

The appellant, Rameshwar Birdhichand Sarda, Ramvilas Rambagas Sarda, were accused 1, 2 and 3 respectively in Sessions Case No. 203 of 1982 on the file of the Additional Sessions Judge, Pune. The appellant and the second accused are the sons of one Birdhichand of Pune whose family has a cloth business. In addition, the appellant, a graduate in Chemical Engineering had started a chemical factory at Bhosari, a suburb of Pune. The third accused is uncle of the appellant and the second accused. The appellant is the husband of Manjushree alias Manju while the second accused is the husband of Anuradha (P.W. 35). Birdhichand's family has its residential house at Ravivar Peth in Pune and owns a flat in a building known as Takshasheela Apartments in Mukund Nagar area of Pune. All the three accused were charged for the alleged offence of murder by poisoning on the night of 11/12.6.1982 of Manju the newly married wife of the first accused and the appellant herein under section 302 I.P.C. read with section 120B.

Accused No, 3 was also charged under section 201 read with section 120B I.P.C. The whole case vested on the circumstantial evidence based on certain letters alleged to have been written by the deceased to some of the witnesses and other statements of the deceased to them and the medical report.

TRIAL COURT:

On an appreciation of the evidence the trial court found all the three accused guilty as charged, convicted them accordingly and sentenced the appellant to death under Section 302 I.P.C.

and all the three accused to rigorous imprisonment for two years and a fine of Rs. 2,000 each under s.120B I.P.C. but did not award any sentence under s.201 read with s.120B.

HIGH COURT:

The appellant and the other two accused file Criminal Appeal No. 265/83 against their conviction and the sentences Awarded to them. The State filed a Criminal Revision application for enhancement of the sentence awarded to accused 2 and 3. The appeal as well as Criminal Revision application was heard along with confirmation case No. 3 of 1983 together by the Division Bench of the Bombay High Court which allowed the appellants appeal in part regarding his conviction and sentence under s.120B I.P.C. but confirmed his conviction and sentence of death awarded under section 302 I.P.C., allowed the appeal of accused 2 and 3 in full and acquitted them and dismissed the Criminal Revision Application.

Hence the appellant alone has come up before the Supreme Court after obtaining Special Leave

SUPREME CPPORT:-

Allowed the appeal,

APPELLANT`S ARGUMENT:

It was argued before the High Court that it was highly improbable that if the betrothal ceremony of appellant's sister, which was as important as the marriage itself, was going to be performed on the 13th of June, would the appellant choose a day before that for murdering his wife and thereby bring disgrace and destruction not only to his family but also to her sister.

We have already adverted to this aspect of the matter but it is rather interesting to note how the High Court has tried to rebut this inherent improbability, on the ground that in a case of administration of poison the culprit would just wait for an opportunity to administer the same and once he gets the opportunity he is not expected to think rationally but would commit the murder at once.

With due respect to the Judges of the High Court, we are not able to agree with the somewhat complex line of reasoning which is not supported by the evidence on record. There is clear evidence, led by the prosecution that except for a week or few days of intervals, Manju always used to live with her husband and she had herself complained that he used to come late at night. Hence, as both were living alone in the same room for the last four months there could be no dearth of any opportunity on the part of the appellant to administer poison if he really wanted to do so. We are unable to follow the logic of the High Court's reasoning that once the appellant got an opportunity he must have clung to it. The evidence further shows that both Manju and appellant had gone for a honeymoon outside Pune and even at that time he could have murdered her and allowed the case to pass for a natural death. However, these are matters of conjectures.

ADDITIONAL SOLICITOR-GENERAL / RESPONDENT`S ARGUMENT:

The Additional Solicitor-General realising the hollowness of the High Court's argument put it in a different way.

1. He submitted that as the deceased was 4-6 weeks pregnant the appellant realised that unless the deceased was murdered at the behest it would become very difficult for him to murder her, even if he had got an opportunity, if a child was born and then he would have to maintain the child also which would have affected his illicit connections with Ujvala.

This appears to be an attractive argument but on close scrutiny it is untenable. If it was only a question of Manju's being 4-6 weeks pregnant before her death, the appellant could just as well have waited just for another fortnight till the marriage of his sister was over which was fixed for

30th June, 1982 and then either have the pregnancy terminated or killed her. Moreover, it would appear from the evidence of PW 2 (P.176) that in his community the Kohl ceremony is not merely a formal betrothal but a very important ceremony in which all the near relations are called and invited to attend the function and a dinner is hosted. We might extract what PW 2 says about this:

"At the time of Kohl celebration of Manju, on 2.8.1981 my relatives i.e. my sister from outside had attended this function and many people were invited for this function. A dinner was also hosted by me. In that function the father of the bridegroom is required to spend for the dinner while the presentations made to the bride are required to be given or donned at the expenses of the side of bridegroom This programme is not attended by the bridegroom." (P.176) As Birdichand and others were made co-accused in the case they were unable to give evidence on this point but it is the admitted case of both the parties that the accused belonged to the same community as PW 2. In these circumstances, it is difficult to accept the argument that the appellant would commit the murder of his wife just on the eve of Kohl ceremony, which he could have done the same long before that ceremony or after the marriage as there was no hurry nor any such impediment which would deny him any opportunity of murdering his wife.

"But in a case like this where the various links as started above have been satisfactorily made out and the circumstances point to the appellant as the probable assailant, with reasonable definiteness and in proximity to the deceased as regards time and situation-such absence of explanation of false explanation would itself be an additional link which completes the chain."

before a false explanation can be used as additional link, the following essential conditions must be satisfied:

(1) various links in the chain of evidence led by the prosecution have been satisfactorily proved. (2) the said circumstance point to the guilt of the accused with reasonable definiteness, and (3) the circumstance is in proximity to the time and situation.

"Another golden thread which runs through the web of the administration of justice in criminal cases is that if two views are possible on the evidence adduced in the case one pointing to the guilt of the accused and the other to his innocence, the view which is favourable to the accused should be adopted This principle has a special relevance in cases where in the guilt of the accused is sought to be established by circumstantial evidence."

So far as this matter is concerned, in such cases the court must carefully scan the evidence and determine the four important circumstances which alone can justify a conviction:

(1) there is a clear motive for an accused to administer poison to the deceased, (2) that the deceased died of poison said to have been administered, (3) that the accused had the poison in his possession, (4) that he had an opportunity to administer the poison to the deceased.

In the instant case, while two ingredients have been proved but two have not. In the first place, it has no doubt been proved that Manju died of potassium cyanide and secondly, it has also been proved that there was an opportunity to administer the poison. It has, however, not been proved by any evidence that the appellant had the poison in his possession. On the other hand, as indicated above, there is clear evidence of PW 2 that potassium cyanide could have been available to Manju from the plastic factory of her mother, but there is no evidence to show that the accused could have procured potassium cyanide from any available source. We might here extract a most unintelligible and extra-ordinary finding of the High Court-

"It is true that there is no direct evidence on these two points, because the prosecution is not able to lead evidence that the accused had secured potassium cyanide poison from a particular source. Similarly there is no direct evidence to prove that he had administered poison to Manju. However, it is not necessary to prove each and every fact by a direct evidence. Circumstantial evidence can be a basis for proving this fact."

(P.160) The comment by the High Court appears to be frightfully vague and absolutely unintelligible. While holding in the clearest possible terms that there is no evidence in this case to show that the appellant was in possession or poison, the High Court observes that this fact may be proved either by direct or indirect (circumstantial) evidence. But it fails to indicate the nature of the circumstantial or indirect evidence to show that the appellant was in possession of poison. If the court seems to suggest that merely because the appellant had the opportunity to administer poison and the same was found in the body of the deceased, it should be presumed that the appellant was in possession of poison, than it has committed a serious and gross error of law and has blatantly violated the principles laid down by this Court. The High Court has not indicated as to what was the basis for coming to a finding that the accused could have procured the cyanide. On the other hand, in view of the decision in Ramgopal's case (supra) failure to prove possession of the cyanide poison with the accused by itself would result in failure of the prosecution to prove its case. We are constrained to observe that the High Court has completely misread and misconstru-ed the decision in Ramgopal's case. Even prior to Ramgopol's case there are two decisions of this Court which have taken the same view. In Chandrakant Nyalchand Seth's case (Criminal Appeal No. 120 of 1957 decided on 19.2.58) this Court observed thus:

"Before a person can be convicted of murder by poisoning, it is necessary to prove that the death of the deceased was caused by poison, that the poison in question was in possession of the accused and that poison was administered by the accused to the deceased. There is no direct evidence in this case that the accused was in possession of Potassium Cyanide or that he administered the same to the deceased."

JUDGMENT:

1. Constitution of India, 1950, Articla 136- Interferenc by the Supreme Court with the concurrent findings of fact of the courts below, normally not permissible-Special circumstance like errors of law, violation of well established principles of criminal jurisprudence etc. would be necessary for interference.

2. Evidence-Circumstantial evidence, nature and proof of- Conditions precedent for conviction-Evidence ActSection 3 (Act 1 of 1972).

Evidence-Circumstantial evidence- Onus of proof- Prosecution must prove every link of the chain and complete chain-Infirmity or lacuna in the prosecution cannot be cured by false defence or plea-A person cannot be convicted on pure moral conviction-False explanation can be used as additional link to fortify the prosecution case, subject to satisfaction of certain conditions.

3. Doctrine of Proximity, concept of, nature and limits

explained-Admissibility of statements and dying declarations under sections 8, 32 of the Evidence Act.

Murder by administration of poison-Circumstances that should be looked into before a conviction-Penal Code (Act XLV of 1860) Section 300.

Evidence, appreciation of-Evidence of interested witnesses, especially that of close relatives of the deceased- Duty of the Court-Evidence Act (Act I of 1872)

Section 3.

4. Benefit of doubt- When two views are possible, one leading to the guilt of the accused and the other leading to his innocence, the benefit of doubt

should go to the accused entitling his acquittal- Evidence Act (Act I of 1872) Sections 101-104. Examination of the accused under Section 313 of Crl. P.C.-Circumstances not put to the accused to explain, cannot be considered for conviction-Code of Criminal Procedure, 1973 (Act II of 1974) Section 313.

3:2. Before a false explanation can be used as additional link, the following essential conditions must be satisfied: [165E]

1. Various links in the chain of evidence led by the prosecution have been satisfactorily proved; [165E]

2. The said circumstance point to the guilt of the accused with reasonable definiteness and; [165G]

3. The circumstances is in proximity to the time and situation.[165H]

If these conditions are fulfilled only then a Court can use a false explanation or a false defence as an additional link to lend as assurance to the Court and not otherwise.

3:3. Before a case against an accused vesting on circumstantial evidence can be said to be fully established the following conditions must be fulfilled as laid down in Hanumat's v. State of M.P. [1953] SCR 1091. [163C]

1. The circumstances from which the conclusion of guilt is to be drawn should be fully established; [163D]

2. The facts so established should be consistent with the hypothesis of guilt and the accused, that is to say, they should not be explainable on any other hypothesis except that the accused is guilty; [163G]

3. The circumstances should be of a conclusive nature and tendency;[163G]

4. They should exclude every possible hypothesis except the one to be proved; and [163H]

5. There must be a chain of evidence so complete as not to leave any reasonable ground for the conclusion consistent with the innocence of the accused and must show that in all human probability the act must have been done by the accused. [164B]

These five golden principles constitute the panchsheel of the proof of a case based on circumstantial evidence and in the absence of a corpus deliciti. [164B]

CHAPTER FIVE

A.R. Antulay V/s R.S Nayak & Anr.[1988] 1 Suppl. SCR 1 : (1988) 2 SCC 602 : 1988 AIR 1531.

(The jurisdiction to try a case could only be conferred by law enacted by the legislature and this Court could not confer jurisdiction if it does not exist in law. The SC held that the Apex Court were without jurisdiction and as such void. There was no jurisdiction or power to transfer a case from the Court of the Special Judge to any High Court. The bench pointed that the directions of the Court were given per incuriam.)

FACTS OF THE CASE:

1. A.R. Antulay became Chief Minister of the State of Maharashtra on 9th June 1980. On 1st September 1981, R. S. Naik a member of opposition applied to the Governor of the State under sec 197 of the Criminal Procedure Code, 1973 and sec 6 of the Prevention of Corruption Act, 1947 for sanction to prosecute the C.M.

2. On 11th of September, 1981, Naik filed a complaint before the Additional Metropolitan Magistrate, Bombay against the C.M. and other known and unknown persons for alleged offence under sections 161 and 165 of the Indian Penal Code and section 5 of the Act as also under sections 384 and 420 read with sections 109 and 120B of the Indian Penal Code and his character and integrity came under a cloud.

3. But the learned magistrate due to absence of sanction refused to take cognizance. The said order was appealed before the Bombay High Court, which held that sanction was necessary for the prosecution of the appellant

and also an order in a writ petition all wired against A.R. Antulay which resulted in his resignation from the post of C.M. on 12th January, 1982. But, continued as the member of legislative assembly.

4. On 28th of July, 1982, the Governor of Maharashtra granted sanction under section 197 of the Code and section 6 of the Act in respect of five items relating to three subjects only and refused sanction in respect of all other items.

5. Finally, On 9th August, 1982 a fresh case was instituted by R.S. Naik against A.R. Antulay before the learned Special Judge bringing in many more allegations including those for which sanction was refused by the Governor reasoning it that the person is seized to be a C.M.

6. The State Government on 15th of January, 1983 notified the appointment of Shri R.B. Sule as the Special Judge to try the offence. On 25th of July 1983, Shri R.B. Sule, Special Judge discharged A.R. Antulay holding that a member of the Legislative Assembly is a public servant and there was no valid sanction for prosecuting the appellant.

7, An appeal filed by complainant under Article 136, the Constitution Bench held that a member of the Legislative Assembly is not a public servant and set aside the order of Special Judge Sule. The court also ordered that the cases against A.R. Antulay and others be transferred to the High Court Bombay withdrawing from the special judge and request to the learned Chief Justice to assign these two cases to a sitting Judge of the High Court for holding the trial from day to day, for expeditious disposal in accordance with law.

8. An Special leave petition was filed by A.K. Antulay for S.C. Questioning the jurisdiction of the special judge to try the case in violating his Fundmental Right under Article 21 and 14 and provision of Criminal law.

9. And also another SLP was filed against the order of special judge stating that the 79 charges against the Appellant need no sanction and a writ petition was filed questioning the validity of sec 197(1) CRPC.

ISSUE BEFORE THE COURT:

- Whether the directions of this court in the last order were legally proper?
- Whether the action and the trial proceedings pursuant to those directions, are legal and valid?

- Can those directions be recalled or set aside or annulled in those proceedings and trial be proceeded according to CRPC?

PETITIONER'S ARGUMENT

a. The proceedings initiated against the appellant were not sustainable in law as no sanction was obtained from the competent authority before cognizance was taken in the matter.
b. Mr. Rao for Antulay argued at length and Brother Mukharji has noticed all those contentions that by the change of the forum of the trial the accused has been prejudiced. Undoubtedly, by this process he misses a forum of appeal because if the trial was handled by a Special Judge, the first appeal would lie to the High Court and further appeal by special leave could come before this Court. If the matter is tried by the High Court there would be only one forum of appeal being this Court, whether as of right or by way of special leave. The appellant has also contended that the direction violates Article 14 of the Constitution because he alone has been singled out and picked up for being treated differently from similarly placed accused persons. Some of these aspects cannot be overlooked with ease. I must, however, indicate here that the argument based upon the extended meaning given to the contents of Article 21 of the Constitution, though attractive have not appealed to me.
c. Appellant contends that the earlier bench had no jurisdiction to issue the impugned directions which were without any visible legal support, that they are 'void' as violative of the constitutional-rights of the appellant, and, also as violating the Rules of natural justice.
d. appellant has been prejudiced by a mistake of the Court and it is not only within power but a duty as well, H of the Court to correct its own mistake, so that no party is prejudiced by the Court's mistake: Actus Curiae Neminem Gravabid.
e. In issuing the impugned direction, the Bench violated the principles of natural justice, as mentioned above. It also overlooked that, as a result thereof, the petitioner (a) was discriminated against by being put to trial before a different forum as compared to other public servants accused of similar offences and (b) lost valuable rights of revision and first appeal to the High Court which he would have had, if tried in the normal course.
f. Learned counsel for the appellant contends that the language of section 7(1) of the Act is mandatory; it directs that offences specified in the

Act can be tried only by persons appointed, under section 6(2) of the Act, by the State Government, to be special judges, No other Judge, it is said, has jurisdiction to try such a case, even if he is a Judge of the High Court. In this context, it is pointed out that a person, to be appointed as a special Judge, under section 6(2) of the 1952 Act, should be one who is, or has been, a Sessions Judge (which expression in this context includes an Additional Sessions Judge and/or an Assistant Sessions Judge). All High Court Judges may not have been Sessions Judges earlier and, it is common ground, Shah, J. who has been nominated by the Chief Justice for trying this case does not fulfill the qualifications prescribed for appointment as a Special Judge. But, that consideration apart, the argument is that, while a High Court can transfer a case from one special judge to another, and the Supreme Court, from a special judge in one State to a special judge in another State, a High Court cannot withdraw a case from a Special Judge to itself and the Supreme Court cannot transfer a case from a Special Judge to the High Court.

RESPONDENT'S ARGUMENT

a. Mr. Jethmalani had told us during arguments that if there was interference in this case there was possibility of litigants thinking that the Court had made a direction by going out of its way because an influential person like Antulay was involved.
b. The submissions of Shri Ram Jethmalani that the exclusivity of the jurisdiction claimed for the special forum under the 1952 Act is in relation to Courts which would, otherwise, be Courts of competing or co-ordinate jurisdictions and that such exclusivity does not effect the superior jurisdiction of the High Court to withdraw, in appropriate situations, the case to itself in exercise of its extraordinary original criminal jurisdiction; that canons of Statutory- construction, appropriate to the situation, require that the exclusion of jurisdiction implied in the 1952 amending Act should not be pushed beyond the purpose sought to be served by the amending law; and that the law while creating the special jurisdiction did not seek to exclude the extra- ordinary jurisdiction of the High Court are not without force.
c. power of transfer contained in the Criminal Procedure Code can be availed of to transfer a case from a Special Judge to any other criminal court or even the High Court.

d. the Supreme Court, as an appellate or revisional court, could have done was either (a) to direct the High Court to consider whether this was a fit case for it to exercise its power under section 407(1)(iv) to withdraw the case to itself and try the same with a view to expeditiously dispose it of or (b) to have withdrawn the case to itself for trial.
e. where a case is thus withdrawn and tried by the Court, the High Court will be conducting the trial in the exercise of its extraordinary original criminal jurisdiction.

JUDGMENT:

1. The jurisdiction to try a case could only be conferred by law enacted by the legislature and this Court could not confer jurisdiction if it does not exist in law. The SC held that the Apex Court were without jurisdiction and as such void. There was no jurisdiction or power to transfer a case from the Court of the Special Judge to any High Court.

2. The bench pointed that the directions of the Court were given per incuriam, that is to say without awareness of or advertence to the exclusive nature of the jurisdiction of the Special Court and without reference to the possibility of the violation of the fundamental rights in a case of this nature as observed by a seven Judges Bench decision in The State of West Bengal v. Anwar Ali Sarkar [1952].

3. The court observed that following rights of the appellant have been taken away by the impugned directions;

a. The right to be tried by a Special Judge in accordance with the procedure established by law and enacted by Parliament.

b. The right of revision to the High Court under sec 9 of the Criminal Law Amendment Act.

c. The right of first appeal to the High Court under the same section.

d. The right to move the Supreme Court under sec 136 thereafter by way of a second appeal, if necessary.

e. The appellant has also a right not to be singled out for special treatment by a Special Court created for him alone. This right is implicit in the right to equality stated by the bench. Also he has also a right not to suffer any order passed behind his back by a Court in violation of the basic principles of natural justice, violating Art. 21.

4. The court held that the learned Special Judge was clearly in error in holding that M.L.A. is a public servant within the meaning of the expression in section 12(a) and further erred in holding that a sanction of the

Legislative Assembly of Maharashtra or majority of the members was a condition precedent to taking cognizance of offences committed by the accused.

5. The Court infringed the Constitutional safeguards granted to a citizen or to an accused and injustice results therefrom. It is just and proper for the Court to rectify and recall that injustice, in the peculiar facts and circumstances of this case. The appellant accused has held an important position in this country, being the Chief Minister of a premier State of the country. He has been charged with serious criminal offences. His trial must be in accordance with law and the procedure established by law would have to be in accordance with the 1952 Act.

6. The apex court observed that the legal wrong that has been caused to the appellant should be remedied. Let that wrong be therefore remedied. Let right be done and in doing so let no more further injury be caused to public purpose

7. And all proceedings to this matter subsequent to the directions of this Court on 16th February, 1984 are set aside and quashed. The trial shall proceed in accordance with law, that is to say, under the Act of 1952.

8. The direction was thus also violative of natural justice as well as the fundamental rights of the petitioner under Article 14 and 21 of the Constitution.

CHAPTER SIX

Kihoto Hollohon v. Zachilhu, 1992 SCR (1) 686.

(The Judgement in Kihoto Hollohon vs Zachillhu and Others upholding the constitutional validity of this 52nd amendment, the court observed that the anti-defection law seeks to recognise the practical need to place the proprieties of political and personal conduct...above certain theoretical assumptions". The court finally held that the law does not violate any rights of free speech or basic structure of the parliamentary democracy. Another important aspect of this judgment is the final decision making authority on declaring the defection. The court made it clear that the presiding officer is the one to make the decision and it is final subject to judicial review after the decision is pronounced and effected.)

FACT OF THE CASE

The tenth schedule was inserted by the Constitution (fifty-second amendments) Act, 1985. In this case, multiple petitions were heard together. The combined petition aimed to challenge the Constitutional validity of the Tenth Schedule introduced by the Constitution (Fifty Second Amendment) Act, 1985.These cases were brought amongst a batch of Writ Petitions, Transfer Petitions, Civil Appeals, Special Leave Petitions and other similar and connected matters raising common questions which were heard together. Four articles of the Constitution were altered by the Constitution (Fifty-second Amendment) Act. These articles are 101(3)(a), 102(2), 190(3) (a) and 191(2). Also, tenth schedule was added. This Amendment is often referred to as Anti-Defection Law.

ISSUES BEFORE THE COURT

Whether the changes made by 52nd amendment are constitutionally valid or not?

PETITIONERS ARGUMENTS

1. The basic underlying contention of the petitioners was that every parliamentarian must have the right to follow his own spirit and sense of judgment and not necessarily with the policy of his political party. This according to the petitioners is deemed to be a fundamental principle of parliamentary democracy, freedom of speech and the right to dissent and the freedom of conscience.

Hon'ble Justice Venkata Chaliah said that*"in such areas of experimental legislation what is constitutionally valid and what is constitutionally invalid is marked by a 'hazy grey line' and thus there is no litmus test of constitutionality."* The majority then went on to decide in favour of the Constitutional validity saying that the Constitution is flexible to provide for the compulsions of the changing times, that the freedom of speech of a member is not an absolute freedom and also that the political party functions on the strength of shared beliefs, it being the cost of the label of the party under which their representative has been elected that he must not vote against it.

2. The right of a parliamentarian is indeed not an absolute right and is thus subject to reasonable restrictions. The right of a parliamentarian to the freedom of speech is provided for under the Article 105(2). This, as contended by Shri Sharma, arguing on the side of the petitioners, is places even above the fundamental right as guaranteed under the Article 19(1)(a) of the Constitution. Political defections in lure of power and money inducements is also clearly a corrupt practice, therefore not falling within the immunity granted to a member of the house.

2. Another contention raised by counsel for petitioners, is that the distinction between 'defection' and 'split' in the Tenth Schedule is very minimal. The differences on which the distinction rests are indeed an outrageous defiance of logic. Appreciating the argument of the counsel the Court has opined that the rule for exemption of split is justified in terms that as much as $1/3^{rd}$ members at the same time cannot be driven dishonest intentions.

However, the arguments of the counsel sound more convincing than the ruling given by the court. These provisions give blanket exemption to splits and mergers and frustrate the very purpose of Anti-Defection law. They are dangerous as their abuse can be easily done. They are totally ill-conceived in view of what has happened in the recent past, and illogical because under the Act, the greater the sin, the greater is the immunity. In many a case, defections are effected by groups-big and small. It would not be difficult to stage splits and mergers for ulterior motives.

The second major contention raised by the petitioners is that paragraph 7 in terms and in effect brings about a change in the operation and effect of Articles 136, 226 and 227 thus attracting the clause (2) of the Article 368 requiring ratification. The court subscribing to it has opined that the words of the paragraph 7 are of wide import and leave no constructional options. The same idea is reinforced by looking into the history of the defection law and the debates in the house which suggests that paragraph 7 was introduced with the very purpose of barring jurisdiction. The court has differentiated the present case from the cases of *Shankari Prasad Singh Deo v. Union of India and State of Bihar*[2] and *Sajjan Singh v. State of Rajasthan*[3] that were relied upon to urge that there is no attraction to the clause (2) of the Article 368.

3. The petitioners also contended that the 'finality clause' which was under the para 6 of the Tenth Schedule, excludes the court's jurisdiction which was, in turn, rendering the speaker immune from Judicial Review. In India the position is such that whatever authority decides disputes must be vested with judicial authority. In the present case too, the power to decide disputed disqualification under para 6(1) is pre-eminently a judicial complexion. In the present case, the majority has held that the Speaker or the chairman under the para 6(1) of the Tenth Schedule is tribunal and that the finality clause does not oust the jurisdiction of the courts under Articles. 136,226 and 227. Instead, the finality clause just limits them.

Another contention raised before the court was that there is a violation of the basic feature as independent adjudicatory machinery for resolution of electoral disputes is an essential incident of democracy. The majority and minority have differed at this point with the majority asserting that there is no violation of basic feature of Constitution keeping in mind the pivotal position of the Speaker in a Parliamentary Democracy. The majority has extolled the position of a Speaker and thus rather unconvincingly tried to justify its view saying that there is no violation of the basic structure of the Constitution.

JUDGMENT:

Minority opinion

Per L.M. Sharma and J.S. Verma, JJ.

1. For the reasons to be given in our detailed judgment to follow, our operative conclusions in the minority opinion on the various constitutional issues are as follows

1. Para 7 of the Tenth Schedule, in clear terms and in effect excludes the jurisdiction of all courts, including the Supreme Court under Article 136 and the High Courts under Articles 226 and 227 to entertain any challenge to the decision under para 6 on any ground even of illegality or perversity, not only at an interim stage but also after the final decision on the question of disqualification on the ground of defection.
2. Para 7 of the Tenth Schedule, therefore, in terms and in effect, makes a change in Article 136 in Chapter IV of Part V; and Articles 226 and 227 in Chapter V of Part VI of the Constitution, attracting the proviso to clause (2) of Article 368.
3. In view of para 7 in the Bill resulting in the Constitution (Fifty-Second Amendment) Act, 1985 it was required to be ratified by the Legislature of not less than one-half of the States as a condition precedent before the Bill could be presented to the President for assent, in accordance with the mandatory special procedure prescribed in the Proviso to clause (2) of Article 368 for exercise of the constituent power. Without ratification by the specified number of State Legislatures, the stage for presenting the Bill for assent of the President did not reach and, therefore, the so-called assent of the President was non est and did not result in the Constitution standing amended in accordance with the terms of the Bill.
4. In the absence of ratification by the specified number of State Legislatures before presentation of the Bill to the President for his assent, as required by the Proviso to clause (2) of Article 368, it is not merely para 7 but, the entire Constitution (Fifty-Second Amendment) Act, 1985 which is rendered unconstitutional, since the constituent power was not exercised as prescribed in Article 368, and therefore, the Constitution did not stand amended in accordance with the terms of the Bill providing for the amendment.
5. Doctrine of Severability cannot be applied to a Bill making a constitutional amendment where any part thereof attracts the Proviso to clause (2) of Article 368.
6. Doctrine of Severability is not applicable to permit striking down para 7 alone saving the remaining provisions of the Bill making the Constitutional Amendment on the ground that para 7 alone attracts the proviso to clause (2) of Article 368.
7. Even otherwise, having regard to the provisions of the Tenth Schedule of the Constitution inserted by the Constitution (Fifty-Second Amendment) Act, 1985, the Doctrine of Severability does not apply to it.

8. Democracy is a part of the basic structure of the Constitution and free and fair elections with provision for resolution of disputes relating to the same as also for adjudication of those relating to subsequent disqualification by an independent body outside the House are essential features of the democratic system in our Constitution. Accordingly, an independent adjudicatory machinery for resolving disputes relating to the competence of Members of the House is envisaged as an attribute of this basic feature. The tenure of the Speaker who is the authority in the Tenth Schedule to decide this dispute is dependent on the continuous support of the majority in the House and, therefore, he (the Speaker) does not satisfy the requirement of such an independent adjudicatory authority; and his choice as the sole arbiter in the matter violates an essential attribute of the basic feature.
9. Consequently, the entire Constitution (Fifty-Second Amendment) Act, 1985 which inserted the Tenth Schedule together with clause (2) in Articles 102 and 191, must be declared unconstitutional or an abortive attempt to so amend the Constitution.
10. It follows that all decisions rendered by the several Speakers under the Tenth Schedule must also be declared nullity and liable to be ignored.
11. On the above conclusions, it does not appear necessary or appropriate to decide the remaining questions urged.

Majority opinion

Per M.N. Venkatachaliah, K. Jayachandra Reddy and S.C. Agrawal, JJ.

A) That having regard to the background and evolution of the principles underlying the Constitution (52nd Amendment) Act, 1985, in so far as it seeks to introduce the Tenth Schedule in the Constitution of India, the provisions of Paragraph 7 of the Tenth Schedule of the Constitution in terms and in effect bring about a change in the operation and effect of Articles 136, 226 and 227 of the Constitution of India and, therefore, the amendment would require to be ratified in accordance with the proviso to sub-Article (2) of Article 368 of the Constitution of India.
B) That there is nothing in the said proviso to Article 368 (2) which detracts from the severability of a provision on account of the inclusion of which the Bill containing the Amendment requires ratification from the rest of the provisions of such Bill which do not attract and require such ratification. Having regard to the mandatory language of Article 368 (2) that "thereupon the constitution shall stand amended" the operation of the proviso should not be extended to constitutional amendments in a Bill which can stand by themselves without such ratification.

C) That, accordingly, the Constitution (52nd Amendment) Act, 1985, in so far as it seeks to introduce the Tenth Schedule in the Constitution of India, to the extent of its provisions which are amenable to the legal-sovereign of the amending process of the Union Parliament cannot be overborne by the proviso which cannot operate in that area. There is no justification for the view that even the rest of the provisions of the Constitution (52nd Amendment) Act, 1985 excluding Paragraph 7 of the Tenth Schedule become constitutionally infirm by reason alone of the fact that one of its severable provisions which attracted and required ratification under the proviso to Article 368(2) was not so ratified.

D) That Paragraph 7 of the Tenth Schedule contains a provision which is independent of, and stands apart from, the main provisions of the Tenth Schedule which are intended to provide a remedy for the evil of unprincipled and unethical political defections and, therefore, is a severable part. The remaining provisions of the Tenth Schedule can and do stand independently of Paragraph 7 and are complete in themselves workable and are not truncated by the excision of Paragraph 7.

E) That the Paragraph 2 of the Tenth Schedule to the Constitution is valid. Its provisions do not suffer from the vice of subverting democratic rights of elected Members of Parliament and the Legislatures of the States. It does not violate their freedom of speech, freedom of vote and conscience as contended.

The provisions of Paragraph 2 do not violate any rights or freedom under Articles 105 and 194 of the Constitution.

The provisions are salutary and are intended to strengthen the fabric of Indian parliamentary democracy by curbing unprincipled and unethical political defections.

F) The contention that the provisions of the Tenth Schedule, even with the exclusion of Paragraph 7, violate the basic structure of the Constitution in that they affect the democratic rights of elected members and, therefore, of the principles of Parliamentary democracy is unsound and is rejected.

G) The Speakers / Chairmen while exercising powers and discharging functions under the Tenth Schedule act as Tribunal adjudicating rights and obligations under the Tenth Schedule and their decisions in that capacity are amenable to judicial review.

However, having regard to the Constitutional Scheme in the Tenth Schedule, judicial review should not cover any stage prior to the making of a decision by the Speakers / Chairmen. Having regard to the Constitutional intendment and the status of the repository of the adjudicatory power, no quia timet actions are permissible, the only exception for any interlocutory interference being cases of interlocutory disqualifications or suspensions which may have grave, immediate and irreversible repercussions and consequence.

H) That Paragraph 6(1) of the Tenth Schedule, to the extent it seeks to impart finality to the decision of the Speakers / Chairmen is valid. But the concept of statutory finality embodied in Paragraph 6(1) does not detract from or abrogate judicial review under Articles 136, 226 and 227 of the Constitution in so far as infirmities based on violations of constitutional mandates, malafides, non-compliance with Rules of Natural Justice and perversity, are concerned.

I) That the deeming provision in Paragraph 6(2) of the Tenth Schedule attracts an immunity analogous to that in Articles 122(1) and 212(1) of the Constitution as understood and explained in Keshav Singh's Case (Spl.Ref.No.1, (1965 (1) SCR 413) to protect the validity of proceedings from mere irregularities of procedure. The deeming provision, having regard to the words "be deemed to be proceedings in Parliament" or "proceedings in the Legislature of a State" confines the scope of the fiction accordingly.

J) That contention that the investiture of adjudicatory functions in the Speakers / Chairmen would be itself vitiate the provision on the ground of likelihood of political bias is unsound and is rejected. The Speakers / Chairmen hold a pivotal position in the scheme of Parliamentary democracy and are guardians of the rights and priviledges of the House. They are expected to and do take far reaching decisions in the functioning of Parliamentary democracy. Vestiture of power to adjudicate questions under the Tenth Schedule in such a constitutional functionaries should not be considered exceptionable.

K) In the view we take of the validity of Paragraph 7 it is unnecessary to pronounce on the contention that judicial review is a basic structure of the Constitution and Paragraph 7 of the Tenth Schedule violates such basic structure.

6. The factual controversies raised in the Writ Petition will, however, have to be decided by the High Court applying the principles declared and laid down by this judgment. The Writ Petition is, accordingly, remitted to the High Court for such disposal in accordance with law.

CONCLUSION:

1. The Judgement in Kihoto Hollohon vs Zachillhu and Others upholding the constitutional validity of this 52nd amendment, the court observed that the anti-defection law seeks to recognise the practical need to place the proprieties of political and personal conduct...above certain theoretical assumptions". The court finally held that the law does not violate any rights of free speech or basic structure of the parliamentary democracy.
2. Another important aspect of this judgment is the final decision making authority on declaring the defection. The court made it clear that the presiding officer is the one to make the decision and it is final subject to judicial review after the decision is pronounced and effected.
3. It was held by the minority judges held that the basic feature of the Constitution has been violated as the Constitutional scheme for decisions on questions on disqualification of members after being duly elected, contemplates adjudication of such disputes by an independent authority outside the House, namely President or Governor in accordance with the opinion of the Election Commission, all of which who high Constitutional functionaries are. The Election Commission had a similar opinion as that of the minority judges in the present case. In the year 1977, it made recommendations and suggested that the disqualification on grounds of defection could also be referred to the Election Commission for tendering opinion to the President or the Governor, as the case may be, and the President or the Governor shall act on such opinion tendered by the Election Commission, as it was in the case of other disqualifications referred to in articles 102 and 191 of the constitution.

It was thus held that the para 6 of the Tenth Schedule does not introduce a non-justiciable area. The power to resolve the disputes of the Speaker/ Chairman is a judicial power. The important construction is that of the 'finality clause' which paved a way for the majority to reach the judgment.

The anti-defection law enabled the political parties to have stronger grip on their members which many times has resulted into preventing them to vote for the lure of money of minister ship. However, it is also resulted into its unintended outcome i.e. the curtailing to a certain extent the role of the MP or member of state legislature. It is culminated into absence of constructive debates on critical policy issues. The whip has become all the more powerful and has to be followed in all circumstances

CHAPTER SEVEN

Indra Sawhney & Ors v. Union of India & Ors [1992] 2 Suppl. SCR 454 : (1992) Supp (3) SCC 217

(Also known as the Mandal verdict. Supreme Court, in its verdict, upheld the government order, being of the opinion that caste was an acceptable indicator of backwardness. The Supreme Court of India gave verdict that 27% central government reservation for OBCs is valid. This judgement also overruled General Manager Southern Railway v. Rangachari and Akhil Bharatiya Soshit Karamchari Sangh (Railway) v. Union of India verdicts, which said that reservations could be made in promotions as well as appointments. Indra Sawhney v. Union of India held that reservations cannot be applied in promotions. 1992 Indra Sawhney & Others v. Union of India judgment laid down the limits of the state's powers: it upheld the ceiling of 50 per cent quotas, emphasized the concept of "social backwardness", and prescribed 11 indicators to ascertain backwardness. The nine-Judge Bench judgement also established the concept of qualitative exclusion, such as "creamy layer".**)**

FACTS OF THE CASE :-

1. On January 1, 1979, the Government headed by the PM Sri Morarji Desai designated the second Backward Classes commission u/a 340 of the Constitution to research the SEBCs inside the region of India and prescribe ventures to be taken for their progressions.

2. The commission presents its report in December 1980 and recognized 3743 stations as socially and instructively in backward classes and prescribe

a booking for their 27 % Government employments for them.

3. Due to inward disagreements, Janta Government fallen and Congress party headed by PM Smt. Indira Gandhi came to control at the middle. The Congress government didn't execute the commission report till 1989.

4. In 1989 the Congress party vanquished and Janta government again came to control and issued Office Memoranda to execute the commission report as it guaranteed to the electorate. In the wake of passing this reminder tossed the country into unrest and a rough hostile to reservation development shook the country for three months bringing about tremendous loss of people and property.

5. On 1 October 1990 a writ request of for the benefit of the Supreme Court Bar Association was filled testing the legitimacy of the O.M. furthermore, to stay its task. The five-judge seat of the court remained the task of OM till the last transfer of the case. •Unfortunately, the Janta Government again fallen because of rebellions and Congress party again came to control at the inside headed by P.V. Narasimha Rao issued another O.M. on September 25, 1991 by presenting the financial standard in conceding reservation by offering inclination to the poorer areas of SEBCs in the 27 % quantity and saved another 10% of opportunities for different SEBCs monetarily in backward segments of higher rank.

ISSUE RAISED BEFORE THE COURT :-

1. Whether the classification is based on the caste or economic basis?
2. Whether the Article 16 (4) is exception of article 16 (1) or not?
3. Whether in Article 16 (4) backward classes are similiar as SEBCS in Article 15 (4) or not?
4. Would making "any provision" under Article 16(4) for reservation "by the state" necessarily have to be by law made by the legislatures of the state or by law made by parliament? Or could such provisions be made by an executive order?
5. Whether the classification between backward class into backward or more back ward class is valid or not?

PETITIONER`S ARGUMENT:

The extension of reservation violated the Constitutional guarantee of equality of opportunity.

Caste was not a reliable indicator of backwardness.

The efficiency of public institutions was at risk.

RESPONDENT`S ARGUMENT:

The respondent State said that the report merely gives the backward classes a means to fulfil their just claims. They argued that the report was a continuation of the first minorities commission which also recommended affirmative action to right the wrongs that backward classes have faced for centuries together.

JUDGMENT:-

Five-judge Bench of Supreme Court referred the issue to a Nine Judge Constitution Bench of Supreme Court in perspective of the significance of the issue to at long last settle the lawful position identifying with reservation. Decision given by the 6:3 majority held that the decision of the Union Government to hold 27% Government occupations for SEBCs gave them Creamy layer among them dispensed with is constitutionally valid. Apex Court struck down the second provision of Office Memoranda and held that holding 10% Government occupations for monetarily in backward classes among higher class is not valid.

Following were the significant proclamations.

1. Backward classes in Article 16(4) were not like as socially and educationally backward in article 15(4).

2. Creamy layer must be barred from the backward classes.

3. Article 16(4) grants characterization of backward classes into backward & more backward classes.

4. A backward class of citizen can't be distinguished just and solely with reference to financial criteria.

5. Reservation should not exceed 50%.

6. Reservation can be made by the Executive Order.

7. No reservation in promotion.

8. Permanent Statutory body to look at whines of over – inclusion /under – inclusion.

9. Majority held that there is no need to express any opinion on the accuracy or ampleness of the activity done by the Mandal Commission.

10. Disputes with respect to new criteria can only be raised in the Supreme Court. Commonly, the reservations kept both under Article 16(1) and 16(4) together ought not to surpass 50% of the appointments in a grade, unit or administration in a specific year. It is just for additional normal reasons that this rate might be surpassed.

1.

CHAPTER EIGHT

S.R. Bommai & Ors. v. Union of India & Ors. [1994] 2 SCR 644 : (1994) 3 SCC 1

(The exercise of power by the President under Article 356(1) to issue Proclamation is subject to the judicial review The Court described Federalism and Secularism as a part of the Basic Structure. It also overruled the judgement given in State of Rajasthan, which stated that the President's decision is not fit to be a subject matter of Judicial review and strengthens the federal structure)

BENCH: S. Ratnavel Pandian, A.M. Ahmadi, P.B. Sawant, K. Ramaswamy, S.C. Agrawal, YogeshwarDayal, B.P. Jeevan Reddy, Kuldip Singh.

FACTS OF CASE:-

1. S.R. Bommai was the Chief Minister in Karnataka between August 13, 1988, and April 21, 1989, representing the Janta Dal. His government was dismissed on April 21, 1989, under Article 356 of the Constitution and President's Rule was imposed on grounds that the incumbent government does not have majority due to the defection of a large number of MLAs.

2. Then-Governor, despite receiving 19 letters from Bommai refused to give him an opportunity to prove his party's majority in the Assembly. Bommai went to court against the Governor's decision to dismiss his government and impose President's Rule under the said Article. He approached the High Court first, which dismissed his writ petition as a result of which, he sought remedy from the Supreme Court.

3. On the other hand, Indira Gandhi had constituted a commission in 1983 headed by Justice Ranjeet Singh Sarkaria on Centre-State relations which submitted its report in 1988. The Sarkaria commission suggested that Article 356 must be used only in extreme cases, as a measure of last resort where all other alternatives have been exhausted or fail to prevent or rectify a breakdown of constitutional machinery in the States, which was also what the intention of the Constitution framers all along. The report of the commission was obviously not binding on the legislature but the Supreme Court took the recommendation into consideration it in the S.R. Bommai case.

4. Apart from the central issue of the political misuse of Article 356 and federalism, the judgement also discussed the idea of Secularism.

ISSUES RAISED BEFORE THE COURT:

There were 3 main issues raised in this case, which are as follows-

1. Is the Proclamation issued by the President under Article 356, amenable to judicial review?
2. If yes, what is the scope of judicial review in this respect?
3. What is the meaning of the expression "A situation has arisen in which the Government of the State cannot be carried on in accordance with the provisions of this Constitution" used in Art. 356(1)?

JUDGMENT:

1. The court held that "*the exercise of power by the President under Article 356(1) to issue Proclamation is subject to the judicial review at least to the extent of examining whether the conditions precedent to the issuance of the Proclamation have been satisfied or not. This examination will necessarily involve the scrutiny as to whether there existed material for the satisfaction of the President that a situation had arisen in which the Government of the State could not be carried on in accordance with the provisions of the Constitution.*"[2]

2. It also held that "*the President has no power to dissolve the Legislative Assembly of the State by using his power under Art. 356(1) till the Proclamation is approved by both the Houses of Parliament under clause (3) of the said article. He may have power only to suspend the Legislative Assembly under sub-clause (c) of clause (1) of the said article.*"[3] Hence, it can be said that clause (3) keeps the powers of the President in check.

3. The power to overrule the Proclamation issued by the President whether it is approved by Parliament or not. This will mean that the courts

also have the power to restore the status quo and, therefore, "*to restore the Council of Ministers and the Legislative Assembly as they stood on the date of the issuance of the Proclamation.*" In other words, the proclamation comes under the purview of Judicial Review. When called upon, the Union of India has to produce the material on the basis of which action was taken.

4. The courts also stated that they do not agree with the opinion given in *State of Rajasthan* judgment, hence overruling it by this judgement.

5. The Court supported the finding of the Sarkaria Commission by endorsing the guidelines given in its report, including the issuance of "*warning to the errant State that it is not carrying on the government of the State in accordance with the provisions of the Constitution*"(except in cases of urgency), along with other procedural recommendations.

6. If the Ministry of State resigns or dismissed or loses majority then Governor can't advise President to impose President's Rule until enough measures are taken by Governor for formation an alternative Government. The court will have the liberty to provide a suitable relief according to the facts of the case and the political circumstances of the time and declare as void action taken by the president till date.

7. The court also reiterated that, "*Secularism is one of the basic features of the Constitution. Any State Government which pursues unsecular policies or unsecular course of action acts contrary to the Constitutional mandate and renders itself amenable to action under Article 356.*"

7. The Court set aside the judgment of the Karnataka High Court and restored the dismissed state government of Karnataka and Meghalaya, declaring that the proclamations issued in both the states are unconstitutional. The proclamations issued for the states of Madhya Pradesh, Himachal Pradesh and Rajasthan were not declared unconstitutional. The Court also issued appropriate directives in relation to the proclamation issued for the State of Nagaland.

CASES OF ALLEGED MISUSE:

1. Arunachal Pradesh government - In 2016, the incumbent government was locked down by the Governor, under Article 356, when the 21 MLAs of the majority party defected to another party and the Governor summoned the Assembly earlier than scheduled with the intention to topple the State government. Supreme Court restored the NabamTuki Government in Arunachal Pradesh and criticised the Governor for "humiliating the elected Government of the day." It also demanded a floor test to ascertain Government's majority.[10]

2. Uttarakhand goverment - In the same year, the Central Government imposed President's Rule in the state just a day before the floor test in the State assembly was scheduled. The Centre justified its actions on the basis of a sting operation showing the Chief Minister indulging in bribery with some of the MLAs. The Supreme Court ordered a floor test, which ultimately led the dismissed government being reinstated.

3. Jammu and Kashmir goverment -The State of Jammu and Kashmir was under President's Rule since June 2018 and on 30th October, 2019 it was lifted so that the Jammu and Kashmir Reorganisation Act, 2019 could be passed. The state was divided into 2 Union Territories of Jammu-Kashmir and Ladakh. The passing of the Act was enabled by amending Article 367. After this amendment, Constituent Assembly was made equal to the state legislature. The state was under President's rule at this time, making the Governor the representative of the State Legislature. So, the Central Government with due consent of the Governor, passed the said Act bifurcating the state into 2 Union Territories. Many legal analysts and lawyers hailed this as misuse of Article 356 and a loophole in the law. They claimed that this disregarded the wishes of the State Legislature completely, while handing over all the powers related to Article 370 to the Central government.

4. Maharashtra goverment - The State of Maharashtra was under President's Rule from 12th November, 2019 to 23rd November, 2019. The proclamation was revoked early in the morning without any meeting or recommendation by the Union Cabinet, by invoking Rule 12 of the Government of India (Transaction of Business) Rules. The Rule says that the Prime Minister may, in any case or classes of cases, permit or condone a departure from these rules, to the extent he deems necessary." The prime minister gave this approval, which acts as post-facto approval of the Union Cabinet. It has been alleged that the invocation as well as revocation of President's Rule was done to benefit the Ruling Party at the Centre.

IMPORTANCE OF THE JUDGMENT:

1. The judgement given in S.R. Bommai strengthens the federal structure in India.

2. Due autonomy to states and barring the interference of Central government in the functioning of government machinery.

3. The judgement specifies the extent of Judicial review, thereby keeping the scale of checks and balances.

3. It aimed to curb the political misuse of Article 356, but recent events demonstrate how these provisions are used for political gains by the parties in power.

4. These events have been repeatedly observed even after the pronouncement of this landmark judgement but the judiciary has actively preserved the federal system. An amendment to the Article is required to reduce the frequency of imposition of President's Rule in states.

CHAPTER NINE

L. Chandra Kumar v. Union of India & Others [1994] 6 Suppl. SCR 261 : (1995) 1 SCC 400

(Tribunals cannot act as substitutes for High-Courts and the Supreme Court. Their decisions will be subject to scrutiny by a Division Bench of the respective High-Courts i.e. all decisions of these tribunals. Section 28 of the Administrative Tribunals Act, 1985 which states "exclusion of jurisdiction" would be ultra-vires the Constitution.)

FACTS OF THE CASE:-

1. Law Commission in 1958 recommended for the establishment of tribunals consisting of judicial and administrative members to decide service matters to relieve the courts, including High Courts and the Supreme Court, from the burden of service litigation which formed a substantial portion of pending litigation. In 1969 Administrative Reform Commission also recommended for the establishment of civil service tribunals both for the Central and State civil servants.

2. In 1975, Swarn Singh Committee again recommended for setting up of service tribunals. It was against this backdrop that Parliament passed Constitution (Forty- Second Amendment) Act, 1976, which added Part-XIV- A in the Constitution. This Part is entitled as 'Tribunals' and consists of only two Articles- Article 323- A, dealing with administrative tribunals and Article 323-B, dealing with tribunals for other matters .

BRIEF INTRODUCTION TO ART.323:-

While Article 323-A contemplates establishment of tribunals for public service matters only, Article 323-B contemplates establishment of tribunals for certain other matters (taxation, foreign exchange, industrial and labour disputes, land reforms, elections to Parliament and State Legislatures etc.)

While tribunals under Article 323-A can be established only by the Parliament, tribunals under Article 323-B can be established both by Parliament and State Legislatures with respect to matters falling within their legislative competence.

Under Article 323-A, only one tribunal for the Centre and one for each State or two or more States may be established, there is no question of hierarchy of tribunals; whereas under Article 323-B a hierarchy of tribunals may be created.

There were special leave petitions, civil appeals and writ petitions pertaining to the constitutional validity of subclause (d) of clause (2) of Article 323-A and sub-clause (d) of clause (3) of Article 323-B of the Constitution of India, 1950; and also in regards to the constitutional validity of the Administrative Tribunals Act, 1985; moreover what was also the subject of challenge was whether the Tribunals constituted under Part XIV-A of the Constitution of India can be effective substitutes for the High-Courts in discharging the power of judicial review.

ISSUES BEFORE THE COURT:-

1. Whether the Tribunals, constituted either under Article 323-A, or under Article 323-B of the Constitution, possess the competence to test the constitutional validity of a statutory provision/rule?
2. Whether these Tribunals, as they are functioning at present, can be said to be effective substitutes for the High-Courts in discharging the power of judicial review? If not, what are the changes required to make them conform to their founding objectives?
3. Whether the power conferred upon Parliament or State Legislatures, as the case may be, by sub-clause (d) of clause (2) of Article 323-A or by sub-clause (d) of clause (3) of Article 323-B of the Constitution, totally exclude the jurisdiction of all courts, except that of the Supreme Court under Article 136, in respect of disputes and complaints referred to in clause (1) of Article 323-A or with regard to all or any of the matters specified in clause (2) of Article 323-B, runs counter to the power of judicial review conferred on the High-Courts under Articles 226/227 and on the Supreme Court under Article 32 of the Constitution?

In pursuance of the power conferred upon it by Clause

1. of Article 323- A of the Constitution, the Parliament enacted the Administrative Tribunals Act, 1985.
2. Pursuant to the provisions of the Administrative Tribunals Act 1985, the Central Administrative Tribunal (CAT) comprising of five Benches was established on 1 November 1985. However, even before CAT had been established, several writ petitions had been filed in various high-courts as well as the Supreme Court challenging the constitutional validity of Article 323- A, as also the provisions of the Administrative Tribunals Act 1985.
3. The exclusion of judicial review under Articles 226, 227 and 32 was questioned as violating the basic structure of the Constitution in S.P. Sampath Kumar v.UOI.
4. In S.P. Sampath Kumar v. UOI, in the final decision the Court held that Section 28 which excludes jurisdiction of the High-Courts under Articles 226/227 is not unconstitutional. The Court ruled that this section does not totally bar judicial review. It also said that Administrative Tribunals under the 1985 Act are substitute of High- Courts and will deal with all service matters even involving Articles 14, 15 and 16. It also advised for changing the qualifications of Chairman of the tribunal.
5. In J.B. Chopra and Ors v. UOI, AIR 1987 SC 357, a Division Bench of the Supreme Court held that "the Administrative Tribunal being a substitute power of the High Court had the necessary jurisdiction, power and authority to adjudicate upon all disputes relating to service matters including the power to deal with all questions pertaining to the Constitutional validity or otherwise of such laws as offending Articles 14 and 16(1) of the Constitution."
6. In M.B. Majumdar v. UOI, AIR 1990 SC 2263, The court, after analysing-the text of Article 323-A of the Constitution, the provisions of the impugned Act, and the decision in Sampath Kumar, rejected the contention that the tribunals were the equals of the high-courts in respect of their service conditions.
7. In R.K. Jain v. UOI, (1993) 4 SCC 119, Justice Ramaswamy analysed the relevant constitutional provisions; the decision in Sampath Kumar, J.B. Chopra and M.B. Majumdar, and held that the tribunals created under Articles 323-A and 323-B could not be held to be substitutes of High-Courts for the purpose of exercising jurisdiction under Articles 226 and

227 of the Constitution.

8. In L. Chandra Kumar v. UOI, (1995) 1 SCC 400, a Division Bench of the Supreme Court expressed the view that the decision rendered by the Constitutional Bench of five Judges in Sampath Kumar case needed to be "comprehensively reconsidered", and a "fresh look by a larger Bench over all the issues adjudicated in Sampath Kumar case was necessary". In the light of the opinion of the Division Bench, the matter was placed before a larger Bench of seven Judges.

JUDGMENT:-

The power of judicial review is a basic and essential feature of the Constitution and the jurisdiction conferred on High Courts under Articles 226 and 227 and on Supreme Court under Article 32 of the Constitution is a part of the basic structure of the Constitution.

For securing independence of judiciary, the judges of superior courts have been entrusted with the power of judicial review. Though the Parliament is empowered to amend the Constitution, the power of amendment cannot be exercised so as to damage the essential feature of the Constitution or to destroy its basic structure.

The High Courts and the Supreme Court have been entrusted with the task of upholding the Constitution (i.e. furthering the ends of the Constitution) and with a view to achieving that end, they have to interpret the Constitution.

1. The Court held that Section 28 of the Administrative Tribunals Act, 1985 and the "exclusion of jurisdiction" clauses in all other legislations enacted under the aegis of Articles 323-A and 323-B would, to the extent that they exclude the jurisdiction of the High-Courts (under Articles 226 and 227) and the Supreme Court (under Article 32) would be ultra-vires the Constitution.
2. The Court held that there was no Constitutional prohibition against administrative tribunals in performing a supplemental as opposed to a substitutional role; that is in exercising their powers such tribunals cannot act as substitutes for High-Courts and the Supreme Court. Their decisions will be subject to scrutiny by a Division Bench of the respective High-Courts i.e. all decisions of these tribunals (tribunals created under Articles 323-A and 323-B of the Constitution of India) will be subject to scrutiny before a Division Bench of the High Court within

whose jurisdiction the concerned tribunal falls.

3. Lastly, the Court upheld Section 5(6) of the Administrative Tribunals Act, 1985 as valid and constitutional and held that Sections 5(2) and 5(6) of the Act must operate together and must be harmoniously construed i.e. where a question involving the interpretation of a statutory provision or rule in relation to the Constitution arises for consideration of a single Member Bench of the Administrative Tribunal, the proviso to section 5(6) will automatically apply and the Chairman or the Member concerned shall refer the matter to a Bench consisting of at least two Members, one of whom must be a Judicial Member.

CHAPTER TEN

Vellore Citizens Welfare Forum vs Union of India & Ors. [1996] 5 Suppl. SCR 241 : (1996) 5 SCC 647

Top of Form

on 28 August, 1996

(Looking on sustainable development, "precautionary principle" and the "polluter pays" principle was implemented.)

Bench: Kuldip Singh, Faizan Uddin, K. Venkataswami

FACTS OF THE CASE:

1. This petition - public interest – under Article 32 of the Constitution of India has been filed by Vellore Citizens Welfare Forum and is directed against the pollution which is being caused by enormous discharge of untreated effluent by the tanneries and other industries in the State of Tamil Nadu . It is stated that the tanneries are discharging untreated effluent into agricultural fields to, road-Sides, Water ways and open lands. The untreated effluent is finally discharged in river Palar which is the main source of water supply to the residents of the area.

2. According to the petitioner the entire surface and sub-soil water of river Palar has been polluted resulting in non availability Potable water to the residents of the area. It is stated that the tanneries in the State of Tamil Nadu have caused environmental degradation in the area. According to the preliminary survey made by the Tamil Nadu Agricultural University Research Center Vellore nearly 35,000 hectares of agricultural land in the Tanneries Belt, has become either partially or totally unfit for cultivation.

It has been further stated in the petition that the tanneries use about 170 types of chemicals in the chrome tanning processes.

3. The said chemicals include sodium chloride, lime, sodium sulphate, chlorium sulphate, fat liquor Amonia and sulphuric acid besides dyes which are used in large quantities. Nearly 35 litres of water is used for processing one kilogram of finished leather, resulting in dangerously enormous quantities of toxic effluents being let out in the open by the tanning industry.

4. Thus these effluents have spoiled the physico-chemical properties of the soil, and have contaminated ground water by percolation.

JUDGMENT:

In the Government Order first read above, the Government have ordered, among other things, that no industry causing serious water pollution should be permitted with in one kilometer from the embankments of rivers, streams, dams etc, and that the Tamil Nadu Pollution Control Board Should furnish a list of such industries to all local bodies. It has been suggested that it is necessary to have a sharper definition for water sources so that ephemeral water collections like rein water ponds, drains, sewerages (bio-degradable) etc. may be excluded form the purview of the above order. The Chairman, Tamil Nadu Pollution Control Board has stated that the scope of the Government Order may be restricted to reservoirs, rivers and public drinking water sources.

He has also stated that there should be a complete ban on location of highly polluting industries within 1 Kilometer of certain water sources.

2. The Government have carefully examined the above suggestions. The Government impose a total ban on the setting up of the highly polluting industries mentioned in Annexure - I to this order ' within one Kilometer from the embankments of the water sources mentioned in Annexure-II to this order.

3. The Government direct that under any circumstance if any highly polluting industry is proposed to be set up within one kilometer from the embankments of water sources other than those mentioned in Annexure-II to this order, the Tamil Nadu Pollution Control Board should examine the case and obtain the approval of the Government for it".

Annexure-I to the Notification includes Distilleries, tanneries, fertilizer, steel plants and foundries as the highly polluting industries. We have our doubts whether the above quoted government order is being enforced by the Tamil Nadu Government. The order has been issued to control pollution and protect the environment. We are of the view that the order should be strictly enforced and no industry listed in Annexure-l to the order should be permitted to be set up in the prohibited area.

Learned counsel for the tanneries raised an objection that the standard regarding total dissolved solids (TDS) fixed by the Board was no. justified. This Court by the order date April 9, 1996 directed the NEERI to examine this aspect and give its opinion. In its report dated June 11, 1996 NEERI has justified the standards stipulated by the Board. The reasoning of the NEERI given in its report dated June 11, 1996 is as under:

"The total dissolved solids in ambient water have phisiological, industrial and economic significance. The consumer acceptance of mineralized water decreases in direct proportion to increased mineralization as indicated by Bruvold (1). High Total dissolved solids (TDS), including chlorides and sulphates, are objectionable due to possible physiological effect and mineral taste that they impart to water. High levels of total dissolved solids produce Laxative/cathartic/purgative effect in consumers. the requirement of soap and other detergents in household and industry is directly related to water hardness as brought out by DeBoer and Larsen (2). High concentration of mineral salts, particularly sulphates and chlorides, are also associated with costly corrosion damage in wastewater treatment systems, as detailed by patterson and Banker (3). Of par particular importance is the tendency of scale deposits with high TDS thereby resulting in high fuel consumption in boilers. The Ministry of Environment and forests (MEF) has not categorically laid down standards for inland surface water discharge for total dissolved solids (TDS), sulphates and chlorides. The Decision on these standards rests with the respective state Pollution Control Boards as per the requirements based on local site conditions. The standards stipulated by the TNPCB are justified on the aforereffered considerations.

The prescribed standards of the TNPCB for inland surfaces water discharge can be met for tannery wastewaters cost-effectively through proper implant control measures in tanning operation, and rationally designed and effectively operated wastewater treatment plants (ETPs & CETPs). Tables 3 and 5 depict the quality of groundwater in some areas around tanneries during peak summer period (June 3- 5, 1996). Table 8 presents the data collection by TNPCB at individual ETPs indicating that TDS, sulphates and chlorides concentrations are below the prescribed standards for inland surface water discharge. The quality of ambient waters needs to the maintained through the standards stipulated by TNPCB."

The Board has Power under the Environment Act and the Rules to lay down standards for emissions or discharge of environmental Pollutants. Rule 3(2) of the Rules even permit the Board to specify more stringent standards from those provided under the Rules. The NEERI having justified the standards stipulated by the Board, We direct that these standards are to be maintained by the tanneries and other industries in the State of Tamil Nadu.

DIRECTIONS OF COURT:

1. The Central Government shall constitute an authority under Section 3(3) of the Environment (Protection) Act, 1986 and shall confer on the said authority all the powers necessary to deal with the situation created by the tanneries and other polluting industries in the State of Tamil Nadu. The Authority shall be headed by a retired judge of the High Court and it may have other members- preferably with expertise in the field of pollution control and environment protection- to be appointed by the Central Government. The Central Government shall confer on the said authority the powers to issue directions under Setion 5 of the Environment Act and for taking measures with respect to the matters referred to in Clause (v), (vi) (vii) (viii) (ix) (x) and (xii) of Sub-Section (2) of Setion 3. The Central Government shall consitute the authority before September 30, 1996.

2. The authority so constituted by the Central Government shall implement the "precautionary principle" and the "polluter pays" principle. The authority shall, with the help of expert opinion and after giving opportunity to the concerned polluters assess the loss to the ecology\ environment in the affected areas and shall also identify the individuals/ families who have suffered because of the pollution and shall assess the compensation to be paid to the said individuals/families. The authority shall further determine the compensation to be recovered from the polluters as cost of reversing the damaged environment. The authority shall lay down just and fair procedure for completing the exercise.

3. The authority shall compute the compensation under two heads namely, for reversing the ecology and for payment to individuals. A statement showing the total amount to be recovered, the names of the polluters from who the amount is to be recovered, the amount to be recovered from each polluter, the persons to who the compensation is to be paid and the amount payable to each of them shall be forwarded to the Collector\District Magistrates of the area concerned. The Collector\ District magistrate shall recover the amount from the polluters, if necessary,

as arrears of land revenue. He shall disburse the compensation awarded by the authority to be affected persons/families.

4. The authority shall direct the closure of the industry owned/managed by a polluter in case he evades or refuses to pay the compensation awarded against him. This shall be in addition to the recovery from his as arrears of land revenue.

5. An industry may have set up the necessary pollution control device at present but it shall be liable to pay for the past pollution generated by the said industry which has resulted in the environmental degradation and suffering to the residents of the area.

6. We impose pollution fine of Rs. 10,000/- each on all the tanneries in the districts of North Arcot Ambedkar, Erode Periyar, Dindigul Anna, Trichi and Chengai M.G.R. The fine shall be paid before October 31, 1996 in the office of the Collector/District Magistrate concerned. We direct the Collectors/District Magistrates of these districts to recover the fines from the tanneries. The money shall be deposited, alongwith the compensation amount recovered from the polluters, under a separate head called "Environment protection Fund" and shall be utilised for compensating the affected persons as identified by the authorities and also for restoring the damaged environment. The pollution fine is liable to the recovered as arrears of land revenue. The tanneries which fail to deposit the amount by October 31, 1996 shall be closed forthwith and shall also be liable under the Contempt of Court Act.

7. The authority, in consultation with expert bodies like NEERI, Central Board, Board shall frame scheme/schemes for reversing the damage caused to the ecology and environment by pollution in the State of Tamil Nadu. The scheme/schemes so framed shall be executed by the State Government under the supervision of the Central Government. The expenditure shall be met from the "Environment protection fund" and from other sources provided by the state Government and the Central Government.

8. We suspend the closure orders in respect of all the tanneries in the five districts of North Arcot Ambedkar, Erode Periyar, Dindigul Anna, Trichi and Chengai M.G.R. We direct all the tanneries in the above five districts to set up CETPs or Individual Pollution control Devices on or before November 30, 1996. Those connected with CETPs shall have to install in addition the primary devices in the tanerries. All the tanneries in the above five districts shall obtain the consent of the Board to function and operate with effect from December 15, 1996. The tanneries who are refused

consent or who fail to obtain the consent of the Board by December 15, 1996 shall be closed forthwith.

9. We direct the Superintendent of Police and the Collector/district Magistrate/Deputy Commissioner of the district concerned to close all those tanneries with immediate effect who fail to obtain the consent from the Board by the said date. Such tanneries shall not be reopened unless the authority permits them to do so. It would be open to the authority to close such tanneries permanently or to direct their relocation.

10. The Government Order No. 213 dated March 30, 1989 shall be enforced forthwith. No. new industry listed in Annexure-I to the Notification shall be permitted to be set up within the prohibited area. The authority shall review the case of all the industries which are already operating in the prohibited area and it would be open to authority to direct the relocation of any of such industries.

11. The standards stipuated by the Board regarding total dissolved solids (TDS) and approved by the NEERI shall be operative. All the tanneries and other industries in the State of Tamil Nadu shall comply with the said standards. The quality of ambient waters has to be maintained through the standards stipulated by the Board.

We have issued comprehensive directions for achieving the end result in this case. It is not necesary for this Court to monitor these matters any further. we are of the view that the Madras High Court would be in a better position to monitor these matters hereinafter. We, therefore, request the Chief Justice of the Madras High Court to constitute a special Bench "Green bench" to deal with this case and other environmental matters. We make it clear that it would be open to the Bench to pass any appropriate order/ orders keeping in view the directions issued by us. We may mention that "Green Benches" are already functioning in Calcutta, Madhya Pradesh and some other High Courts. We Direct the Registry of this Court to send the records to the registry of the Madras High matter as a petition under Article 226 of the Constitution of India and deal with it in accordance with law and also in terms of the directions issued by us. We give liberty to the parties to approach the High Court as and when necessary.

Mr. M.C. Mehta has been assisting this Court to our utmost satisfaction. We place on record our appreciation for Mr. Mehta. We direct the State of Tamil Nadu to pay Rs. 50,000/- towards legal fees and other out of pocket expenses incurred by Mr. Mehta.

CHAPTER ELEVEN

Shri D.K. Basu v. State of West Bengal [1996] 10 Suppl. SCR 284 : (1997) 1 SCC 416

On 18 December, 1996

(Due to custodial violence and deaths in police lock up, court has formulated certain guideline for police to check atrocities on accused / victim and compensation was also awarded by

Author: A. S. Anand

Bench: Kuldip Singh, A.S. Anand

FACT OF THE CASE:-

1. The Executive Chairman, Legal Aid Services, West Bengal, a non-political organisation registered under the Society Registration Act, on 26th August, 1986 addressed a letter to the Chief Justice of India drawing his attention to certain news items published in the Telegraph dated 20, 21 and 22 of July, 1986 and in the Statesman and Indian express dated 17th August, 1986 regarding deaths in police lock-ups and custody.
2. The Executive Chairman after reproducing the new items submitted that it was imperative to examine the issue in depth and to develop "custody jurisprudence" and formulate modalities for awarding compensation to the victim and /or family members of the victim for attrocities and death caused in police custody and to provide for accountability of the efforts are often made to hush up the matter of lock-up deaths and thus the crime goes unpunished and "flourishes". It was requested that the letter alongwith the new items be treated as a writ petition under "public interest litigation" category.

3. Considering the importance of the issue raised in the letter being concerned by frequent complaints regarding custodial violence and deaths in police lock up, the letter was treated as a writ petition and notice was issued on 9.2.1987 to the respondents.
4. In response to the notice, the State of West Bengal filed a counter. It was maintained that the police was no hushing up any matter of lock-up death and that where ever police personnel were found to be responsible for such death, action was being initiated against them. The respondents characterised the writ petition as misconceived, misleading and untenable in law.
5. While the writ petition was under consideration a letter addressed by Shri Ashok Kumar Johri on 29.7.87 to the Hon'ble Chief Justice of India drawing the attention of this Court to the death of one Mahesh Bihari of Pilkhana, Aligarh in police custody was received. That letter was also treated as a writ petition and was directed to be listed alongwith the writ petition filed by Shri D.K. Basu. On 14.8.1987 this Court made the following order :
6. Mr. D. K. Basu was one of the Petitioners in this case. He was Judge of Calcutta High Court and the Chairman of Legal Aid Services West Bengal (LASWEB). DK Basu, Executive Chairman of Legal Aid Services, West Bengal, a non-political organization on 26/08/1986 addressed a letter to the Supreme Court of India calling his attention to certain news published in the Telegraph Newspaper about deaths in police custody and custody. He requested that the letter be treated as a Writ Petition within the "Public Interest Litigation". Considering the importance of the issues raised in the letter, it was treated as a written Petition and the Defendants were notified.

JUDGMENT:

"Custodial torture" is a naked violation of human dignity and degradation with destroys, to a very large extent, the individual personality. IT is a calculated assault on human dignity and whenever human dignity is wounded, civilisation takes a step backward-flag of humanity must on each such occasion fly half-mast.

In all custodial crimes that is of real concern is not only infliction of body pain but the mental agony which a person undergoes within the four walls of police station or lock-up. Whether it is physical assault or rape in police custody, the extent of trauma a person experiences is beyond the purview of law.

"Custodial violence" and abuse of police power is not only peculiar to this country, but it is widespread. It has been the concern of international community because the problem is universal and the challenge is almost global. The Universal Declaration of Human Rights in 1984, which market the emergency of worldwide trend of protection and guarantee of certain basic human rights, stipulates in Article 5 that "No one shall be subjected to torture or to curel, inhuman or degrading treatment or punishment." Despite the pious declaration, the crime continues unabated, though every civilised nation shows its concern and takes steps for its eradication.

It was considering these aspects that the Law Commission in its 113th Report recommended the insertion of Section 114B in the Indian Evidence Act. The Law Commission recommended in its 113th Report that in prosecution of a police officer for an alleged offence of having caused bodily injury to a person, if there was evidence that the injury was caused during the period when the person was in the custody of the police, the Court may presume that the injury was caused by the police officer having the custody of the person during that period. The Commission further recommended that the court, while considering the question of presumption, should have regard to all relevant circumstances including the period of custody statement made by the victim, medical evidence and the evidence with the Magistrate may have recorded. Change of burden of proof was, thus, advocated.

Police is, no doubt, under a legal duty and has legitimate right to arrest a criminal and to interrogate him during the investigation of a an offence but it must be remembered that the law does not permit use of third degree methods or torture of accused in custody during interrogation and investigation with that view to solve the crime. End cannot justify the means. The interrogation and investigation into a crime should be in true sense purpose full to make the investigation effective. By torturing a person and using their degree methods, the police would be accomplishing behind the closed doors what the demands of our legal order forbid. No. society can permit it.

How do we check the abuse of police power? Transparency of action and accountability perhaps are tow possible safeguards which this Court must insist upon. Attention is also required to be paid to properly develop work culture, training and orientation of police force consistent with basic human values. Training methodology of the police needs restructuring. The force needs to be infused with basic human values and made sensitive to the constitutional ethos. Efforts must be made to change the attitude and approach of the police personal handling investigations so that they do not sacrifice basic human values during interrogation and do not resort to questionable form of interrogation. With a view to bring in transparency, the presence of the counsel of the arrestee at some point of time during the interrogation may deter the police from using third degree methods during interrogation.

Apart from the police, there are several other governmental authorities also like Directorate of Revenue Intelligence, Directorate of Enforcement, Costal Guard, Central Reserve Police Force (CRPF), Border Security Force (BSF), the Central Industrial Security Force (CISF), the State Armed Police, Intelligence Agencies like the Intelligence Bureau, R.A.W, Central Bureau of Investigation (CBI) , CID, Tariff Police, Mounted Police and ITBP which have the power to detain a person and to interrogated him in connection with the investigation of economic offences, offences under the Essential Commodities Act, Excise and Customs Act. Foreign Exchange Regulation Act etc. There are instances of torture and death in custody of these authorities as well, In re Death of Sawinder Singh Grover [1995 Supp (4) SCC, 450], (to which Kuldip Singh, j. was a party) this Court took suo moto notice of the death of Sawinder Singh Grover during his custody with the Directorate of Enforcement. After getting an enquiry conducted by the additional District Judge, which disclosed a prima facie case for investigation and prosecution, this Court directed the CBI to lodge a FIR and initiate criminal proceeding against all persons named in the report of the Additional District Judge and proceed against them. The Union of India/ Directorate of Enforcement was also directed to pay sum of Rs. 2 lacs to the widow of the deceased by was of the relevant provisions of law to protect the interest of arrested persons in such cases too is a genuine need.

There is one other aspect also which needs out consideration, We are conscious of the fact that the police in India have to perform a difficult and delicate task, particularly in view of the deteriorating law and order situation, communal riots, political turmoil, student unrest, terrorist activities, and among others the increasing number of underworld and armed gangs and criminals, Many hard core criminals like extremist, the terrorists, drug peddlers, smugglers who have organised gangs, have taken strong roots in the society. It is being said in certain quarters that with more and more liberalisation and enforcement of fundamental rights, it would lead to difficulties in the detection of crimes committed by such categories of hardened criminals by soft peddling interrogation. It is felt in those quarters that if we lay to much of emphasis on protection of their fundamental rights and human rights such criminals may go scot-free without exposing any element or iota or criminality with the result, the crime would go unpunished and in the ultimate analysis the society would suffer. The concern is genuine and the problem is real. To deal with such a situation, a balanced approach is needed to meet the ends of justice. This all the more so, in view of the expectation of the society that police must deal with the criminals in an efficient and effective manner and bring to book those who are involved in the crime. The cure cannot, however, be worst than the disease itself.

In addition to the statutory and constitutional requirements to which we have made a reference, we are of the view that it would be useful and effective to structure appropriate machinery for contemporaneous recording and notification of all cases of arrest and detention to bring in transparency and accountability. It is desirable that the officer arresting a person should prepare a memo of his arrest on witness who may be a member of the family of the arrestee or a respectable person of the locality from where the arrest is made. The date and time of arrest shall be recorded in The memo which must also be counter signed by The arrestee.

We therefore, consider it appropriate to issue the following requirements to be followed in all cases of arrest or detention till legal provisions are made in that behalf as preventive measures :

(1) The police personnel carrying out the arrest and handling the interrogation of the arrestee should bear accurate, visible and clear identification and name togs with their designations. The particulars of all such police personnel who handle interrogation of the arrestee must be recorded in a register.

(2) That the police officer carrying out the arrest of the arrestee shall prepare a memo of arrest at the time of arrest a such memo shall be attested by atleast one witness. who may be either a member of the family of the arrestee or a respectable person of the locality from where the arrest is made. It shall also be counter signed by the arrestee and shall contain the time and date of arrest. (3) A person who has been arrested or detained and is being held in custody in a police station or interrogation centre or other lock-up, shall be entitled to have one friend or relative or other person known to him or having interest in his welfare being informed, as soon as

practicable, that he has been arrested and is being detained at the particular place, unless the attesting witness of the memo of arrest is himself such a friend or a relative of the arrestee. (4) The time, place of arrest and venue of custody of an arrestee must be notified by the police where the next friend or relative of the arrestee lives outside the district or town through the legal Aid Organisation in the District and the police station of the area concerned telegraphically within a period of 8 to 12 hours after the arrest.

(5) The person arrested must be made aware of this right to have someone informed of his arrest or detention as soon he is put under arrest or is detained.

(6) An entry must be made in the diary at the place of detention regarding the arrest of the person which shall also disclose the name of he next friend of the person who has been informed of the arrest an the names and particulars of the police officials in whose custody the arrestee is. (7) The arrestee should, where he so requests, be also examined at the time of his arrest and major and minor injuries, if any present on his/her body, must be recorded at that time. The "Inspection Memo" must be signed both by the arrestee and the police officer effecting the arrest and its copy provided to the arrestee.

(8) The arrestee should be subjected to medical examination by trained doctor every 48 hours during his detention in custody by a doctor on the panel of approved doctors appointed by Director, Health Services of the concerned Stare or Union Territory. Director, Health Services should prepare such a penal for all Tehsils and Districts as well. (9) Copies of all the documents including the memo of arrest, referred to above, should be sent to the illaga Magistrate for his record.

(10) The arrestee may be permitted to meet his lawyer during interrogation, though not throughout the interrogation.

(11) A police control room should be provided at all district and state headquarters, where information regarding the arrest and the place of custody of the arrestee shall be communicated by the officer causing the arrest, within 12 hours of effecting the arrest and at the police control room it should be displayed on a conspicuous notice board.

Failure to comply with the requirements hereinabove mentioned shall apart from rendering the concerned official liable for departmental action, also render his liable to be punished for contempt of court and the proceedings for contempt of court may be instituted in any High Court of the country, having territorial jurisdiction over the matter.

The requirements, referred to above flow from Articles 21 and 22 (1) of the Constitution and need to be strictly followed. These would apply with equal force to the other governmental agencies also to which a reference has been made earlier.

These requirements are in addition to the constitutional and statutory safeguards and do not detract from various other directions given by the courts from time to time in connection with the safeguarding of the rights and dignity of the arrestee.

The requirements mentioned above shall be forwarded to the Director General of Police and the Home Secretary of every Stare/Union Territory and it shall be their obligation to circulate the same to every police station under their charge and get the same notified at every police station at conspicuous place. It would also be useful and serve larger interest to broadcast the requirements on the All India Radio besides being shown on the National network of Doordarshan and by publishing and distributing pamphlets in the local language containing these requirements for information of the general public. Creating awareness about the rights of the arrestee would in out opinion be a step in the right direction to combat the evil of custodial crime and bring in transparency and accountability. It is hoped that these requirements would help to curb, if not totally eliminate, the use of questionable methods during interrogation and investigation leading to custodial commission of crimes.

PUNITIVE MEASURES UBI JUS IBI REMEDIUM - There is no wrong without a remedy. The law will that in every case where man is wronged and undamaged he must have a remedy. A mere declaration of invalidity of an action or finding of custodial violence or death in lock-up does not by itself provide any meaningful remedy to a person whose fundamental right to life has been infringed. Much more needs to be done.

A similar approach of redressing the wrong by award of monetary compensation against the State for its failure to protect the fundamental rights of the citizen has been adopted by the Courts of Ireland, which has a written constitution, guaranteeing fundamental rights, but which also like the Indian Constitution contains no provision of remedy for the infringement of those rights. That has, however, not prevented the Court in Ireland from developing remedies, including the award of damages, not only against individuals guilty of infringement, but against the State itself.

Thus, to sum up, it is now a well accepted proposition in most of the jurisdictions, that monetary or pecuniary compensation is an appropriate and indeed an effective and sometimes perhaps the only suitable remedy for redressal of the established infringement of the fundamental right to life of a citizen by the public servants and the State is vicariously liable for their acts. The claim of the citizen is based on the principle of strict liability to which the defence of sovereign immunity is not available and the citizen must revive the amount of compensation from the State, which shall have the right to be indemnified by the wrong doer. In the assessment of compensation, the emphasis has to be on the compensatory and not on punitive element. The objective is to apply balm to the wounds and not to punish the transgressor or the offender, as awarding appropriate punishment for the offender, as awarding appropriate punishment for the offence (irrespective of compensation) must be left to the criminal courts in which the offender is prosecuted, which the State, in law, is duty bound to do, That award of compensation in the public law jurisdiction is also without prejudice to any other action like civil suit for damages which is lawfully available to the victim or the heirs of the deceased victim with respect to the same matter for the tortious act committed by the functionaries of the State. The quantum of compensation will of course, depend upon the peculiar facts of each case and no strait jacket formula can be evolved in that behalf. The relief to redress the wrong for the established invasion of the fundamental rights of the citizen, under the public law jurisdiction is, in addition to the traditional remedies and not it derrogation of them. The amount of compensation as awarded by the Court and paid by the State to redress the wrong done, may in a given case, be adjusted against any amount which may be awarded to the claimant by way of damages in a civil suit.

CHAPTER TWELVE

Mafatlal Industries Ltd. Etc. Etc. v. Union Of India Etc. Etc [1996] 10 Suppl.SCR 585 : (1997) 5 SCC 536

On 19 December, 1996

Author: Paripoornan

Bench: Ahmadi A.M. (Cj), Verma, J.S. (J) Agrawal, S.C. (J), Jeevan Reddy, B.P. (J) Anand, A.S. (J), Hansaria B.L. Sen, S.C. (J), Paripoornan, K.S.(J) & (J)

FACTS OF THE CASE:-

1. Civil Appeal No.3255 of 1984 – Mafatlal Industries Ltd., Ahmdabad v Union of India. The appellant is a textile mill situate at Ahmedabad. The appellant and a few other mills manufacture "blended yarn". The said blended yarn was captively consumed by the various mills for manufacture of fabric, popularly known as "art silk" fabric. For the period prior to March 16/17, 1972, the mills paid excise duty on blended yarn manufactured for captive consumption under Tariff Item 18 or 18A of the First Schedule to the Excise Act.

2. In Special Application No.1058/72 filed by M/s. Calico Mills, who manufactured fabrics and was captively consuming blended yarn, produced by it for manufacturing fabric known as "art silk fabric", a Division Bench of the Gujarat High Court by judgment dated 15.1.1976, held that the levy of the excise duty on blended yarn prior to March 16/17, 1972, under tariff Item 18 or 18A was clearly ultra vires. The High Court directed refund of the excise duty levied for 3 years prior to institution of the petition, which

was instituted on 6.5.1972.

3. The appellant and other mill-owners stated that as a result of the declaration of the law as aforesaid by the Court, they were not liable to pay excise duty on blended yarn up to March 16/17, 1972 and that they had paid the excise duty on the same upto that date under mistake of law. They requested for refund of the excise duty so paid till March 16/17, 1972, stating that such duty was illegally recovered from them. The Revenue did not refund the excise duty as claimed. So, the appellant and others filed suits within three years of the aforesaid judgment (15.1.1976) for refund of excise duty illegally recovered from them, with interest.

4. The trial court decreed the suits. In the appeals filed by the Union of India against the aforesaid decrees passed by the trial court, the High Court of Gujarat allowed the appeals and set aside the decrees passed by the trial courts, by judgment dated 6.4.1984. It was held that in order to successfully sustain the claim of restitution based on Section 72 of the Contract Act, the person claiming restitution should prove "loss or injury" to him, and in the cases before them, the excise duty paid on blended yarn was ultimately passed on to the buyer of the fabric, and so the claim for restitution will not lie. In other words, in cases where an assessee has "passed on" the duty paid by or realised from him, he has suffered no loss or injury, and the action for restitution is unsustainable. The aforesaid statement of the law is seriously disputed by the appellants in Civil Appeal No.3255/84 and others.

QUESTION OF LAW BEFORE THE COURT :-

1. whether in an action claiming refund of excise duty (tax) paid under mistake of law, is it essential for the person claiming such refund, to establish "loss or injury" to him? In other words, in cases where the person from whom the excise duty (tax) is collected, has "passed on" the liability or deemed to have passed on the liability, is it open to him to claim refund of the duty paid by him, placing reliance on Section 72of the Indian Contract Act?

2. The further question as to whether an action by way of civil suit or a writ petition under Article 226 of the Constitution will lie, in the light of various amendments to the Act, claiming "refund" or "restitution", also arises for consideration.

JUDGMENT

1. The nine-Judge verdict of the Supreme has decided by a majority of 8:1 as to what rights and remedies are available to a citizen against the State in the matter of refund of unlawfully recovered taxes and imposts. The

court relied on the decisions of the courts which have applied the doctrine of unjust enrichment. Reliance was based on ***State of Madhya Pradesh v. Vyankatlal & Anr.[1985 (3)***

S.C.R. 561] and ***Shiv Shanker Dal Mills etc. v. State of Haryana & Ors. Etc. [1979 (3) S.C.R. 1217]*** wherein court held that though refund of fee so collected may be legally due to the traders, the traders may be repaid amounts only to the extent that they have not passed on the burden to their customers. To the extent they have passed on, it held, they were not entitled.

2. Where burden of duty is not passed on to third party, refund is admissible but no civil suit for refund is maintainable. No automatic refund to be granted under section 11B of Central Excise Act & Section 27 of Customs Act unless it is proved that duty has not been passed on to third party. (CA. No. 3255 of 1984 dt. 19-12-1996)

3. It is held that if the person claiming the refund has passed on the burden of duty to another and has not really suffered any loss or prejudice, there is no question of reimbursing him and he cannot successfully sustain an action for restitution, based on Section 72 of the Indian Contract Act. With great respect, I fully concur with the aforesaid conclusion of my learned brother. But, in view of the importance of the question raised, I would like to record my own reasons for the aforesaid conclusion.

4. I shall separately deal with the maintainability of the action either by way of suit or petition under Article 226 of the Constitution -- the extent to which there is ouster of jurisdiction of Courts.

CHAPTER THIRTEEN

Vishakha and Ors. v State of Rajasthan and Ors. [1997] 3 Suppl. SCR 404 : (1997) 6 SCC 241

(In 1997, the Supreme Court laid down guidelines in the Vishaka case, pending formal legislation, for dealing with sexual harassment of women at the workplace. Later on The Sexual Harassment of Women at Workplace (Prevention, Prohibition and Redressal) Act, 2013 ("Sexual Harassment Act") has been made effective on April 23, 2013 by way of publication in the Gazette of India.)

BENCH: J. S. Verma (then C.J.I), Sujata Manohar and B. N. Kripal.

FACTS OF THE CASE:

1. **Vishakha and others v State of Rajasthan** was case where Vishakha and other women groups filed Public Interest Litigation (PIL) against State of Rajasthan and Union of India to enforce the fundamental rights of working women under Articles 14, 19 and 21 of the Constitution of India.

2. The petition was filed after Bhanwari Devi, a social worker in Rajasthan was brutally gang raped for stopping a child marriage.

JUDGMENT:

1. The court decided that the consideration of "International Conventions and norms are significant for the purpose of interpretation of the guarantee of gender equality, right to work with human dignity in Articles 14, 15 19(1)(g) and 21 of the Constitution and the safeguards

against sexual harassment implicit therein."

2. The judgment has given guideline what are popularly known as the Vishaka guideline.

3. The judgment provided the basic definitions of Sexual Harassment at the workplace and provided guidelines to deal with it. It is seen as a significant legal victory for women's groups in India.

4. In India before 1997, There was no formal guidelines for how an incident involving sexual harassment at workplace should be dealt by an employer. Women experiencing sexual harassment at workplace had to lodge a complaint under Section 354 of the Indian Penal Code that deals with the 'criminal assault of women to outrage women's modesty', and Section 509 that punishes an individual or individuals for using a 'word, gesture or act intended to insult the modesty of a woman'. These sections left the interpretation of 'outraging women's modesty' to the discretion of the police officer.

5. The court decided that the consideration of "International Conventions and norms are significant for the purpose of interpretation of the guarantee of gender equality, right to work with human dignity in Articles 14, 15 19(1)(g) and 21 of the Constitution and the safeguards against Sexual Harassment implicit therein." Supreme Court of India defined sexual harassment and set guidelines for employers.

What is sexual harassment

6. Sexual harassment includes such unwelcome sexually determined behaviour (whether directly or by implication) as:

a) physical contact and advances;

b) a demand or request for sexual favours;

c) sexually coloured remarks;

d) showing pornography;

e) any other unwelcome physical verbal or non-verbal conduct of sexual nature.

7. Where any of these acts is committed in circumstances where under the victim of such conduct has a reasonable apprehension that in relation to the victim's employment or work whether she is drawing salary, or honorarium or voluntary, whether in government, public or private enterprise such conduct can be humiliating and may constitute a health and safety problem.

8. It is discriminatory for instance when the woman has reasonable grounds to believe that her objection would disadvantage her in connection with her employment or work including recruiting or promotion or when it creates a hostile work environment. Thus, sexual harassment need NOT involve physical contact. Any act that creates a hostile work environment - be it by virtue of cracking lewd jokes, verbal abuse, circulating lewd rumours etc. counts as sexual harassment.

8. The creation of a hostile work environment through unwelcome physical verbal or non-verbal conduct of sexual nature may consist not of a single act but of pattern of behaviour comprising many such acts.

9. Thus, it is important that the victim report such behaviour as soon as possible and not wait for it to become worse. In some cases, the psychological stigma of reporting the conduct of a co-worker might require a great deal of courage on the part of the victim and they may report such acts after a long period of time. The guidelines suggest that the complaint mechanism should ensure time bound treatment of complaints, but **they do not suggest that a report can only be made within a short period of time since the incident occurred**. Often, the police refuse to lodge FIR for Sexual Harassment cases, especially where the harassment occurred some time ago.

From guidelines to Act

The judgement only proposed guidelines to alleviate the problem of Sexual Harassment in 1997. India finally enacted its law on prevention of sexual harassment against female employees at the workplace. The Sexual Harassment of Women at Workplace (Prevention, Prohibition and Redressal) Act, 2013 ("Sexual Harassment Act") has been made effective on April 23, 2013 by way of publication in the Gazette of India.)

CHAPTER FOURTEEN

Githa Hariharan and Anr. Vs. Reserve Bank of India and Anr. [1999] 1SCR 669 : (1999) 2 SCC 228

(**Githa Hariharan** applied to the Reserve Bank of India for 9% Relief Bond to be held in the name of her minor son. RBI Authority advised her to produce the application signed by the father and in the alternative, the bank informed that a certificate of guardianship from a competent Authority in her favour as, as per Section 6 of Hindu Minority and Wards Act, 1956 she may not be considered as guardian as the father of the son is alive. Therefore for challenging the validity of Section 6 of Hindu Minority and Wards Act, 1956 read with Section 19 of the Guardian and Wards Act (1890) Section 19(b)**guardian not be appointed by the court in certain cases,** and declaring it as unconstituonal, she file a writ petition before Supreme Court. Hon'ble Supreme Cour pleased to dismiss the case with certain explanation and direction to the RBI about word 'after" comes under Section 6 of Hindu Minority and Wards Act, 1956 that,...*the word did not necessarily mean after the death of the father, on the contrary, it means 'in the absent off' be it temporary or otherwise or total apathy of the father towards the child or even inability of the father by reason of ailment or otherwise)*

Bench: Anand CJI, Srinivasan J, Banerjee J

Date of Judgement: 17 February 1999

FACTS OF THE CASE

1. The petitioner and Dr. Mohan Ram were married at Bangalore in 1982 and in July 1984, a son named Rishab Bailey was born to them.

2. In December 1984 the petitioners applied to the Reserve Bank of India for 9% Relief Bond to be held in the name of their minor son Rishab along with an intimation that the petitioner No. 1 being the mother, would act as the natural guardian for the purpose of investments.

3. The application, however, was sent back to the petitioner by the RBI Authority advising her to produce the application signed by the father and in the alternative, the bank informed that a certificate of guardianship from a competent Authority in her favour.

4. Second, there was a divorce proceeding pending between the petitioner and her husband in which the husband prayed for the custody of the child.

5. In association with this, he had written many letters to the petitioner asserting that he is the natural guardian of the minor child and they could take no decision without his approval, which has resulted in the present case

6. Further the first respondent has been repeatedly writing to the petitioner, asserting that he was the only natural guardian of the minor and no decision should be taken without his permission. Incidentally, the minor has been staying with the mother. The father has shown total apathy towards the child and as a matter of fact, is not interested in welfare and benefit of the child excepting however claiming the right to be the natural guardian without however discharging any corresponding obligation.

7. It is on these facts that the petitioner moved this honorable court under Article 32 of the constitution praying for the declaration of Section 6(a) **natural guardian of a Hindu minor** read with Section 19(b)**guardian not be appointed by the court in certain cases,** under the light of Article 14 and 15 of the constitution of India as unconstitutional.

8. Two writ petitions one jointly by Githa Hariharan and her husband and another by Githa Hariharan alone herself was filed which was taken together by the ho'ble court. Section 6 of the Hindu Minority and Guardianship Act (1956) and Section 19 of the Guardian and Wards Act (1890) was under challenge. The first of these acts says that the Hindu father is the "natural guardian" of his legitimate minor son and his minor unmarried daughter. He is the guardian of the child's "person and property" to the exclusion of the mother. The mother's rights enter the legal picture only if the father dies; takes to vanaprastha; turns yati or sanyasi; or if a court deems him "unfit" for guardianship. Section 19 of the Guardian and Wards Act debars the court from appointing the guardian of a minor whose

father is living, and is not, in the court's opinion, unfit to be guardian.

LEGAL ISSUE BEFORE THE COURT :

Whether section 6 of the Hindu Minority and Guardianship Act violates the Constitution of India?

ARGUMENTS OFPETITIONER:

The main contention of Ms. Indira Jai Singh, learned senior counsel for the petitioners is that the two sections i.e. Section (6)a of HMG Act and Section 19(b) of GW Act are violative of the equality clause of the Constitution, inasmuch as the mother of the minor is relegated to an inferior position on ground of sex alone since her right, as a natural guardian of the minor, is made cognisable only `after' the father. Hence, according to the learned counsel both the sections must be struck down as unconstitutional.

1. The communication from the RBI is arbitrary and was opposed to the basic concept of justice under Article 32 of the constitution. Therefore challenging the validity of **Section 6 of Hindu Minority and Wards Act, 1956.**

2. Further, they argued that the provision seriously disadvantages women and discriminate against women in the matter of guardianship rights, responsibilities, and authority in relation to their own children.

JUDGEMENT:

On observing the facts and arguments the bench asserted the predominance of the child's welfare in all consideration. The welfare of the child is the most important over all the other, welfare not means only the monetary benefits, it includes love, affection, security, etc for the child. The bench pointed out the precedent Gajre vs. Pathnkhan. In which the father was alive, he was not taking any interest in the affairs of the child. In this case, the mother was ruled to be the natural guardian of her minor daughter. He set out that the Hindu law and the Act held that the father is the natural guardian and after him the mother but in the above cases, the court held the opposite.

In **Jijabai Vithalrao Gajre Vs Pathankhan & Ors** ....*a rigid insistence of strict statutory interpretation may not be conducive* for the growth of the child, and welfare being the predominant criteria, it would be a planning *exercise of the judicial power of interpreting the law so as to be otherwise conducive to a fuller and better development and growth of the child.*

It was felt strongly that a long-established law should not easily be set aside; that a key point was an interpretation of the word **"after"** (Section 6 of Hindu Minority and Wards Act, 1956); and that,

...the word did not necessarily mean after the death of the father, on the contrary, it means 'in the absent off' be it temporary or otherwise or total apathy of the father towards the child or even inability of the father by reason of ailment or otherwise

The bench concluded that the literal meaning of the word [after] should not be taken, instead, it has to be interpreted to the object of the Act and the constitutional guarantee of gender equality since any other interpretation would render the statute void which ought to be avoided. Subsequently, the bench dismissed the petition with the direction to the Reserve Bank of India to formulate appropriate methodology in the light of his observations. The bench also instructed the District Court to take account of the comment when deciding the custody of the minor.

COCLUSION :

From the facts, issues, and the decision of the apex court we learn that fighting for our rights is a vital part in our life. The power judicial review vested in the hand of the judiciary must be used properly without making any over-rule. Simply declaring any provision of an Act as unconstitutional or void is not the right way of judicial review, finding out the purpose of the provision under consideration is a vital part while deciding the constitutionality of any Act. From the decision of the above case, the judiciary plays its role in a proper and perfect manner.

CHAPTER FIFTEEN

Rupa Ashok Hurra vs. Ashok Hurra [2002] 2 SCR 1006 : (2002) 4 SCC 388.

(The court invented Curative Petition which was also incorporate in Supreme Court Rules 2013. The main issue before court was Whether an aggrieved person is entitled to any relief against a final judgment/order of this Court after dismissal of Review Petition either under Article 32 of the Constitution or otherwise. The order passed by this Court and invented Curative Petitioncan for correcting error under its inherent powers under article 142 of constitution even after dismissal of the Review Petition)

FACTS OF THE CASE:

Shri Ashok G. Hurra (the husband), Respondent herein and Rupa Ashok Hurra, (the wife), the Appellant married on 3.12.1970 according to the Hindu rites and custom at Ahmedabad. The couple have one issue. Difference of opinion cropped up between the parties. On 30.6.1983, the wife left the matrimonial home. Thereafter, the couple started residing separately. On 21.8.1984, a joint petition for divorce was filed under Section 13B of the Hindu Marriage Act. It was signed by both the parties and both of them appeared before Court. Both of them are highly educated and intelligent and managing their own affairs and business. In the joint petition, it was averred that all the matters regarding ornaments, clothes and other movables were settled between them and the wife renounced her right to claim maintenance. The parties simply sought a decree of dissolution of the marriage by mutual consent under Section 13B(2) of the Hindu Marriage Act (hereinafter referred to as 'the Act'), on a motion by both the parties, six months after the date of presentation of the petition under sub-section (1) of the Act, and not later than eighteen months, the Court, shall, after enquiry, pass a decree of divorce by mutual consent. On 4.4.1985, the husband alone moved an application praying for passing a decree of divorce. On this motion, the Court issued notice to the wife.

On 27.3.1986, the wife filed an application withdrawing her consent for divorce. She prayed that Petition for divorce by mutual consent may be dismissed. This submission was objected to by the appellant, denying the averments made in the application and also stating further that the wife has no right to revoke the consent which she has legally granted. The husband filed an affidavit-in-reply on 9.4.1986 and contended that the wife has no right to withdraw or revoke the consent after the period of 18 months. He also prayed that consistent with the prayer made in the joint Hindu Marriage Petition filed on 21.8.1984 a decree for divorce by mutual consent may be passed. The wife seems to have filed an objection thereto.

After hearing the parties, the learned City Civil Judge (the Trial Court) held that since consent to be accepted and, in this view, dismissed the petition for divorce by mutual consent. P

In the appeal filed by the husband, a learned Single Judge of the Gujarat High Court in First Appeal No. 1070 of 1987, by judgement dated 15.3.1996, after a review of the entire facts and the relevant laws on the subject, set aside the order passed in Hindu Marriage Petition No. 248 of 1984 dated 17.10.1986 by the Trial Court and passed the decree of dissolution of marriage from the date of the petition.

In the Letters Patent Appeal (LPA) No.373/96, filed by the wife, a Division Bench of the Gujarat High Court, by judgment dated 9.9.1996, set aside the order of the learned Single Judge.

Against the judgment of the Division Bench rendered in the Letters Patent Appeal No. 373 of 1996, the husband, filed Special Leave Petition (SLP) and Special Leave was granted. This Court passed the following Order:

"25. The appeal (filed from S.L.P.20097/96) is allowed. Subject to the fulfilment of the following conditions, a decree of divorce for dissolution of marriage by mutual consent solemnised between the appellant and the respondent is passed under Section 13B of the Act. It is made clear that the decree is conditional and shall take effect only on payment or deposit in this Court of the entire sum of rupees ten lakhs by the appellant to the respondent, as ordered herein and also the cost as assessed below on or before 10.12.1997. The appellant shall pay or remit the amounts ordered before the said date, in two instalments— a sum of Rs.5 Lakhs + Rs.50,000/- (the assessed cost) as ordered hereinbelow, on or before 10.8.1997 and the balance of Rs.5 Lakhs (rupees five lakhs) on or before 10.12.1997. The assessed costs required to be paid by the appellant shall be Rs.50,000/- towards the entire proceedings to the respondent. If default is made in the payment of the instalment due on 10.8.1997 together with cost, then also, this decree shall not take effect and the appeal shall stand dismissed. If the amounts ordered herein are duly deposited in this Court by the appellant, the respondent can withdraw the said amounts, without further orders. We further declare and hold that all pending proceedings, more particularly referred to in para 8 of this judgment, including the proceedings under Section 494 IPC read with Section 17 of Hindu Marriage Act, 1955 between the parties shall stand terminated, but only on payment or deposit of the amounts filed ordered by us in this judgment. This is made clear."

A Review application against aforesaid was also dismissed.

Petition under Article 32 of the Constitution of India filed.

Thereafter reference from Bench of three Judges to Bench of 5 Judges came to be made in the above background to decide a question of Constitutional importance.

LEGAL BACKGROUND OF THE CASE:

The Court noted that—- The Petitioner in these writ petitions seek reconsideration of the final judgments of this Court after they have been unsuccessful in Review Petitions and in that these cases are different from the cases referred to above. The provision of Order XL Rule 5 of the Supreme Court Rules bars further application for Review in the same matter. The concern of the Court now is whether any relief can be given to the petitioner who challenge the final judgment of this Court, though after disposal of review petitions, complaining of the gross abuse of the process of Court and if-remedial injustice. In a State like India, governed by rule of law, certainly of law declared and the final decision rendered on merits in a lis between the parties by the highest Court in the country is of paramount importance. The principle of finality is insisted upon not on the ground that a judgment given by the Apex Court is impeccable but on the maxim "Interest reipublicae ut sit finis litium."

THE ISSUES BEFORE THE COURT:

"Whether the judgment of this Court dated March 10, 1997 in Civil Appeal No.1843 of 1997 can be regarded as a nullify and whether a writ petition under Article 32 of the Constitution can be maintained to question the validity of a judgment of this Court after the petition for review of the said judgment has been dismissed are, in our opinion, questions which need to be considered by a Constitution Bench of this Court.

The other writ petitions were tagged to that case. In these cases the following question of Constitutional law of considerable significance arises for consideration:

Question:

Whether an aggrieved person is entitled to any relief against a final judgment/order of this Court after dismissal of Review Petition either under Article 32 of the Constitution or otherwise ?

Answer: (Para 14) On the analysis of the ratio laid down in the aforementioned cases, we reaffirm our considered view that a final judgment/order passed by this Court cannot be assailed in an application under Article 32 of the Constitution of India by an aggrieved person, whether he was a party to the case or not.

After answering as above laying down the law, it was found a further question arose as under:

Question: Whether an order passed by this Court can be corrected under its inherent powers after dismissal of the Review Petition on the ground that it was passed

(a) either without jurisdiction, Or

(b) in violation of the principle of natural justice, Or

(c) due to unfair procedure giving scope for bias which resulted in abuse of the process of the Court, Or

(d) miscarriage of justice to an aggrieved person.

Answer: To prevent abuse of process and to cure a gross miscarriage of justice, this Court may reconsider its judgment in exercise of its inherent powers. (Para-49)

Methodology and requirement to invoke aforesaid inherent power by way of Curative Petition: (para-50)

The Petitioner is entitled to relief if he establishes

(1). Violation of the principle of natural justice in that he was not a party to the lis but the judgment adversely affected his interest, or if he was a party to the lis, he was not served with notice of the proceedings and the matter proceeded as if he had notice and

(2). Where in the proceedings, a learned Judge failed to disclose his connection with the subject matter or the parties giving scope for an apprehension of bias and the judgment adversely affect the Petitioner.

REQUIREMENT OF CURATIVE PETITION :

1. The Petition shall inter alia aver specifically that the grounds mentioned therein had been taken in the Review Petition and that the same was dismissed by circulation.
2. The Curative Petition shall contain a certification by a Senior Advocate with regard to the fulfilment of the above requirements.

DEALING WITH CURATIVE PETITION BY THE COURT:

1. The Curative Petition has to be first circulated to a Bench of Three Judges and the Judges who passed the Judgement complaint of, if available.
2. It is only when a majority of the learned Judges on this Bench conclude that the matter needs hearing that it should be listed before the same Bench (as for as possible) which may pass appropriate orders.
3. It shall be open to the Bench at any stage of consideration of the Curative Petition to ask a Senior Counsel to assist it as amicus curie.
4. In the event of Bench holding at any stage that the Petition is without any merit and vexatious, it may impose exemplary costs on the Petitioner.

Significance of this Case for being chosen for 4th Paper in Advocate-on-Record Exam may be appreciated in the fact, that the Judgment explains the jurisdiction of Supreme Court under Article 32 of the Constitution of India and other aspects relating to it.

The decision is such that the opinion of Mr. Justice Quadri delivered in Judgment has been endorsed by all other Judges constituting the Bench.

CHAPTER SIXTEEN

Pradeep Kumar Biswas and Ors. v. Indian Institute of Chemical Biology and Ors. [2002] 3 SCR 100 : (2002) 5 SCC 111.

(When a Corporation or any autonomous body can be described as a State for purposes of Article 12 of the Constitution of India ? The body either born statutorily or not made no difference. What mattered was the deep and pervasive control of the government and (i) financial, (ii) functional, (iii) administrative domination by the Government.)

IMPORTANT CASES RELATED TO THIS ISSUES:

1. Sabhajit Tewary vs. union of India (1975)
2. Sukhdev Singh and others vs. union of India (1975)
3. Ramana Dayaram Shetty vs. The International Airport Authority of India, AIR 1979
4. Ajay Hasia vs. Khalid Mujib Sehravardi, AIR 1981
5. Pradeep Kumar Biswas vs. Indian Institute of Chemical Biology (2002)
6. G.Bassi Reddy vs. International Crops Research Institute, AIR 2003

Sukhdev Singh case and the Sabhajit Tewary were the cases that were decided on the same day by the same Bench.

In Sabhajit Tewary 1975), the Court held that CSIR not to be covered under Article 12, because of the reason that its origin or genesis was not from any Statute. This indicta of the Sabhajit Tewary case was followed in various other cases since it was 5-Judge Constitutional Bench judgment which was to be followed by smaller Benches.

However, soon enough, the judgment started to gain criticism. Drastic changes started coming in the proposition of Shabhajit Tewary's judgement starting from Ramana Dayaram Shetty case and then Ajay Hasija case also indicated that statutory genesis is not the basis of the test and the Ajay Hasija judgment held, a Regional College which was not a statutory body but a Society registered under Society Registration Act, to be a "State" under Article 12 of the Constitution.

Finally, in the present case, by a Seven-Judge Bench, the Sabhajit Tewary was overruled.

The settled in this case was then followed in other cases in full length, one of the cases being G.Bassi Reddy vs. International Crops Research Institute, although the institute being International was not observed to have any dominance of the Indian Government and was held not to be a "State".

FACTS OF THE CASE:

1. The appellant filed a Writ Petition before the Calcutta High Court to challenge the termination of their services by 'Indian Institute of Chemical Biology' which is a unit of the Council of Scientific and Industrial Research (CSIR)

2. The Writ was rejected by the High Court because of the decision taken in an earlier case 'Sabhajit Tewary case (1967) in which CSIR was held not to be an 'authority' under Article 12.

3. The case went to the Supreme Court and the 2-Judge Bench referred the matter to a larger 7-Judge Constitutional Bench. This summary is of that 7-Judge Constitutional Bench in which Sabhajit Tewary's case was reconsidered.

ISSUES BEFORE THE COURT:

1. Whether CSIR was a State within the meaning of Article 12.
2. And if yes, whether the Supreme Court should reverse the decision in Sabhajit Tewary.

JUDGMENT :

1. After reviewing the previous cases, Sukhdev (1975), Sabhajit Tewary (1975), Ramana (1979), Ajay Hasija (1981), the Court in the present case concluded, with regard to the test for finding out whether a body is a State or any other authority under Article 12, : "The question in each would be— whether in the light of the cumulative facts as established, the body is financially, functionally and administratively dominated by or under the control of the Government. Such control must be particular to the body in question and must be pervasive. If this is found, then the body is a State within Article 12. On the other hand, when the control is merely regulatory whether under statute or otherwise it would not serve to make the body of a State.
2. The Court also observed that the tests formulated in Ajay Hasija case were not rigid set of principles and it all comes down to the facts of each case and then the test which has mean mentioned in the previous point. (It is important to note down here that the Court removed the confusion with regard to the statutory position of the body. The body either born statutorily or not made no difference. What mattered was the deep and pervasive control of the government and (i) financial, (ii) functional, (iii) administrative domination by the Government.)

IMPORTANT OBSERVATIONS:

The Court observed the following points with respect to CSIR which established that CSIR was financially, functionally and administratively dominated by the Government and such control was deep and pervasive. The Court observed that:

1. CSIR was 'created by the Government to carry on in an organised manner what was being done earlier by the Department of Commerce of the Central Government.
2. CSIR was set up in the National Interest to further the economic welfare of the society by fostering planned industrial development in the country.
3. All CSIR's income and property was to be applied only towards the promotion of the objects as mentioned in CSIR's memorandum with the limitation on expenditure which would be imposed by the Government.
4. The Director General who is ex officio Secretary of the Society was to be appointed by the Government of India. "Furthermore, the members of the Governing Body who are not there ex-offcio are nominated by

the President and their membership could be terminated by him and the Prime Minister is the ex officio President of CSIR.

5. "The Governing Body also has the power to frame, amend or appeal or repeal the bye-laws of CSIR but only with the sanction of the Government of India."
6. Under Bye-laws ...., various service rules and orders, pay scales and reservation rules applicable to the government servants are applicable to the employees of CSIR.
7. CSIR could not lay down or change the terms and conditions of service of its employees and any change in the bye-laws could be carried out only with the approval of the Government of India.
8. The then financial position of CSIR was that at least 70% of the funds of CSIR were available from grants made by the Government of India. The Court observed that "the assets and funds of CSIR thought nominally owned by the Society are in the ultimate analysis owned by the Government.

Held:

1. The Court held that the Sabhajit Tewary decision must be overruled.
2. The Court also held— CSIR to be under Article 12 and therefore Writ Petition was maintainable against the concerned body in this case—Indian Institute of Chemical Biology— which was a unit of CSIR.

CHAPTER SEVENTEEN

P. Ramachandra Rao v. State of Karnataka [2002]3 SCR 60 : (2002) 4 SCC 578

Top of Form

On 16 April, 2002

(Prescribing periods of limitation at the end of which the trial court would beobliged to terminate the proceedings and necessarily acquit or discharge the accused, and further, making such directions applicable to all the cases in the present and for the future amounts to legislation, which cannotbe done by judicial directives and within the arena of the judicial law-makingpower available to constitutional courts, howsoever liberally court may interpretArticles 32, 21, 141 and 142 of the Constitution. The dividing line is fine but perceptible. Courts can declare the law, they can interpret the law, they can remove obvious lacunae and fill the gaps but they cannot entrench upon in the field of legislation properly meant for the Legislature. Thus under Articles 21, 141 and 142--Criminal trials--WhetherSupreme Court can fix time-bars for conclusion or termination of trials in order to effectuate right to speedy trial flowing from and recognised in Article 21?--Held, (per majority of 6:1) "no"--This would amount to legislation--Held, (per minority, Raju, J.) "yes" but it is neither advisable nor practicable". In this case, the Apex Court laid down certain factors to identify whether an accused has been deprived of his Right to Speedy Trial. They are:

length of delay,

the justification for the delay,

the accused assertion of his Right to Speedy Trial, and

prejudice caused to the accused by such delay.

If nothing is shown and there are no circumstances to raise a presumption that the accused had been prejudiced there will be no justification to quash the conviction on the ground of delayed trial only)

Bench: Cji, R.C. Lahoti, N. Santosh Hegde, Ruma Pal, Arijit Pasayat

FACTS OF THE CASE:-

In Criminal Appeal No.535/2000 the appellant was working as an Electrical Superintendent in the Mangalore City Corporation. For the check period 1.5.1961 to 25.8.1987 he was found to have amassed assets disproportionate to his known sources of income. Charge-sheet accusing him of offences under Section 13(1)(e) read with Section 13(2) of the Prevention of Corruption Act, 1988 was filed on 15.3.1994. The accused appeared before the Special Court and was enlarged on bail on 6.6.1994.

TRIAL COURT:-

Charges were framed on 10.8.1994 and the case proceeded for trial on 8.11.1994. However, the trial did not commence. On 23.2.1999 the learned Special Judge who was seized of the trial directed the accused to be acquitted as the trial had not commenced till then and the period of two years had elapsed which obliged him to acquit the accused in terms of the directions of this court in Raj Deo Sharma Vs. State of Bihar (1998) 7 SCC 507 (hereinafter, Raj Deo Sharma-I).

HIGH COURT:-

The State of Karnataka through the D.S.P. Lokayukta, Mangalore preferred an appeal before the High Court putting in issue the acquittal of the accused.

SINGLE JUDGE:- The learned Single Judge of the High Court, vide the impugned order, allowed the appeal, set aside the order of acquittal and remanded the case to the Trial Court, forming an opinion that a case charging an accused with corruption was an exception to the directions made in Raj Deo Sharma-I as clarified by this Court in Raj Deo Sharma (II) Vs. State of Bihar (1999) 7 SCC 604. Strangely enough the High Court not only condoned a delay of 55 days in filing the appeal against acquittal by the State but also allowed the appeal itself both without even issuing notice to the accused.

SUPREME COURT:- The aggrieved accused has filed this appeal by special leave. Similar are the facts in all the other appeals. Shorn of details, suffice it to say that in all the appeals the accused persons who were facing corruption charges, were acquitted by the Special Courts for failure of commencement of trial in spite of lapse of two years from the date of framing of the charges and all the State appeals were allowed by the High Court without noticing the respective accused persons.

The appeals came up for hearing before a Bench of three learned Judges who noticed the common ground that the appeals in the High Court were allowed by the learned Judge thereat without issuing notice to the accused and upon this ground alone, of want of notice, the appeals here at could be allowed and the appeals before the High Court restored to file for fresh disposal after notice to the accused but it was felt that a question arose in these appeals which was likely to arise in many more and therefore the appeals should be heard on their merits. In the order dated September 19, 2000, the Bench of three learned Judges stated:

JUDGMENT:

"The question is whether the earlier judgments of this court, principally, in Common Cause Vs. Union of India (1996 (4) SCC 33), Common Cause Vs. Union of India (1996(6) SCC 775), Raj Deo Sharma Vs. State of Bihar (1998(7) SCC 507) and Raj Deo Sharma (II) Vs. State of Bihar 1999 (7) SCC 604), would apply to prosecutions under the Prevention of Corruption Act and other economic offences.

Having perused the judgments afore-mentioned, we are of the view that these appeals should be heard by a Constitution Bench. We take this view because we think that it may be necessary to sythesise the various guidelines and directions issued in these judgments. We are also of the view that a Constitution Bench should consider whether time limits of the nature mentioned in some of these judgments can, under the law, be laid down".

On 25th April, 2001 the appeals were heard by the Constitution Bench and during the course of hearing attention of the Constitution Bench was invited to the decision of an earlier Constitution Bench in Abdul Rehman Antulay and Ors.Vs. R.S. Nayak & Anr. (1992) 1 SCC 225 and the four judgments referred to in the order of reference dated 19th September, 2000 by the Bench of three learned Judges. It appears that the learned Judges of the Constitution Bench were of the opinion that the directions made in the two Common Cause cases and the two Raj Deo Sharma's cases ran counter to the Constitution Bench directions in Abdul Rehman Antulay's case, the latter being five-Judge Bench decision, the appeals deserved to be heard by a Bench of seven learned Judges. The relevant part of the order dated 26th April, 2001 reads as under:-

"The Constitution Bench judgement in A.R.

Antulay's case holds that "it is neither advisable nor feasible to draw or prescribe an outer time limit for conclusion of all criminal proceedings". Even so, the four judgements afore-mentioned lay down such time limits. Two of them also lay down to which class of criminal proceedings such time limits should apply and to which class they should not.

We think, in these circumstances, that a Bench of seven learned Judges should consider whether the dictum afore-mentioned in A.R. Antulay's case still holds the field; if not, whether the general directions of the kind given in these judgements are permissible in law and should be upheld.

Having regard to what is to be considered by the Bench of seven learned Judges, notice shall issue to the Attorney General and to the Advocates General of the States.

The papers shall be placed before the Hon'ble the Chief Justice for appropriate directions. Having regard to the importance of the matter, the Bench may be constituted at an early date".

On 20.2.2002 the Court directed, "Common Cause", the petitioner in the two Common Cause cases which arose out of writ- petitions under Article 32 of the Constitution, heard and decided by this Court as public interest litigations, to be noticed. "Common Cause" has responded and made appearance through counsel.

We have heard Shri Harish Salve, the learned Solicitor General appearing for Attorney General for India, Mr. Ranjit Kumar, Senior Advocate assisted by Ms. Binu Tamta, Advocate for the appellants, Mr. Sanjay R. Hegde and Mr. Satya Mitra, Advocates for the respondents, Mr. S. Murlidhar, Advocate for "Common Cause" and such other Advocates General and Standing Counsel who have chosen to appear for the States.

We shall briefly refer to the five decisions cited in the order of reference as also to a few earlier decisions so as to highlight the issue posed before us.

The width of vision cast on Article 21 , so as to perceive its broad sweep and content, by seven-Judge Bench of this Court in Mrs. Maneka Gandhi Vs. Union of India & Anr., (1978) 1 SCC 248, inspired a declaration of law, made on February 12, 1979 in Hussainara Khatoon and Ors. (I) Vs. Home Secretary, State of Bihar (1980) 1 SCC 81, that Article 21 confers a fundamental right on every person not to be deprived of his life or liberty, except according to procedure established by law; that such procedure is not some semblance of a procedure but the procedure should be "reasonable, fair and just"; and therefrom flows, without doubt, the right to speedy trial. The Court said __ "No procedure which does not ensure a reasonably quick trial can be regarded as 'reasonable, fair or just' and it would fall foul of Article 21. There can, therefore, be no doubt that speedy trial, and by speedy trial we mean reasonably expeditious trial, is an integral and essential part of the fundamental right to life and liberty enshrined in Article 21" Many accused persons tormented by unduly lengthy trial or criminal proceedings, in any forum whatsoever were enabled, by Hussainara Khatoon(I) statement of law, in successfully maintaining petitions for quashing of charges, criminal proceedings and/or conviction, on making out a case of violation of Article 21 of the Constitution. Right to speedy trial and fair procedure has passed through several milestones on the path of constitutional jurisprudence. In Maneka Gandhi (supra), this Court held that the several fundamental rights guaranteed by Part III required to be read as components of one integral whole and not as separate channels. The reasonableness of law and procedure, to withstand the test of Articles 21, 19 and 14, must be right and just and fair and not arbitrary, fanciful or oppressive, meaning thereby that speedy trial must be reasonably expeditious trial as an integral and essential part of the fundamental right of life and liberty under Article

21. Several cases marking the trend and development of law applying Maneka Gandhi and Hussainara Khatoon(I) principles to myriad situations came up for the consideration of this Court by a Constitution Bench in Abdul Rehman Antulay and Ors. Vs. R.S. Nayak and Ors. (1992) 1 SCC 225, (A.R. Antulay, for short). The proponents of right to speedy trial strongly urged before this Court for taking one step forward in the direction and prescribing time limits beyond which no criminal proceeding should be allowed to go on, advocating that unless this was done, Maneka Gandhi and Hussainara Khatoon(I) exposition of Article 21 would remain a mere illusion and a platitude. Invoking of the constitutional jurisdiction of this Court so as to judicially forge two termini and lay down periods of limitation applicable like a mathematical formula, beyond which a trial or criminal proceeding shall not proceed, was resisted by the opponents submitting that the right to speedy trial was an amorphous one something less than other fundamental rights guaranteed by the Constitution. The submissions made by proponents included that the right to speedy trial flowing from Article 21 to be meaningful, enforceable and effective ought to be accompanied by an outer limit beyond which continuance of the proceedings will be violative of Article 21. It was submitted that Section 468 of the Code of Criminal Procedure applied only to minor offences but the

Court should extend the same principle to major offences as well. It was also urged that a period of 10 years calculated from the date of registration of crime should be placed as an outer limit wherein shall be counted the time taken by the investigation.

The Constitution Bench, in A.R. Antulay's case, heard elaborate arguments. The Court, it its pronouncement, formulated certain propositions, 11 in number, meant to serve as guidelines. It is not necessary for our purpose to reproduce all those propositions. Suffice it to state that in the opinion of the Constitution Bench

(i) fair, just and reasonable procedure implicit in Article 21 of the Constitution creates a right in the accused to be tried speedily;

(ii) right to speedy trial flowing from Article 21 encompasses all the stages, namely, the stage of investigation, inquiry, trial, appeal, revision and re-trial;

(iii) who is responsible for the delay and what factors have contributed towards delay are relevant factors. Attendant circumstances, including nature of the offence, number of accused and witnesses, the work-load of the court concerned, prevailing local conditions and so on what is called the systemic delays must be kept in view;

(iv) each and every delay does not necessarily prejudice the accused as some delays indeed work to his advantage. Guidelines 8, 9, 10 and 11 are relevant for our purpose and hence are extracted and reproduced hereunder:-

"(8) Ultimately, the court has to balance and weigh the several relevant factors 'balancing test' or 'balancing process' and determine in each case whether the right to speedy trial has been denied in a given case.

(9) Ordinarily speaking, where the court comes to the conclusion that right to speedy trial of an accused has been infringed the charges or the conviction, as the case may be, shall be quashed. But this is not the only course open. The nature of the offence and other circumstances in a given case may be such that quashing of proceedings may not be in the interest of justice. In such a case, it is open to the court to make such other appropriate order including an order to conclude the trial within a fixed time where the trial is not concluded or reducing the sentence where the trial has concluded as may be deemed just and equitable in the circumstances of the case.

(10) It is neither advisable nor practicable to fix any time-limit for trial of offences. Any such rule is bound to be qualified one. Such rule cannot

also be evolved merely to shift the burden of proving justification on to the shoulders of the prosecution. In every case of complaint of denial of right to speedy trial, it is primarily for the prosecution to justify and explain the delay. At the same time, it is the duty of the court to weigh all the circumstances of a given case before pronouncing upon the complaint. The Supreme Court of USA too has repeatedly refused to fix any such outer time-limit in spite of the Sixth Amendment. Nor do we think that not fixing any such outer limit ineffectuates the guarantee of right to speedy trial.

(11) An objection based on denial of right to speedy trial and for relief on that account, should first be addressed to the High Court. Even if the High Court entertains such a plea, ordinarily it should not stay the proceedings, except in a case of grave and exceptional nature. Such proceedings in High Court must, however, be disposed of on a priority basis."

During the course of its judgment also the Constitution Bench made certain observations which need to be extracted and reproduced:-

"But then speedy trial or other expressions conveying the said concept are necessarily relative in nature. One may ask speedy means, how speedy? How long a delay is too long? We do not think it is possible to lay down any time schedules for conclusion of criminal proceedings. The nature of offence, the number of accused, the number of witnesses, the workload in the particular court, means of communication and several other circumstances have to be kept in mind". (para 83).

".it is neither advisable nor feasible to draw or prescribe an outer time-limit for conclusion of all criminal proceedings. It is not necessary to do so for effectuating the right to speedy trial. We are also not satisfied that without such an outer limit, the right becomes illusory". (para 83) "even apart from Article 21 courts in this country have been cognizant of undue delays in criminal matters and wherever there was inordinate delay or where the proceedings were pending for too long and any further proceedings were deemed to be oppressive and unwarranted, they were put an end to by making appropriate orders".

(para 65) [emphasis supplied] In 1986, "Common Cause"__ a Registered Society, espousing public causes, preferred a petition under Article 32 of the Constitution of India seeking certain directions. By a brief order ("Common Cause" A Registered Society through its Director Vs. Union of India & Ors. (1996) 4 SCC 32, hereinafter Common Cause (I)), a two-Judge Bench of this Court issued two sets of directions: one, regarding bail, and the other, regarding quashing of trial. Depending on the quantum of imprisonment provided for several offences under the Indian Penal Code and the period of time which the accused have already spent in jail, the undertrial accused confined in jails were directed to be released on bail or on personal bond subject to such conditions as the Court may deem fit to impose in the light of Section 437 of Cr.P.C.. The other set of directions directed the trial in pending cases to be terminated and the accused to be discharged or acquitted depending on the nature of offence by reference to (i) the maximum sentence inflictable whether fine only or imprisonment, and if imprisonment, then the maximum set out in the law, and (ii) the period for which the case has remained pending in the criminal court.

A perusal of the directions made by the Division Bench shows the cases having been divided into two categories: (i) traffic offences, and (ii) cases under IPC or any other law for the time being in force. The Court directed the trial Courts to close such cases on the occurrence of following event and the period of delay:- Category (i) : Traffic Offences:

The Court directed the cases to be closed and the accused to be discharged on lapse of more than two years on account of non-serving of summons to the accused or for any other reason whatsoever. Category (ii) : Cases under IPC or any other law for the time being in force :

The Court directed that in the following sub-categories if the trial has not commenced and the period noted against each sub- category has elapsed then the case shall be closed and the accused shall be discharged or acquitted __ Nature of the cases Period of delay i.e. trial not commenced for Cases compoundable with the permission of the Court More than two years Cases pertaining to offences which are non-cognizable and bailable More than two years Cases in connection with offences punishable with fine only and are not of recurring nature More than one year Cases punishable with imprisonment upto one year, with or without fine More than one year Cases pertaining to offences punishable with imprisonment upto three years with or without fine More than two years The period of pendency was directed to be calculated from the date the accused are summoned to appear in Court. The Division Bench, vide direction 4, specified certain categories of cases to which its directions would not be applicable. Vide direction 5, this court directed the offences covered by direction 4 to be tried on priority basis and observance of this direction being monitored by the High Courts. All the directions were made applicable not only to the cases pending on the day but also to cases which may be instituted thereafter.

Abovesaid directions in Common Cause-I were made on May 1, 1996. Not even a period of 6 months had elapsed, on 15.10.1996, Shri Sheo Raj Purohit __ a public-spirited advocate addressed a Letter Petition to this Court, inviting its attention to certain consequences flowing from the directions made by this Court in Common Cause (I) and which were likely to cause injustice to the serious detriment of the society and could result in encouraging dilatory tactics adopted by the accused. A two-Judge Bench of this court, which was the same as had issued directions in Common Cause (I), made three directions which had the effect of clarifying/modifying the directions in Common Cause (I). The first direction clarified that the time spent in criminal proceedings, wholly or partly, attributable to the dilatory tactics or prolonging of trial by action of the accused, or on account of stay of criminal proceedings secured by such accused from higher courts shall be excluded in counting the time-limit regarding pendency of criminal proceedings. Second direction defined the terminus a quo, i.e. what would be the point of commencement of trial while working out 'pendency of trials' in Sessions Court, warrant cases and summons cases. In the third direction, the list of cases, by reference to nature of offence to which directions in Common Cause (I) would not apply, was expanded.

In Raj Deo Sharma (I), an accused charged with offences under Sections 5(2) & 5 (1) (e) of the Prevention of Corruption Act, 1947 came up to this Court, having failed in High Court, seeking quashing of prosecution against him on the ground of violation of right to speedy trial. Against him the offence was registered in 1982 and chargesheet was submitted in 1985. The accused appeared on 24.4.1987 before the Special Judge. Charges were framed on 4.3.1993. Until 1.6.1995 only 3 out of 40 witnesses were examined. The three-Judge Bench of this Court, which heard the case, set aside the order passed by the High Court and sent the matter back to the Special Judge for passing appropriate orders in the light of its judgment. Vide para 17, the three-Judge Bench issued five further directions purporting to be supplemental to the propositions laid down in A.R. Antulay. The directions need not be reproduced and suffice it to observe that by dividing the offence into two categories those punishable with imprisonment for a period not exceeding 7 years and those punishable with imprisonment for a period exceeding 7 years, the Court laid down periods of limitation by reference to which either the prosecution evidence shall be closed or the accused shall be released on bail. So far as the trial for offences is concerned, for the purpose of making directions, the Court categorized the offences and the nature and period of delay into two, which may be set out in a tabular form as under:-

Nature of offence Nature and period of delay Offence punishable with imprisonment for a period not exceeding seven years, whether the accused is in jail or not Completion of two years from the date of recording the plea of the accused on the charges framed, whether the prosecution has examined all the witnesses or not within the said period of two years Offence punishable with imprisonment for a period exceeding seven years, whether the accused is in jail or not Completion of three years from the date of recording the plea of the accused on the charge framed, whether the prosecution has examined all the witnesses or not within the said period The consequence which would follow on completion of two or three years, as abovesaid, is, the Court directed, that the trial Court shall close the prosecution evidence and can proceed to the next step of trial. In respect of the second category, the Court added a rider by way of exception stating __ "Unless for very exceptional reasons to be recorded and in the interest of justice, the Court considers it necessary to grant further time to the prosecution to adduce evidence beyond the aforesaid time limit" (of three years). The period of inability for completing prosecution evidence attributable to conduct of accused in protracting the trial and the period during which trial remained stayed by orders of the court or by operation of law was directed to be excluded from calculating the period at the end of which the prosecution evidence shall be closed. Further, the Court said that the directions made by it shall be in addition to and without prejudice to the directions issued in Common Cause (I) as modified in Common Cause (II).

Raj Deo Sharma (I) came up once again for consideration of this Court in Raj Deo Sharma Vs. State of Bihar (1999) 7 SCC 604, hereinafter Raj Deo Sharma (II). This was on an application filed by Central Bureau of Investigation (CBI) for clarification (and also for some modification) in the directions issued. The three-Judge Bench which heard the matter consisted of K.T. Thomas, J. and M. Srinivasan, J. who were also on the Bench issuing directions in Raj Deo Sharma (I) and M.B. Shah, J. who was not on the Bench in Raj Deo Sharma (I). In the submission of CBI the directions of the Court made in Raj Deo Sharma (I) ran counter to A.R. Antulay and did not take into account the time taken by the Court on account of its inability to carry on day to day trial due to pressure of work. The CBI also pleaded for the directions in Raj Deo Sharma (I) being made prospective only, i.e., period prior to the date of directions in Raj Deo Sharma (I) being excluded from consideration. All the three learned Judges wrote separate judgments. K.T. Thomas, J. by his judgment, to avert 'possibility of miscarriage of justice', added a rider to the directions made in Raj Deo Sharma (I) that an additional period of one year can be claimed by the prosecution in respect of prosecutions which were pending on the date of judgment in Raj Deo Sharma (I) and the Court concerned would be free to grant such extension if it considered it necessary in the interest of administration of criminal justice. M. Srinivasan, J. in his separate judgment, assigning his own reasons, expressed concurrence with the opinion expressed and the only clarification ordered to be made by K.T. Thomas, J. and placed on record his express disagreement with the opinion recorded by M.B. Shah, J.

M.B. Shah, J. in his dissenting judgment noted the most usual causes for delay in delivery of criminal justice as discernible from several reported cases travelling upto this Court and held that the remedy for the causes of delay in disposal of criminal cases lies in effective steps being taken by the Judiciary, the Legislature and the State Governments, all the three. The dangers behind constructing time-limit barriers by judicial dictum beyond which a criminal trial or proceedings could not proceed, in the opinion of M.B. Shah, J., are (i) it would affect the smooth functioning of the society in accordance with law and finally the Constitution. The victims left without any remedy would resort to taking revenge by unlawful means resulting in further increase in the crimes and criminals. People at large in the society would also feel unsafe and insecure and their confidence in the judicial system would be shaken. Law would lose its deterrent effect on criminals; (ii) with the present strength of Judges and infrastructure available with criminal courts it would be almost impossible for the available criminal courts to dispose of the cases within the prescribed time-limit; (iii) prescribing such time-limits may run counter to the law specifically laid down by Constitution Bench in Antulay's case. In the fore-quoted thinking of M.B. Shah, J. we hear the echo of what Constitution Bench spoke in Kartar Singh Vs. State of Punjab (1994) 3 SCC 569, vide para 351, "No doubt, liberty of a citizen must be zealously safeguarded by the courts; nonetheless the courts while dispensing justice in cases like the one under the TADA Act, should keep in mind not only the liberty of the accused but also the interest of the victim and their near and dear and above all the collective interest of the community and the safety of the nation so that the public may not lose faith in the system of judicial administration and indulge in private retribution."

At the end M.B. Shah, J. opined that order dated 8.10.1998 made in Raj Deo Sharma (I) requires to be held in abeyance and the State Government and Registrars of the High Courts ought to be directed to come up with specific plans for the setting up of additional courts/special courts (permanent/ad hoc) to cope up with the pending workload on the basis of available figures of pending cases also by taking into consideration the criteria for disposal of criminal cases prescribed by various High Courts. In conclusion, the Court directed the application filed by the CBI to be disposed of in terms of the majority opinion.

A perception of the causes for delay at the trial and in conclusion of criminal proceedings is necessary so as to appreciate whether setting up bars of limitation entailing termination of trial or proceedings can be justified. The root cause for delay in dispensation of justice in our country is poor judge-population-ratio. Law Commission of India in its 120th Report on Manpower Planning in Judiciary (July 1987), based on its survey, regretted that in spite of Article 39A added as a major Directive Principle in the Constitution by 42nd Amendment (1976), obliging the State to secure such operation of legal system as promotes justice and to ensure that opportunities for securing justice are not denied to any citizen several reorganisation proposals in the field of administration of justice in India have been basically patch work, ad hoc and unsystematic solutions to the problem. The judge-population-ratio in India (based on 1971 census) was only 10.5 judges per million population while such ratio was 41.6 in Australia, 50.9 in England, 75.2 in Canada and 107 in United States. The Law Commission suggested that India required 107 judges per million of Indian population; however to begin with the judge strength needed to be raised to five-fold, i.e., 50 judges per million population in a period of five years but in any case not going beyond ten years. Touch of sad sarcasm is difficult to hide when the Law Commission observed (in its 120th Report, ibid) that adequate reorganisation of the Indian judiciary is at the one and at the same time everybody's concern and, therefore, nobody's concern. There are other factors contributing to the delay at the trial. In A.R. Antulay's case, vide para 83, the Constitution Bench has noted that in spite of having proposed to go on with the trial of a case, five days a week and week after week, it may not be possible to conclude the trial for reasons, viz. (1) non-availability of the counsel, (2) non- availability of the accused, (3) interlocutory proceedings, and (4) other systemic delays. In addition, the Court noted that in certain cases there may be a large number of witnesses and in some offences, by their very nature, the evidence may be lengthy. In Kartar Singh Vs. State of Punjab (1994) 3 SCC 569 another Constitution Bench opined that the delay is dependent on the circumstances of each case because reasons for delay will vary, such as (i) delay in investigation on account of the widespread ramifications of crimes and its designed network either nationally or internationally, (ii) the deliberate absence of witness or witnesses, (iii) crowded dockets on the file of the court etc. In Raj Deo Sharma (II), in the dissenting opinion of M.B. Shah, J., the reasons for delay have been summarized as, (1) Dilatory proceedings; (2) Absence of effective steps towards radical simplification and streamlining of criminal procedure; (3) Multi-tier appeals/revision applications and diversion to disposal of interlocutory matters; (4) Heavy dockets; mounting arrears; delayed service of process; and (5) Judiciary, starved by executive by neglect of basic necessities and amenities, enabling smooth functioning.

Several cases coming to our notice while hearing appeals, petitions and miscellaneous petitions (such as for bail and quashing of proceedings) reveal, apart from inadequate judge strength, other factors contributing to the delay at the trial. Generally speaking, these are: (i) absence of, or delay in appointment of, public prosecutors proportionate with the number of courts/cases; (ii) absence of or belated service of summons and warrants on the accused/witnesses;

(iii) non-production of undertrial prisoners in the Court; (iv) presiding Judges proceeding on leave, though the cases are fixed for trial; (v) strikes by members of Bar; and (vi) counsel engaged by the accused suddenly declining to appear or seeking an adjournment for personal reasons or personal inconvenience. It is common knowledge that appointments of public prosecutors are politicized. By convention, government advocates and public prosecutors were appointed by the executive on the recommendation of or in consultation with the head of judicial administration at the relevant level but gradually the executive has started bypassing the merit based recommendations of, or process of consultation with, District and Sessions Judges. For non- service of summons/orders and non-production of undertrial prisoners, the usual reasons assigned are shortage of police personnel and police people being busy in VIP duties or law and order duties. These can hardly be valid reasons for not making the requisite police personnel available for assisting the Courts in expediting the trial. The members of the Bar shall also have to realize and remind themselves of their professional obligation __ legal and ethical, that having accepted a brief for an accused they have no justification to decline or avoid appearing at the trial when the case is taken up for hearing by the Court. All these factors demonstrate that the goal of speedy justice can be achieved by a combined and result-oriented collective thinking and action on the part of the Legislature, the Judiciary, the Executive and representative bodies of members of Bar.

Is it at all necessary to have limitation bars terminating trials and proceedings? Is there no effective mechanisms available for achieving the same end? The Criminal Procedure Code, as it stands, incorporates a few provisions to which resort can be had for protecting the interest of the accused and saving him from unreasonable prolixity or laxity at the trial amounting to oppression. Section 309, dealing with power to postpone or adjourn proceedings, provides generally for every inquiry or trial, being proceeded with as expeditiously as possible, and in particular, when the examination of witnesses has once begun, the same to be continued from day to day until all the witnesses in attendance have been examined, unless the Court finds the adjournment of the same beyond the following day to be necessary for reasons to be recorded. Explanation-2 to Section 309 confers power on the Court to impose costs to be paid by the prosecution or the accused, in appropriate cases, and putting the parties on terms while granting an adjournment or postponing of proceedings. This power to impose costs is rarely exercised by the Courts. Section 258, in Chapter XX of Cr.P.C., on Trial of Summons- cases, empowers the Magistrate trying summons cases instituted otherwise than upon complaint, for reasons to be recorded by him, to stop the proceedings at any stage without pronouncing any judgment and where such stoppage of proceedings is made after the evidence of the principal witnesses has been recorded, to pronounce a judgment of acquittal, and in any other case, release the accused, having effect of discharge. This provision is almost never used by the Courts. In appropriate cases, inherent power of the High Court, under Section 482 can be invoked to make such orders, as may be necessary, to give effect to any order under the Code of Criminal Procedure or to prevent abuse of the process of any Court, or otherwise, to secure the ends of justice. The power is wide and, if judiciously and consciously exercised, can take care of almost all the situations where interference by the High Court becomes necessary on account of delay in proceedings or for any other reason amounting to oppression or harassment in any trial, inquiry or proceedings. In appropriate cases, the High Courts have exercised their jurisdiction under Section 482 of Cr.P.C. for quashing of first information report and investigation, and terminating criminal proceedings if the case of abuse of process of law was clearly made out. Such power can certainly be exercised on a case being made out of breach of fundamental right conferred by Article 21 of the Constitution. The Constitution Bench in A.R. Antulay's case referred to such power, vesting in the High Court (vide paras 62 and 65 of its judgment) and held that it was clear that even apart from Article 21 , the Courts can take care of undue or inordinate delays in criminal matters or proceedings if they remain pending for too long and putting to an end, by making appropriate orders, to further proceedings when they are found to be oppressive and unwarranted.

Legislation is that source of law which consists in the declaration of legal rules by a competent authority. When judges by judicial decisions lay down a new principle of general application of the nature specifically reserved for legislature they may be said to have legislated, and not merely declared the law. Salmond on Principles of Jurisprudence (12th Edition) goes on to say "we must distinguish law-making by legislators from law-making by the courts. Legislators can lay down rules purely for the future and without reference to any actual dispute; the courts, insofar as they create law, can do so only in application to the cases before them and only insofar as is necessary for their solution. Judicial law-making is incidental to the solving of legal disputes; legislative law-making is the central function of the legislator" (page 115). It is not difficult to perceive the dividing line between permissible legislation by judicial directives and enacting law the field exclusively reserved for legislature. We are concerned here to determine whether in prescribing various periods of limitation, adverted to above, the Court transgressed the limit of judicial legislation.

Bars of limitation, judicially engrafted, are, no doubt, meant to provide a solution to the aforementioned problems. But a solution of this nature gives rise to greater problems like scuttling a trial without adjudication, stultifying access to justice and giving easy exit from the portals of justice. Such general remedial measures cannot be said to be apt solutions. For two reasons we hold such bars of limitation uncalled for and impermissible : first, because it tantamounts to impermissible legislation an activity beyond the power which the Constitution confers on judiciary, and secondly, because such bars of limitation fly in the face of law laid down by Constitution Bench in A.R. Antulay's case and, therefore, run counter to the doctrine of precedents and their binding efficacy.

In a monograph " Judicial Activism and Constitutional Democracy in India", commended by Professor Sir William Wade, Q.C. as a "small book devoted to a big subject", the learned author, while recording appreciation of judicial activism, sounds a note of caution "it is plain that the judiciary is the least competent to function as a legislative or the administrative agency. For one thing, courts lack the facilities to gather detailed data or to make probing enquiries. Reliance on advocates who appear before them for data is likely to give them partisan or inadequate information. On the other hand if courts have to rely on their own knowledge or research it is bound to be selective and subjective. Courts also have no means for effectively supervising and implementing the aftermath of their orders, schemes and mandates. Moreover, since courts mandate for isolated cases, their decrees make no allowance for the differing and varying situations which administrators will encounter in applying the mandates to other cases. Courts have also no method to reverse their orders if they are found unworkable or requiring modification". Highlighting the difficulties which the courts are likely to encounter if embarking in the fields of legislation or administration, the learned author advises " the Supreme Court could have well left the decision- making to the other branches of government after directing their attention to the problems rather than itself entering the remedial field".

The primary function of judiciary is to interpret the law. It may lay down principles, guidelines and exhibit creativity in the field left open and unoccupied by Legislation. Patrick Devlin in 'The Judge' (1979) refers to the role of the Judge as lawmaker and states that there is no doubt that historically judges did make law, at least in the sense of formulating it. Even now when they are against innovation, they have never formally abrogated their powers; their attitude is: 'We could if we would but we think it better not.' But as a matter of history did the English judges of the golden age make law? They decided cases which worked up into principles. The judges, as Lord Wright once put it in an unexpectedly picturesque phrase, proceeded 'from case to case, like the ancient Mediterranean mariners, hugging the coast from point to point and avoiding the dangers of the open sea of system and science'. The golden age judges were not rationalisers and, except in the devising of procedures, they were not innovators. They did not design a new machine capable of speeding ahead; they struggled with the aid of fictions and bits of procedural string to keep the machine on the road.

Professor S.P. Sathe, in his recent work (Year 2002) "Judicial Activism in India Transgressing Borders and Enforcing Limits", touches the topic "Directions : A New Form of Judicial Legislation". Evaluating legitimacy of judicial activism, the learned author has cautioned against Court "legislating" exactly in the way in which a Legislature legislates and he observes by reference to a few cases that the guidelines laid down by court, at times, cross the border of judicial law making in the realist sense and trench upon legislating like a Legislature. "Directions are either issued to fill in the gaps in the legislation or to provide for matters that have not been provided by any legislation. The Court has taken over the legislative function not in the traditional interstitial sense but in an overt manner and has justified it as being an essential component of its role as a constitutional court." (p.242). "In a strict sense these are instances of judicial excessivism that fly in the face of the doctrine of separation of powers. The doctrine of separation of powers envisages that the legislature should make law, the executive should execute it, and the judiciary should settle disputes in accordance with the existing law. In reality such watertight separation exists nowhere and is impracticable. Broadly, it means that one organ of the State should not perform a function that essentially belongs to another organ. While law-making through interpretation and expansion of the meanings of open-textured expressions such as 'due process of law', 'equal protection of law', or 'freedom of speech and expression' is a legitimate judicial function, the making of an entirely new law..through directionsis not a legitimate judicial function." (p.250).

Prescribing periods of limitation at the end of which the trial court would be obliged to terminate the proceedings and necessarily acquit or discharge the accused, and further, making such directions applicable to all the cases in the present and for the future amounts to legislation, which, in our opinion, cannot be done by judicial directives and within the arena of the judicial law-making power available to constitutional courts, howsoever liberally we may interpret Articles 32, 21, 141 and 142 of the Constitution. The dividing line is fine but perceptible. Courts can declare the law, they can interpret the law, they can remove obvious lacunae and fill the gaps but they cannot entrench upon in the field of legislation properly meant for the legislature. Binding directions can be issued for enforcing the law and appropriate directions may issue, including laying down of time limits or chalking out a calendar for proceedings to follow, to redeem the injustice done or for taking care of rights violated, in a given case or set of cases, depending on facts brought to the notice of Court. This is permissible for judiciary to do. But it may not, like legislature, enact a provision akin to or on the lines of Chapter XXXVI of the Code of Criminal Procedure, 1973.

The other reason why the bars of limitation enacted in Common Cause (I), Common Cause (II) and Raj Deo Sharma (I) and Raj Deo Sharma (II) cannot be sustained is that these decisions though two or three-judge Bench decisions run counter to that extent to the dictum of Constitution Bench in A.R. Antulay's case and therefore cannot be said to be good law to the extent they are in breach of the doctrine of precedents. The well settled principle of precedents which has crystalised into a rule of law is that a bench of lesser strength is bound by the view expressed by a bench of larger strength and cannot take a view in departure or in conflict therefrom. We have in the earlier part of this judgment extracted and reproduced passages from A.R. Antulay's case. The Constitution Bench turned down the fervent plea of proponents of right to speedy trial for laying down time-limits as bar beyond which a criminal proceeding or trial shall not proceed and expressly ruled that it was neither advisable nor practicable (and hence not judicially feasible) to fix any time-limit for trial of offences. Having placed on record the exposition of law as to right to speedy trial flowing from Article 21 of the Constitution this Court held that it was necessary to leave the rule as elastic and not to fix it in the frame of defined and rigid rules. It must be left to the judicious discretion of the court seized of an individual case to find out from the totality of circumstances of a given case if the quantum of time consumed upto a given point of time amounted to violation of Article 21 , and if so, then to terminate the particular proceedings, and if not, then to proceed ahead. The test is whether the proceedings or trial has remained pending for such a length of time that the inordinate delay can legitimately be called oppressive and unwarranted, as suggested in A.R. Antulay. In Kartar Singh's case (supra) the Constitution Bench while recognising the principle that the denial of an accused's right of speedy trial may result in a decision to dismiss the indictment or in reversing of a conviction, went on to state, "Of course, no length of time is per se too long to pass scrutiny under this principle nor the accused is called upon to show the actual prejudice by delay of disposal of cases. On the other hand, the court has to adopt a balancing approach by taking note of the possible prejudices and disadvantages to be suffered by the accused by avoidable delay and to determine whether the accused in a criminal proceeding has been deprived of his right of having speedy trial with unreasonable delay which could be identified by the factors (1) length of delay, (2) the justification for the delay, (3) the accused's assertion of his right to speedy trial, and (4) prejudice caused to the accused by such delay." (para 92).

For all the foregoing reasons, we are of the opinion that in Common Cause case (I) (as modified in Common Cause (II)) and Raj Deo Sharma (I) and (II), the Court could not have prescribed periods of limitation beyond which the trial of a criminal case or a criminal proceeding cannot continue and must mandatorily be closed followed by an order acquitting or discharging the accused. In conclusion we hold:-

(1) The dictum in A.R. Antulay's case is correct and still holds the field.

(2) The propositions emerging from Article 21 of the Constitution and expounding the right to speedy trial laid down as guidelines in A.R. Antulay's case, adequately take care of right to speedy trial. We uphold and re-affirm the said propositions.

(3) The guidelines laid down in A.R. Antulay's case are not exhaustive but only illustrative. They are not intended to operate as hard and fast rules or to be applied like a strait-jacket formula. Their applicability would depend on the fact-situation of each case. It is difficult to foresee all situations and no generalization can be made.

(4) It is neither advisable, nor feasible, nor judicially permissible to draw or prescribe an outer limit for conclusion of all criminal proceedings. The time-limits or bars of limitation prescribed in the several directions made in Common Cause (I), Raj Deo Sharma (I) and Raj Deo Sharma (II) could not have been so prescribed or drawn and are not good law. The criminal courts are not obliged to terminate trial or criminal proceedings merely on account of lapse of time, as prescribed by the directions made in Common Cause Case (I), Raj Deo Sharma case (I) and (II). At the most the periods of time prescribed in those decisions can be taken by the courts seized of the trial or proceedings to act as reminders when they may be persuaded to apply their judicial mind to the facts and circumstances of the case before them and determine by taking into consideration the several relevant factors as pointed out in A.R. Antulay's case and decide whether the trial or proceedings have become so inordinately delayed as to be called oppressive and unwarranted. Such time-limits cannot and will not by themselves be treated by any Court as a bar to further continuance of the trial or proceedings and as mandatorily obliging the court to terminate the same and acquit or discharge the accused.

(5) The Criminal Courts should exercise their available powers, such as those under Section 309, 311, and 258 of Code of Criminal Procedure to effectuate the right to speedy trial. A watchful and diligent trial judge can prove to be better protector of such right than any guidelines. In appropriate cases jurisdiction of High Court under Section 482 of Cr.P.C. and Articles 226 and 227 of Constitution can be invoked seeking appropriate relief or suitable directions.

(6) This is an appropriate occasion to remind the Union of India and the State Governments of their constitutional obligation to strengthen the judiciary-quantitatively and qualitatively by providing requisite funds, manpower and infrastructure. We hope and trust that the Governments shall act.

We answer the questions posed in the orders of reference dated September 19, 2000 and April 26, 2001 in the abovesaid terms.

The appeals are allowed. The impugned judgments of the High Court are set aside. As the High Court could not have condoned the delay in filing of the appeals and then allowed the appeals without noticing the respective accused-respondents before the High Court, now the High Court shall hear and decide the appeals afresh after noticing the accused-respondent before it in each of the appeals and consistently with the principles of law laid down hereinabove.

Before we may part, we would like to make certain observations ex abundanti cautela :

Firstly, we have dealt with the directions made by this Court in Common Cause Case-I and II and Raj Deo Sharma Case I and II regarding trial of cases. The directions made in those cases regarding enlargement of accused persons on bail are not subject matter of this reference or these appeals and we have consciously abstained from dealing with legality, propriety or otherwise of directions in regard to bail. This is because different considerations arise before the criminal courts while dealing with termination of a trial or proceedings and while dealing with right of accused to be enlarged on bail.

Secondly, though we are deleting the directions made respectively by two and three-Judge Benches of this Court in the cases under reference, for reasons which we have already stated, we should not, even for a moment, be considered as having made a departure from the law as to speedy trial and speedy conclusion of criminal proceedings of whatever nature and at whichever stage before any authority or the court. It is the constitutional obligation of the State to dispense speedy justice, more so in the field of criminal law, and paucity of funds or resources is no defence to denial of right to justice emanating from Articles 21, 19 and 14 and the Preamble of the Constitution as also from the Directive Principles of State Policy. It is high time that the Union of India and the various States realize their constitutional obligation and do something concrete in the direction of strengthening the justice delivery system. We need to remind all concerned of what was said by this Court in Hussainara Khatoon (IV) 1980 (1) SCC 98, "The State cannot be permitted to deny the constitutional right of speedy trial to the accused on the ground that the State has no adequate financial resources to incur the necessary expenditure needed for improving the administrative and judicial apparatus with a view to ensuring speedy trial. The State may have its financial constraints and its priorities in expenditure, but, 'the law does not permit any government to deprive its citizens of constitutional rights on a plea of poverty', or administrative inability."

Thirdly, we are deleting the bars of limitation on the twin grounds that it amounts to judicial legislation, which is not permissible, and because they run counter to the doctrine of binding precedents. The larger question of powers of this court to pass orders and issue directions in public interest or in social action litigations, specially by reference to Articles 32, 141, 142 and 144 of the Constitution, is not the subject matter of reference before us and this judgment should not be read as an interpretation of those Articles of the Constitution and laying down, defining or limiting the scope of the powers exercisable thereunder by this Court.

And lastly, it is clarified that this decision shall not be a ground for re-opening a case or proceeding by setting aside any such acquittal or discharge as is based on the authority of 'Common Cause' and 'Raj Deo Sharma' cases and which has already achieved finality and re-open the trial against the accused therein.

CHAPTER EIGHTEEN

18. TMA Pai Foundation and Ors. v. State of Karnataka and Ors.[2002] 3 : (2002) 8 SSC 481 : AIR 2003 SC 355

(11-judge order which laid down the contours of governmental regulations on private institutions. It also specifically provides for the educational rights of the **minorities** to 'establish and administer the educational institutions of their choice' under Article 30. The minority-run institutions have the autonomy to recruit their teachers as per their preference with just one caveat held by the court that the recruitment must be transparent, fair, and merit-based but no monitoring bodies have been constituted. The court held that the minority status of any religion will be decided state-wise and not nation-wise. It is the fundamental right of the minorities to set up their educational institutions but these rights given to them under Article 30(1) will not be absolute. It must be read with article 29(2) and also concerning all the other fundamental rights. The state can impose reasonable restrictions on such institutions. The minority institutions can admit students as per the criteria decided by them if they are not getting any aid from the state. The admission process should be transparent, merit-based, and fair. Merit should not be compromised even if it is an unaided minority institution. In the case of aided institutions, the state can regulate the admission process for the forward classes. It was also recommended that the primary criteria for admissions should be merit while keeping in mind the need to make special provisions for candidates of the backward classes. The admissions policy of the state should be redrafted and implemented accordingly. Even the recruitment of the teaching staff should be fair. Basic provisions to regulate the aforesaid things can be made by the state but the independence of the minority institutions should not get damaged. Fees charged by unaided minority institutions cannot be regulated, however it shouldn't be higher than what is approved by the regulatory norms.

Moreover, State can regulate the service conditions of the teaching and administrative staff without impeding general administrative control. If minority institutions get any financial aid and grants from the state then they should reserve some seats for the open category also to a reasonable extent based upon merit. The minority institutions are of two categories i.e., aided and unaided educational institutions. Unaided educational institutions have more autonomy than aided ones. Since the minority institutions allow non-minority students for admissions based upon merit, it will not amount to a contravention of Article 29(2) despite the institution admitting minority students of their choice. Finally, it was held by the court that 50 percent of the total seats of the petitioner's educational institutes will be selected by the state government based on competitive exams or some other alternative tests. The candidates will pay fees as per the limit sanctioned by the state governmen)

Article 30: Right of minorities to establish and administer educational institutions

(1) All minorities, whether based on religion or language, shall have the right to establish and administer educational institutions of their choice

(2) The state shall not, in granting aid to educational institutions, discriminate against any educational institution on the ground that it is under the management of a minority, whether based on religion or language.

BENCH: Quadri, S.S.M. (J), Pal, Ruma (J), Variava, S.N. (J), Balakrishnan, K.G. (J) Reddi, P.V. (J), Bhan, Ashok (J) Pasayat, Arijit (J)

FACTS OF THE CASE:

1. T.M.A Pai is a trust whereas Manipal Institute of Technology is an educational institution which is owned and administered by the trust. An academic institution called 'The Academy of General Education' was formed by Dr. T.M.A Pai which was registered as a society under the Societies Registration Act in the place called Manipal which was in the state of Madras but after the recognition of the states, it has become a part of the state of Karnataka.

2. Many institutions were formed under the name of the same academy including Manipal Engineering College Trust. The object of the trust as indicated in the trust deed is to promote Konkani language, culture and also for the educational advancement of the students speaking in Konkani language in addition to all casts and communities.

3. With the object of prohibiting the evil collection of the fee in excess amount, the governor of the state promulgated an ordinance called the **Karnataka Educational Institutions Ordinance, 1984** under the prohibition of the capital fee.

4. Questioning the validity of the said ordinance and the order of the state government which was dated on 19.07.1984 fixing the total intake of college and also earmarking 40% of the seats thereof as government seats, therefore, a writ petition was presented regarding the same. Thereof during the pendency of the petition, an act came into force fixing the rates of capitation fee and tuition fee chargeable to private unaided educational institutions.

As the college is not receiving any financial aid from the state government it is declared under the category of a private unaided educational institution.'

ISSUES BEFORE THE COURT:

1. Whether there exists a fundamental right to set up educational institutions and if so, under which provision?
2. To what extent government may impose regulations upon private institutions?
3. What is to be the unit to determine the existence of a religious or linguistic **minority** in relation to Article 30?

PETITIONER`S ARGUMENTS:

1. The petitioners contended that the Karnataka Educational Institutions (Prohibition of Capitation Fee) Act is violative of Article 30 of the constitution which conferred a fundamental right on the linguistic and religious **minorities** to establish and administer the educational institutions of their choice.
2. The petitioners contended that Konkani is a language of a section of people in the state which constitutes a **minority.**

3. The petitioners contended that TMA PAI was a Konkani speaking person by birth therefore after his demise to commemorate his memory and to promote his objectives a Konkani speaking institution was established. As Konkani being a **minority** speaking the language in Karnataka they are entitled to protection under article 30 of the constitution.
4. The petitioners contended that government cannot impose any restrictions on unaided **minority** institutions, as they are protected under Article 30.

RESPONDENT`S ARGUMENTS:

1. The Respondents contended that the Manipal institution was not established by a **minority** and for the benefit of Konkani speaking people.
2. The respondents contended that the Act has been enacted to destroy the practice of collecting capitation fee and commercialisation of education. Therefore the provisions of the Act are not violative of Article 30, 14 and 19 of the Constitution.
3. The respondent contended that Article 30 is applicable to professional education.
4. The respondent contention that Article 30 is not an absolute right, therefore the government can impose restrictions.

JUDGMENT:

The majority judgement consisting of 6 judges held that:-

1. With regard to State law, the unit to determine a religious or linguistic **minority** can only be the State.
2. The **minorities**' rights under Article 30(1) cover **professional education** as indicated by the use of the words “of their choice”.
3. Any regulation framed in the national interest must necessarily apply to all educational institutions, whether run by the majority or the **minority.** Such a limitation must necessarily be read into Article 30. The right under Article 30(1) cannot be such as to override the national interest or to prevent the Government from framing regulations on that behalf.
4. Article 30(2) only means that a **minority** institution shall not be discriminated against where aid to educational institutions is granted. If an abject surrender of the right to management is made a condition of

aid, the denial of aid would violate Article 30(2).

5. The right conferred on the **minorities** by Art. 30(1) is not absolute. It has to be read subject to Art. 29(2) and other fundamental rights. **Minority** educational institutions thus become divisible into two categories, viz.: aided educational institutions and unaided educational institutions. The unaided institutions enjoy much greater autonomy than aided institutions.
6. As long as the **minority** educational institution permits the admission of citizens belonging to the **non-minority** class to a reasonable extent based upon merit, it will not be an infraction of Article 29(2), even though the institution admits students of the **minority** group of its own choice for whom the institution was meant.
7. Right of **minorities** includes right to determine the procedure and method of admission and selection of students which must be fair and transparent and based on merit for professional and higher education colleges.
8. Even unaided **minority** institution cannot ignore merit. In the case of an aided institution, for non-**minority** students, the State can regulate the admission which has to be merit-based subject to the reservation policy of the State. Merit to be determined by an entrance test or by any other method with consideration for weaker sections.
9. In the case of unaided **minority** institutions, the regulatory measure of control by the State should be minimal though the condition of recognition and of affiliation have to be complied with, and though matters of appointment of teaching and non-teaching staff and administrative control over them would be beyond regulation. Fees charged by unaided institutions cannot be regulated but they cannot charge capitation fee.
10. In the case of aided **minority** institutions, regulations can be provided for conditions of service of teaching and other staff without interfering with the overall administrative control.
11. Fifty percent of the total seats in the educational institutions of the petitioner should select the candidates selected by the state government on the basis of a competitive examination or a test. The candidates who get selected in such a way should pay scales of fee as applicable to this class of students as determined by the State Government from time to time.

CHAPTER NINETEEN

P. A. Inamdar & Ors. v. State of Maharashtra, (2005) 6 SCC 537

(The seven-member Bench comprising Chief Justice R.C. Lahoti and Justices Y.K. Sabharwal, D.M. Dharmadhikari, Arun Kumar, G.P. Mathur, Tarun Chatterjee and P.K. Balasubramanian, held unanimously that enforcing the reservation policy of the State on seats in unaided professional institutions constitutes a serious encroachment on the right and autonomy of these institutions. The Bench held that merely because the State's resources in providing professional education are limited, it cannot force private educational institutions, which intend to provide better professional education, to make admissions on the basis of its reservation policy to less meritorious candidates.)

TWO CASES :P. A. Inamdar & Ors. v. State of Maharashtra

1. DECIDED BY 2 JUDGES

P.A. Inamdar & Ors. v. State of Maharashtra, (2004) 8 SCC 139

It is a case decided by a 2-Judge Bench of the Supreme Court, in which the dispute related to the fixation of quota in respect of unaided professional institutions and to the holding of examinations for admission into such colleges. The interpretation put by a 5-Judge Bench in the case of Islamic Academy of Education v. State of Karnataka, (2003) 6 SCC 697, on the 11-Judge Bench decision in the case of T.M.A. Pai Foundation v. State of Karnataka, (2002) 8 SCC 481, was also in question. The 2-Judge Bench decided that the issues raised should be referred to a larger Bench for final determination having regard to the nature of the controversy involved in this case.

2. DECIDED BY 7 JUDGES

P.A. Inamdar & Ors. v. State of Maharashtra, (2005) 6 SCC 537

FACTS OF THE CASE:

This is a case decided by a 2-Judge Bench of the Supreme Court, in which the dispute related to the fixation of quota in respect of unaided professional institutions and to the holding of examinations for admission into such colleges. The interpretation put by a 5-Judge Bench in the case of ***Islamic Academy of Education* v. *State of Karnataka*, (2003) 6 SCC 697**, on the 11-Judge Bench decision in the case of ***T.M.A. Pai Foundation* v. *State of Karnataka*, (2002) 8 SCC 481**, was also in question. The 2-Judge Bench decided that the issues raised should be referred to a larger Bench for final determination having regard to the nature of the controversy involved in this case.

As an interim measure, for the academic year 2004-05, for the State of Karnataka, it was *prima facie* held in this case that the seats should be filled up by the institutions concerned in the ratio of 50:50 purely as a temporary measure and without prejudice to the contentions of the parties for the purpose of the final disposal. Likewise, Interim orders were issued for certain colleges in State of Maharashtra

In this way 2 judges bencch case was raffered to 7 judges bench for adjudication.

ISSUES BEFORE THE COURT:

1. Is there a fundamental right to set up educational institutions?
2. Does Unni Krishnan require reconsideration?
3. In case of private institutions, can there be government regulations and, if so, to what extent?

JUDGMENT BY 2 JUDGES :

The setting up of the committees in *Islamic Academy,* the extent of quotas and state reservation in private institutions, and the regulation of fees was once again challenged before the Supreme Court and a larger bench of seven judges was set up in *PA Inamdar v. State of Maharashtra,*(2005) 6 SCC 537,in order to clarify the ratio of the judgment in *TMA Pai*. The Court in *Inamdar* held:

a. The policy of reservation cannot be enforced by the state nor can a quota or percentage of admissions be carved out to be appropriated by the state.

b. A common entrance test can be held by a group of similarly placed institutions provided that it is fair, transparent, and non-exploitative. The state may itself or through an agency, arrange for holding such tests and students can be admitted on the basis of merit out of these common entrance tests. However, the state may only take over if the three criteria mentioned above are not satisfied.

c. Every institution is free to devise its own fee structure subject to the limitation that there can be no profiteering and no capitation fee can be charged directly or indirectly, or in any form. NRI seats are permissible to the extent of 15 per cent in all institutions.

d. The two committees for *monitoring admission procedure* and *determining fee structure* under the judgment of *Islamic Academy* are permissible as regulatory measures.

e. In the absence of any central legislation, it is for the central and state governments to come out with a detailed, well-thought-out legislation on the subject.

***T.M.A. Pai Foundation v. State of Karnataka*, (2002) 8 SCC 481 : AIR 2003 SC 355:**

This is a case decided by a Constitution Bench of 11-Judges of the Supreme Court mainly on the question of scope of right of minorities to establish and administer educational institutions of their choice under Article 30(1) read with Article 29(2) of the Constitution. This judgment deals with the rights of and permissible restrictions upon minority (aided and unaided) institutions. The majority opinion is on behalf of six Judges with one more Judge concurring with the majority by a separate opinion. Remaining four Judges gave three separate opinions in which they party dissented from the majority opinion.

JUDGMENT BY 7 JUDGES :

The Supreme Court held as under:

1. With regard to a State law, the unit to determine a religious or linguistic minority can only be the State.
2. Even for a Central law, for the purpose of determining the minority, the unit will be the State and not the whole of India; thus, religious and linguistic minorities, who have been put on a par in Article 30, have to be considered State-wise.
3. The question, whether followers of a sect or denomination of a particular religion can claim minority status even though followers of that religion

are in majority in that State, was left unanswered to be decided by a regular Bench.

4. The question as to what are the indicia for treating an educational institution as a minority educational institution, whether the fact that it was established by or is administered by person(s) belonging to a religious or linguistic minority is determinative of its character, was also left unanswered to be decided by a regular Bench.
5. The minorities' rights under Article 30(1) cover **professional education** as indicated by the use of the words "of their choice".
6. Any regulation framed in the national interest must necessarily apply to all educational institutions, whether run by the majority or the minority. Such a limitation must necessarily be read into Article 30. The right under Article 30(1) cannot be such as to override the national interest or to prevent the Government from framing regulations in that behalf. It is, of course, true that government regulations cannot destroy the minority character of the institution or make the right to establish and administer a mere illusion; but the right under Article 30 is not so absolute as to be above the law.
7. Even though the words of Article 30(1) are unqualified, at least certain other laws of the land pertaining to health, morality and standards of education apply. The right under Article 30(1) is not absolute or above other provisions of the law. Regulations or conditions concerning, generally, the welfare of students and teachers may be made applicable in order to provide a proper academic atmosphere, as such provisions do not in any way interfere with the right of administration or management under Article 30(1).
8. Article 30(2) only means that a minority institution shall not be discriminated against where aid to educational institutions is granted. If an abject surrender of the right to management is made a condition of aid, the denial of aid would be violative of Article 30(2). However, conditions of aid that do not involve a surrender of the substantial right of management would not be inconsistent with constitutional guarantees, even if they indirectly impinge upon some facet of administration. The implication of Article 30(2) is also that it recognizes that the minority nature of the institution should continue, notwithstanding the grant of aid.
9. Although the right to administer includes within it a right to grant admission to students of their choice under Article 30(1), when such

a minority institution is granted the facility of receiving grant-in-aid, Article 29(2) would apply, and necessarily, therefore, one of the rights of administration of the minorities would be eroded to some extent. As long as the minority educational institution permits admission of citizens belonging to the non-minority class to a reasonable extent based upon merit, it will not be an infraction of Article 29(2), even though the institution admits students of the minority group of its own choice for whom the institution was meant. What would be a reasonable extent would depend upon variable factors, and it may not be advisable to fix any specific percentage. The situation would vary according to the type of institution and the nature of education that is being imparted in the institution. Even if it is possible to fill up all the seats with students of the minority group, the moment the institution is granted aid, the institution will have to admit students of the non-minority group to a reasonable extent. Observing that a ceiling of 50% would not be proper, the Supreme Court held that it will be more appropriate that, depending upon the level of the institution, whether it be a primary or secondary or high school or a college, professional or otherwise, and on the population and educational needs of the area in which the institution is to be located, the State properly balances the interests of all by providing for such a percentage of students of the minority community to be admitted, so as to adequately serve the interest of the community for which the institution was established.

10. For unaided schools and undergraduate colleges, where scope for merit-based selection is practically nil, State or University can provide for the qualifications and minimum eligibility conditions. Admission has to be on a transparent basis and merit considered.
11. Right to administer is not absolute and so regulatory measures can be imposed for ensuring educational standards and maintaining excellence thereof especially in professional institutions.
12. An aided minority institution remains so despite receiving grant-in-aid from the Government. It has a right over admitting its minority students on merit basis. It must also admit a reasonable number of non-minority students. What is a reasonable number is to be decided by State Govt. on consideration of type of institution, the courses of education, population and educational needs etc.
13. Right of minorities includes right to determine the procedure and method of admission and selection of students which must be fair and

transparent and based on merit for professional and higher education colleges. Even unaided minority institution cannot ignore merit. In case of aided institution, for non-minority students, the State can regulate the admission which has to be merit-based subject to reservation policy of the State. Merit to be determined by an entrance test or by any other method with consideration for weaker sections.

14. In case of unaided minority institutions, the regulatory measure of control by the State should be minimal though condition of recognition and of affiliation have to be complied with, and though matters of appointment of teaching and non-teaching staff and administrative control over them would be beyond regulation. Fees charged by unaided institutions cannot be regulated but they cannot charge capitation fee.
15. In case of aided minority institutions, regulations can be provided for conditions of service of teaching and other staff without interfering with the overall administrative control.
16. But, both in aided and unaided minority institutions, management must evolve a rational procedure for selection of teaching staff and for taking disciplinary action. State or controlling authority can always prescribe the minimum qualification, experience and other conditions bearing on the merit of an individual for being appointed as a teacher or a principal of any educational institution.

CHAPTER TWENTY

Technip Sa vs Sms Holding (Pvt.) Ltd. & Ors [2005] 1 Suppl. SCR 223 : (2005) 5 SCC 46

Top of Form

(Securities and Exchange Board of India Act, 1992 Section 15Z – SEBI (Substantial Acquisition of Shares and Takeover) Regulations, 1997 – Regulations 10 and 12 – French Companies Act, 1966 – Article 355-1 – Substantial acquisition/takeover – Prerequisite conditions and procedural compliances – Takeover without making any public offer – Consequence – Technip and Coflexip were companies incorporated in France – SEAMEC was a company incorporated and registered in India – Coflexip, through a chain of wholly owned subsidiaries was controlling the majority shareholding of SEAMEC – Thus SEAMEC was a subsidiary of Coflexip – Price of SEAMEC shares in April 2000 was Rs 238 but in July 2001 the price was Rs. 43.12 – Technip acquiring control over SEAMEC without making any public announcement – On a complaint SEBI taking the view that the French law applied to the takeover of Coflexip and consequently SEAMEC by Technip and holding that Technip obtained control of Coflexip in July 2001 and had violated Regulations 10 and 12 thereby acquiring 58.24 per cent of the shares/voting rights and control of SEAMEC in July 2001 without making public offer – SEBI accordingly directing Technip to make a public announcement within 45 days of its order taking 3.7.2001 as specified date for calculation of the offer price – Technip also directed to pay 15 per cent interest to willing minority shareholders of SEAMEC for the delayed public announcement – Minority shareholders of SEAMEC appealing to Securities Appellate Tribunal (SAT) – Said Tribunal while concurring with the finding of the SEBI regarding violation of the Takeover Regulations, holding that the Indian law was applicable and that the relevant date on which control of SEAMEC was taken over by Technip was April 2000 and accordingly directing 12.4.2000 to be taken as the date for calculating the offer price – Validity. Setting aside the order of SAT and restoring the decision of SEBI held that there was no evidence to show that Technip obtained de facto control of Coflexip in April 2000 and therefore SEBI was correct in coming to the conclusion that Technip obtained control of Coflexip in July 2001 and consequently the acquisition of controlling interest of SEAMEC was only in July 2001 and accordingly specifying 3.7.2001 as the specified date for calculation of the offer price)

On 11 May, 2005

Author: R Pal

Bench: Ruma Pal, Arijit Pasayat, C.K. Thakker

FACTS OF THE CASE:-

There are five main protagonists in these appeals, the appellant,

Technip, a company incorporated in France,

Coflexip, also incorporated in France,

the Institut Francais du Petrol (referred to as IFP) which through its subsidiary ISIS, a company incorporated in France,

was a shareholder in Technip and Coflexip,

South East Asia Marine Engineering and Construction Ltd. (referred to as SEAMEC), a company incorporated and registered in India and finally the respondents who are the shareholders of SEAMEC.

SEAMEC is a subsidiary of Coflexip in the sense that Coflexip through a chain of wholly owned subsidiaries controls the majority shareholding in SEAMEC.

QUESTION OF LAW:-

1. whether Technip acquired control of SEAMEC through Coflexip in April, 2000, or in July, 2001? There is no dispute that if Technip controls Coflexip then it also controls SEAMEC and if there has been a change of control of SEAMEC then Technip would be bound to offer to purchase the shares of the minority shareholders in SEAMEC in accordance with the provisions of the Securities And Exchange Board of India (Substantial Acquisition of Shares and Takeover)Regulations, 1997 (hereinafter referred

to as the Regulations). The importance of the date of control/acquisition is because of the price of the shares payable on such public offer. In this case the price of SEAMEC shares in April 2000 was Rs.238 per share which was much higher than the price of Rs.43.12 per share in July, 2001. Technip had not made any public announcement at all, either in April 2000 or in July, 2001.

On the complaint of certain shareholders of SEAMEC before the Securities and Exchange Board of India (SEBI), proceedings were initiated against Technip under the Securities and Exchange Board of India Act, 1992 (referred as 'the Act'). SEBI held that French law applied to the takeover of Coflexip and consequently SEAMEC by Technip for the purpose of determining when such takeover was effected. It found that the Technip had obtained control of Coflexip in July 2001 and had violated Regulations 10 and 12 of the Regulations thereby acquiring 58.24% of the shares/voting rights and control in SEAMEC in July 2001 without making any public offer. Technip was accordingly directed by SEBI to make a public announcement as required under the Regulations within 45 days of its order taking 3rd July, 2001 as the specified date for calculation of the offered price. Technip was also directed to pay interest at the rate of 15% per annum to the willing minority shareholders of SEAMEC, for the delayed public announcement.

The minority shareholders of SEAMEC preferred an appeal from SEBI's order before the Securities Appellate Tribunal (SAT) constituted under the Act. Their grievance was that the date of control of Coflexip by Technip was 12.4.2000 and not 3rd July, 2001 as held by SEBI. While the appeal was pending, pursuant to an interim order passed by the Tribunal, Technip implemented the order of SEBI by making a public announcement to acquire the shares of SEAMEC by taking 3rd July, 2001 as the specified date. Technip has also made payment of the share consideration together with the interest thereon to the shareholders of SEAMEC who accepted the public offer.

The Tribunal held that the applicable law to the question as to when control of SEAMEC had been taken over by Technip, was Indian Law. The Tribunal affirmed SEBI's conclusion that the Regulations had been violated by Technip by its failure to make a public announcement but decided that the relevant date on which the control of SEAMEC was taken over by Technip was April, 2000. The Tribunal accordingly directed Technip to treat the relevant date for calculating the offer price as 12th April, 2000 and to pay SEAMEC shareholders the difference between the price of the shares between 3.7.2001 and 12th April, 2000 together with the interest on such difference at the rate of 15%. One of the grounds on which the Tribunal came to the conclusion that Technip had taken over Coflexip in April, 2000 was based on the fact that both the companies had been promoted by IFP and that IFP through ISIS acting in concert with Technip had brought about the takeover of Coflexip by Technip.

According to Technip, since Technip and Coflexip are both registered in France and the takeover of Coflexip by Technip also took place in France, the applicable law is French. In terms of French Law, according to Technip, there was no control of Coflexip by Technip in April, 2000 and as such there was no change in control of SEAMEC on that date but in July 2001. It is further submitted that in any event Regulation 12 did not apply to the takeover because SEAMEC was not the target company and that while taking over Coflexip, Technip neither had the common objective nor was there any agreement between Technip and Coflexip with regard to SEAMEC. The rate of interest has also been challenged. It is said that although there was no challenge to the rate which was fixed by SEBI, if the Tribunal's order is upheld, then the impact of interest would be much greater. It is submitted that in any event, the dividend paid must be adjusted against the interest claimed. It is the final submission of Technip that if April 2000 is to be taken as the date of control, then only those shareholders who were shareholders of SEAMEC on the specified date and continued as such till the offer was made are entitled to the benefit of the Tribunal's order. A separate appeal has been preferred by IFP from the decision of the Tribunal being CA No.10092/98. The grievance of IFP is that it is a professional body created by decree of the French Government and has been set up as a centre for research and industrial development, education, professional training and information for the oil and gas and automotive industries in France. IFP does not carry on any industry or commercial activities nor does it manage or control any listed company. It promotes companies to apply the results of its own research. IFP says that an unnecessary stigma has been cast by the Tribunal's decision on a Government organization even though the show cause notice issued by SEBI did not make any allegation against IFP.

The respondents have on the other hand argued that the law applicable to SEAMEC was Indian Law and to determine if there was a change in the management and control of SEAMEC the provisions of the Regulations would apply. In terms of Regulations 10, 11 and 12 read with Regulation 2, any person, who acquires shares or voting rights in a registered company (described as a target company under the Regulations) above 15% or acquires control over the target company is required to make a public announcement offering to purchase the shares of the other shareholders in the target company. It is the submission of the respondents that according to Indian and French Law de facto control of Coflexip and therefore SEAMEC was taken over by Technip in April, 2000. The respondents also claim that Technip had in fact applied to SEBI to exempt them from the operation of the Regulations. The application had been rejected. This issue according to the respondent could not, therefore be reopened. It is said that SEAMEC was very much in the contemplation of Technip when it decided to take over Coflexip. It is asserted that therefore Regulations 10,11 and 12 applied in full measure. Technip had not only acted in concert with ISIS, another shareholder of Coflexip, but even by itself was in a position to exercise and in fact exercised control over Coflexip and therefore SEAMEC in April 2000.

The shareholders of SEAMEC may be classified into three groups;

a) Those, who were shareholders of SEAMEC in April, 2000 and continued as such;

b) Those, who were not shareholders in April, 2000 but were shareholders during the public offer having purchased the shares of SEAMEC before July, 2001.

c) Those shareholders, who were shareholders on the date of the public offer holding shares purchased in April 2000 and more shares after April, 2000 but before July, 2001.

The respondents who belong to group (b) have said that the public offer made by Technip after SEBI's order was unconditional. It was made to the shareholders who were shareholders as on the date of the public offer. On the question of interest it is said that it was not open to Technip to question either its liability to pay interest or the rate of interest and that Technip had already paid interest to the present shareholders without protest. Finally it is said that the finding of fact by the Tribunal should not be interfered with unless this Court came to the conclusion under Section 15Z of the Act that it was perverse.

We will start with this final submission. Section 15Z of the SEBI Act, 1992 allows any person aggrieved by the decision or the order of the Securities Appellate Tribunal to file an appeal to the Supreme Court on any question of law arising out of such order. Now the primary dispute in this appeal is whether the impugned transaction is to be judged according to French Law or Indian Law. That is a question of law. Furthermore, the determination as to what French Law is, is doubtless a question of fact but it is "a question of fact of a peculiar kind". As has been commented in Cheshire and North's Private International Law (12th Edn.) "To describe it (foreign law) as one of fact is no doubt apposite, in the sense that the applicable law must be ascertained according to the evidence of witnesses, yet there can be no doubt that what is involved is at bottom a question of law. This has been recognized by the courts".

Admittedly both Coflexip and Technip were incorporated according to and under the laws of France. They are therefore 'domiciled' in France. Normally, we would resolve any issue relating to their internal affairs by applying the law of their domicil, in this case French Law (See: Hazard Brothers & Co. v. Midland Bank Ltd. 1933 AC 289, 297; Metliss v. National Bank of Greece & Athens, SA: [1961] AC 255). But by that token it is equally true that SEAMEC which was incorporated in India would be governed by Indian law and that is what SAT held:

"SEBI has viewed (sic) that since Technip and Coflexip are French companies, matters relating to them should be decided in accordance with French law. To the said extent SEBI is correct. SEBI has no jurisdiction to regulate takeovers and acquisitions taking place outside India. But certainly SEBI has jurisdiction to regulate substantial acquisition and takeovers of companies in India".

But then it came to the conclusion that even the question "whether Technip acquired control over Coflexip on 12.4.2000 and consequently over SEAMEC need be tested in the light of 2(c) definition". In other words Indian law would apply to determine whether the control of Coflexip was taken over by Technip. According to SAT any view to the contrary would "lead to absurd consequences even defeating the very objective of the Takeover Regulations". SAT's conclusion as to the applicable law is questioned by the appellant and that cannot be considered as a question of fact. As held in Dalmia Dairy Industries Ltd. Vs. National Bank of Pakistan , the role of the appellate Court is such cases is:

"..to examine the evidence of foreign law which was before the justices and to decide for ourselves whether that evidence justifies the conclusion to which they came ".

The respondent's preliminary objection to the maintainability of the appeal is accordingly rejected.

The jurisdiction of SEBI or SAT or indeed this Court to apply foreign law has not been questioned at any stage. What is referred to as "private international law" by some authorities is referred to as conflict of laws by others . Whatever the nomenclature, it is based on the 'just disposal of proceedings having a foreign element'. To quote from Kuwait Airways Corp. v. Iraqi Airways Co. (2002) UKHL 19.

"The jurisprudence is founded on the recognition that in proceedings having connections with more than one country an issue brought before a court in one country may be more appropriately decided by reference to the laws of another country even though those laws are different from the law of the forum court."

We have already said and it must be taken to be a generally accepted rule of private international law, that questions of status of a person's domicile ought in general to be recognized in other countries unless it is contrary to public policy. Questions of status of an individual would include matters such as legal competence, marriage and custody. (See in re Langley's Settlement Trusts (1962) Ch. 541); Russ v. Russ (1962) 3 All E.R.; Smt. Surinder Kaur Sandhu v. Harbax Singh Sandhu: AIR 1984 SC 1224; Oppenheimer v. Cattermole (1975) 1 All ER 538). Questions as to the status of a corporation are to be decided according to the laws of its domicil or incorporation subject to certain exceptions including the exception of domestic public policy. This is because "a corporation is a purely artificial body created by law. It can act only in accordance with the law of its creation". Therefore, if it is a corporation, it can be so only by virtue of the law by which it was incorporated and it is to this law alone that all questions concerning the creation and dissolution of the corporate status are referred unless it is contrary to public policy. [See: In the matter of American Fibre Chair Seat Corporation. William Daum et al. v. Arthur J Kinsman 265 N.Y.416; 193 N.E.253; McDermott Inc. v. Harry Lewis, 531 A.2d 206; Richard Reid Rogers v. Guaranty Trust Company of New York (288 US 123- 151(S.C.(U.S.) Carl Zeiss Stiftung v. Rayner and Keller Ltd. (1966)2 ALL ER 536; Gaudiya Mission & Ors. v. Brahmachari & Ors. 1998 Ch. 341; Kuwait Airways Corp. V. Iraqi Airways Co. (No. 3) 2002 UKHL 19; Lazard Brothers & Co. v. Midland Bank Ltd. (1933) AC 289 at 297; Cheshire and North's Private International Law (12th Edn.) p.174].

This general rule regarding determination of status by the lex incorporationis will not apply when the issue relates to the discharge of obligations or assertion of rights by a corporation in another country whether such obligation is imposed by or right arises under statute or contract which is governed by the law of such other country. The distinction is brought out in the case of National Bank of Greece and Athens S.A. and Metliss: 58 A.C. 509. A Greek Bank had issued mortgage bonds to persons in U.K. in pounds sterling. The bonds were guaranteed by another bank. Both the issuing bank and the guaranteeing bank were incorporated under Greek Law. The guaranteeing bank was subsequently amalgamated with a third Greek company and a new company was formed. A bond holder sued the new company seeking to enforce the guarantee. Under the Greek law there was a moratorium imposed on payments by the new bank. It was held by the House of Lords that the status of the new bank would be decided according to the law of the domicile of the original guarantor company and the new company which was Greek law. It was found that according to Greek law the new company succeeded to the assets and liabilities of the guarantor company. The question then was whether the English Courts would recognize the moratorium as debarring the bond holder from enforcing his rights under the bond. It was not in dispute that the bond was governed by English law. It was held that the evidence of the effect of the Greek moratorium in Greece was therefore irrelevant. "This was an English debt and the obligation to pay it, its quantum and the date of payment, are all governed by English law which will not give effect to the Greek Moratorium." (pg. 529) The claim of the bond holder was accordingly allowed. Consequent upon the decision of the House of Lords a new Greek law was passed retrospectively modifying the terms of the amalgamation, so that the new bank was no longer required to discharge the original guarantor's dues to the bond holders. The House of Lords in Adams vs. National Bank of Greece S.A. 1961 A.C. 255, 282 again rejected the new bank's submission that it was not liable on the bonds. It was held that what was sought to be enforced was not "a Greek right, but a right arising under a contract under English law". It was held:

"It is well settled that English law cannot give effect to a foreign law which discharges an English liability to pay money in England and the appellants' contracts were English contracts under which they were to be paid in England".

Although the law of the Bank's domicile determined its status as a debtor, it could not determine the liability of the defendant on a contract subject expressly to English law. The relationship of Technip to Coflexip whether one of control or not is really a question of their status. The applicable law would therefore be the law of their domicil, namely, French law. Having determined their status according to French Law, the next question as to their obligation under the Indian Law vis a vis SEAMEC would have to be governed exclusively by Indian law (in this case the Act and the Regulations). SAT's error lay in not differentiating between the two issues of status and the obligation by reason of the status and in seeking to cover both under a single system of law. But, contend the respondents, the French law even if applicable, was contrary to the Act and Regulations and is thereby contrary to the public policy underlying the Indian enactment. In our view, domestic public policy which can justify a disregard of the applicable foreign law must relate to basic principles of morality and justice and the foreign law amount to a flagrant or gross breach of such principles. As far back as in 1918, Cardozo J, speaking for the Bench in Fannie F. Loucks et al., as Administrators of the Estate of Everett A. Loucks, Deceased, Appellants, V. Standard Oil Company of New York, Respondent. 224 N.Y.99; said:

"The courts are not free to refuse to enforce a foreign right at the pleasure of the judges, to suit the individual notion of expediency or fairness. They do not close their doors unless help would violate some fundamental principle of justice, some prevalent conception of good morals, some deep-rooted tradition of the common weal".

Similarly the House of Lords in Kuwait Airways Corp. v. Iraqi Airways Co.(No.3): (2002) UKHL 19 said: "Exceptionally and rarely, a provision of foreign law will be disregarded when it would lead to a result wholly alien to fundamental requirements of justice as administered by an English court".

In other words the power to disregard a provision in the foreign law must be exercised exceptionally and with the greatest circumspection "when to do otherwise would affront basic principles of justice and fairness which the courts seek to apply in the administration of justice in this country. Gross infringements of human rights are one instance, and an important instance, of such provision". (ibid) The issue in the latter case arose out of an Iraqi law which confiscated Kuwaiti aeroplanes and vested them in the Iraqi Airlines Corporation. The Court refused to recognize the Iraqi law because:

"a legislative act by a foreign state which is an flagrant breach of clearly established rules of international law ought not to be recognized by the courts of this country as forming part of the lex situs of that state".

This Court in Renusagar Power Co. Ltd. Vs. General Electric Co. 1994 Supp.(1) SCC 644 while construing Section 7 (1) (b) of the Foreign Awards Act which allows Indian Courts the power to refuse to enforce foreign awards which are contrary to public policy, has held that:- ".defence of public policy which is permissible under Section 7(1) (b) (ii) should be construed narrowly. It must be held that the enforcement of a foreign award would be refused on the ground that it is contrary to public policy if such enforcement would be contrary to (i) fundamental policy of Indian law; or (ii) the interests of India; or (iii) justice or morality. (pg.682) In that case it had been argued by the appellant that the expression "public policy" in Section 7(1) (b) (ii) of the Act has to be construed in a liberal sense and not narrowly and it would include within its ambit disregard of the provisions of the Foreign Exchange Regulations Act, 1973. This Court accepted the argument on the ground that the provisions contained in FERA have been enacted to safeguard the economic interests of India and any violation of the said provisions would be contrary to the public policy of India as envisaged in Section 7(1)(b)(ii) of the Act. However on the facts it was held that the enforcement of the award would not involve violation of any of the provisions of FERA and for that reason it not would be contrary to public policy of India so as to render the award unenforceable in view of Section 7(1)(b)(ii) of that Act. In a sense all statutes enacted by Parliament or the States can be said to be part of Indian public policy. But to discard a foreign law only because it is contrary to an Indian statute would defeat the basis of private international law to which India undisputedly subscribes.[See: Surinder Kaur Sandhu v Harbax Singh Sandhu (supra)]. To quote again from the Kuwait Airways case (supra).

"The laws of the other country may have adopted solutions, or even basic principles, rejected by the law of the forum country. These differences do not in themselves furnish reasons why the forum court should decline to apply the foreign law. On the contrary, the existence of differences is the very reason why it may be appropriate for the forum court to have recourse to the foreign law. If the laws of all countries were uniform there would be no 'conflict' of laws".

The Bhagwati Committee Report on Takeovers (1997) which was prepared after examining the principles and practices and the regulatory framework governing takeovers in as many as fourteen countries noted that while the practice and procedures vary from country to country, the principles and the concerns- cardinal among which are equality of opportunity to all shareholders, protection of minority interest, transparency and fairness-have remained more or less common. The aim of French Law like Indian Law is to ensure that all parties to a public tender offer respect the principles of shareholder equality, market transparency and integrity, fair trading and fair competition. All this is culled from the opinions of the experts relied upon by all the parties. Under Section 45 of the Evidence Act, 1972, the Court can take the admitted position into consideration in order to form an opinion as to the text of the relevant French law. [See: De Beeche and Ors. Vs. The South American Stores (Gath and Chaves Limited and the Chilian Stores Gath and Chaves Limited) 1934 LR A.C. 148] Undisputedly, in April 2000, the relevant law in force in France was Article 355-1 of the French Companies Act 1966 (LOI No.66-537, du 24 Juillet 1966, Sur les Societas Commerciales). It read as follows:-

"I. A company shall be regarded as controlling another:

(1) When it directly or indirectly holds a percentage of the capital conferring on it the majority of the voting rights in the general meetings of this company;

(2) When it alone holds the majority of the voting rights in this company pursuant to an agreement concluded with other members or shareholders and which is not contrary to the interests of the company;

(3) When it actually makes, due to the voting rights which it holds, the decisions in the general meetings of this company.

"II. It shall be presumed to exercise this control when it directly or indirectly holds a percentage of the voting rights higher than 40% and when no other member or shareholder directly or indirectly holds a percentage higher than its own."

Sub-clauses (1) and (2) of Clause (1) of Article 355-1, deal with de jure acquisition of control by one company of another. The third sub-clause deals with de facto control. All three sub-sections deal with the position of a company acting on its own. Clause II of Article 355.1 provided for statutory presumption of control when the acquiring company directly or indirectly held more than 40% of the voting rights and was the largest shareholder.

In May, 2001, Article 355-1 of the 1996 Act was amended to include the following Sub-section:-

"III. In order to apply the same sections of this chapter, two or more persons acting in concert shall be regarded as jointly controlling another when they actually make, under an agreement to implement a common policy, the decisions taken in the general meetings of the latter."

Clause III provides for control being acquired by persons acting in concert under an agreement to implement a common policy if they actually take decisions in furtherance of such agreement at general meetings of the "controlled company". The entire Article was incorporated in the French Commercial Code as Article L 233-3 in 2002. The second relevant Article is Article 356-1. Roughly translated it provided:-

"Any individual or legal entity, acting alone or in concert, that becomes the owner of a number of shares representing more than one twentieth, one tenth, one fifth, one third, one half or two thirds of the capital or the voting rights of a company having its registered office in France and whose shares are admitted for trading on a regulated market or are traded on the over-the- counter market as stated in article 34 of law no.96-597 dated July 2nd, 1996 relating to the modernization of financial activities, shall inform such company in a period of 15 days as of the crossing upwards of the threshold of the total number of shares that such person holds.

The owner also informs the Conceil de Marches Financiers (CMF) within a period of 5 trading days as of the day of crossing upwards of the threshold when the shares are listed on a regulated market. The CMF makes public such information.

The notifications referred to in the two proceeding paragraphs are also to be provided in the same period when the equity interest falls below the thresholds provided in the first paragraph.

The owner who is required to disclose the information in accordance with the first paragraph above specifies the number of securities that it possesses giving access to the capital of the company as well as the voting rights attached thereto.

The by-laws of the company can provide for additional disclosure obligations relating to holdings of fractions of the capital or voting rights that are less than the one-twentieth mentioned in the preceding paragraph. The obligation relates to holding each such fraction, which cannot be less than 0.5% of the capital or voting rights.

In the event of a failure to satisfy the disclosure obligations mentioned in the preceding paragraph, the by-laws of the company may stipulate that the provisions of the first two paragraphs of article 356-4 shall apply only if requested and duly recorded in the minutes of the general meeting, by one or more shareholders holding a fraction of the capital or the voting rights of the issuing company at least equal to the smallest fraction of the capital held which must be declared. This percentage shall nevertheless not be greater than 5%.

The owner who is required to disclose according to the first paragraph must declare upon exceeding the thresholds of one tenth or one fifth of the capital or the voting rights the objectives that he intends to pursue over the coming twelve months. This declaration shall state whether the acquirer is acting alone or in concert, whether he intends to make further purchases, whether he intends to acquire control of the company, and whether he intends to seek his appointment or that of one or more other persons to the board of directors, management committee or surveillance committee. It is sent to the company whose shares have been acquired and to the CMF who publishes it, and to the Commission des Operations de Bourse (COB), within fifteen trading days of surpassing the threshold. Should those intentions change, and this is admissible only in the event of substantial changes in the environment, the financial situation or the shareholder base of the persons concerned, a new declaration must be made and published in the same way.

The last paragraph of Section 356-I provides that, upon crossing the thresholds of 10% of share capital or voting rights in the target company, and again of 20% of share capital or voting rights in the target company, the purchaser is required to file with the Stock Exchange Authorities, with copy to the target company, a Statement of Intent, specifying (i) whether the purchaser acts alone or in concert with third parties, (ii) whether the purchaser intends to continue acquiring shares in the target company, (iii) whether the purchaser intends to acquire control of the target company and (iv), whether the purchaser intends to seek representation on the Board of Directors of the target. The Section has been re-enacted as L 233-7 of the 2002, French Commercial Code.

Therefore, French Law at the relevant time provided that a company holds control over another (the Target Company) in the following cases.

(i) the Company holds, directly or indirectly, title to a number of shares granting to such holder a majority of voting rights in the general meetings of shareholders of the Target.

(ii) the Company holds the majority of voting rights in the Target pursuant to an agreement with a third party or as a result of acting in concert with such third party.

(iii) the Company in effect determines, through the votes it holds, the decisions taken in the general meetings of shareholders of the Target (what is known as 'de facto' control).

The Stock Exchange authorities in France are the Conceil des Marches Financiers or the French Financial Markets Authority (referred to as the 'CMF') and the Commission des Operations de Bourse viz. the French Stock Exchange Authority (referred to as the 'COB'). They are regulatory bodies with powers of inspection, supervision and disciplinary action. The supervisory role of CMF is itself subject to the Commission Bancaire or the French Banking Commission and the COB. Article 1 and Article 2 of Decree No. 96-869 dated October 3, 1996 also provide for appeals from the decisions taken by the CMF before the Paris Courts of Appeals. Article 33 of Chapter- I Title-II provides that the CMF shall set forth the Rules governing public offers including the conditions under which a natural or legal person, acting alone or in concert within the meaning of Article 356-1-3 of Law 66-37 dated July 24, 1966 aforesaid and who directly or indirectly comes to hold a certain percentage of the capital stock or voting rights in a company whose shares are traded on a regulated market to forthwith inform the CMF and file a proposed tender offer with a view to acquiring a specified quantity of the company's securities. If this filing is not made, the securities that the person holds in excess of the aforementioned percentage of the capital stock or voting rights shall be deprived of voting rights.

The provisions in French law relating to takeovers as we see them are, therefore, rigorous. The Indian law is no less rigorous and differs only marginally with the French law on the subject.

The three relevant Regulations which were alleged to have been violated by Technip are Regulations 10,11 and 12. Regulations 10,11 and 12 are contained in Chapter III of the Regulations which deals with substantial acquisition of shares or voting rights in and acquisition of control over a listed company:-

"10. No acquirer shall acquire shares or voting rights which (taken together with shares or voting rights if any, held by him or by persons acting in concert with him), entitle such acquirer or exercise fifteen percent or more of the voting right in a company, unless such acquirer makes a public announcement to acquire shares of such company in accordance with the Regulations.

11(1) No acquirer who, together with persons acting in concert with him, has acquired, in accordance with the provisions of law, not less than 15% not more than 75% of the shares or voting rights in a company, shall acquire either by himself or through or with persons acting in concert with him, additional shares or voting rights entitling him to exercise more than 2% of the voting rights, in any period of 12 months, unless such acquirer makes a public announcement to acquire shares in accordance with the Regulations.

(2) No acquirer shall acquire shares or voting rights which (taken together with shares or voting rights, if any, held by him or by persons acting in concert with him), entitle such acquirer to exercise more than 51% of the voting rights in a company, unless such acquirer makes a public announcement to acquire share of such company in accordance with the Regulations.

Explanation: For the purposes of Regulation 10 and Regulation 11, acquisition shall mean and include;

(b) direct acquisition in a listed company to which the Regulations apply;

(c) indirect acquisition by virtue of acquisition of holding companies, whether listed or unlisted, whether in India or abroad.

12. Irrespective of whether or not there has been any acquisition of shares or voting rights in a company, no acquirer shall acquire control over the target company, unless such person makes a public announcement to acquire shares and acquires such shares in accordance with the Regulations.

Explanation.

Where any person or persons has given joint control, such control shall not be deemed to be a change in control so long as the control given is equal as the control given is equal to or less than the control exercises by person(s) presently having control over the company."

The difference between the French law and their regulations relates to the prescribed limits of share holding for control by one company over another. This cannot conceivably make the French law violative of any public policy underlying the Acts and Regulations so as to persuade us to disregard the French Law.

Thus it is the French law which we must apply to decide whether Technip took over the control of Coflexip in April 2000 or July 2001. Incidentally, the opinions of various persons claiming to be experts in French Commercial Law have expressed diametrically opposing views as to whether Technip could be said to have taken control of Coflexip applying the relevant French law, in April 2000. We do not propose to rely upon either of the views expressed as none of them was subjected to cross examination. According to Technip their expert affirmed an affidavit and was offered for cross examination by SEBI and that SEBI declined to do so.

But the affidavit unlike the opinion expressed by the same firm earlier to Technip on 15th November 2001 did not express any opinion as to whether Technip did or did not acquire control of Coflexip either in April or July 2001 but only gave evidence of the applicable French law and highlighted the consequences of failure to comply with the statement of intent which was required to be filed with CMF. Therefore, ultimately it is for this Court to resolve the conflict by looking at the admitted text of the French law and the material on record to decide the proper application of the provisions. According to the show cause notice issued by SEBI to Technip, Technip had acquired control of Coflexip by acting in concert with ISIS. Technip has said that in April, 2000 there was no concept of acting in concert under French Law since the extended meaning of 'controlled company' was introduced by amendment to Article 355-1 only in May, 2001. The submission ignores Article 356-1. The concept of a takeover by acting in concert was there in 2000. In fact Article 355-1 of the French Companies Act merely sets out factors determining when a company could be said to hold control over another. It does not, as Article 356.1 does, speak of the method for acquiring such control. At this stage and before we apply the law to the facts we may note one aspect that has been lost sight of by SAT and that is that irrespective of the status of Coflexip and Technip to each other, in order to trigger Regulations 10 to 12, it would have to be established that the purchase of the 29.68% shares by Technip in Coflexip was with the object of taking control of SEAMEC. That is what the relevant Regulations provide and also what is alleged in the Show Cause Notice issued to Technip by SEBI. The allegation in the show cause notice was that Technip, the acquirer and ISIS as a shareholder of Coflexip acted in concert to acquire control over Coflexip and therefore SEAMEC treating SEAMEC as the target company. The emphasis is on the target company whether the case is of direct or indirect acquisition under the Regulations. Thus Regulation 2(b) of the Regulations defines 'acquirer' as meaning any person who, directly or indirectly, acquires or agrees to acquire shares or voting rights in the target company and 'acquirer' also means a person who acquire or agrees to acquire control over the target company either by himself or with any person acting in concert with the acquirer.

The word 'control' has been defined in Regulation 2(c) in the following manner:

"control" shall include the right to appoint majority of the directors or to control the management or policy decisions exercisable by a person or persons acting individually or in concert, directly or indirectly, including by virtue of their shareholding or management rights or shareholders agreements or voting agreements or in any other manner".

The other definition which is relevant is Regulation 2(e) defining the phrase 'person acting in concert'. We are concerned with sub section (i) which says that it comprises "persons who, for a common objective or purpose of substantial acquisition of shares or voting rights or gaining control over the target company, pursuant to an agreement or understanding (formal or informal), directly or indirectly co-operate by acquiring or agreeing to acquire shares or voting rights in the target company or control over the target company". Finally is the definition of the word 'target company' in Regulation 2(o) as meaning a listed company whose shares or voting rights or control is directly or indirectly acquired or is being acquired. If the Indian Law were to be invoked in April 2000 it would have to be shown that Technip acquired or agreed to acquire the right to control SEAMEC (in this case the alleged target company) either by itself or acting in concert with any other shareholder or Coflexip.

According to the Bhagwati Committee Report to be acting in concert with an acquirer, persons must fulfill certain 'bright line' tests. They must have commonality of objectives and a community of interest and their act of acquiring the shares or voting rights in company must serve this common objective. The commonality of objective which should be established between the acquirer and a shareholder in order to trigger off Regulations 10,11 and 12 with respect to a subsidiary company is referred to as the "chain principle" in the Report which enunciates that an offer should be made to the shareholders of such a target company if

(a) the shareholding in the second company constitutes a substantial part of the assets of the first company; or

(b) one of the main purposes of acquiring control of the first company was to secure control of the second company.

This is evident also reading the definitions of 'acquirer' 'control' 'acting in concert' and 'target company' in Regulations 2 (b)(c) (e) and (o) together.

A similar position obtains in England where Note 7 to Rule 9.1 of the City Code on Takeovers and Mergers likewise provides:-

"Occasionally, a person or group of persons requiring statutory control of a company (which need not be a company to which the Code applies) will thereby acquire or consolidate control, as defined in the Code, of a second company because the first company itself holds a controlling block of shares in the second company, or holds shares which, when aggregated with those already held by the person or group, secure or consolidate control of the second company. The Panel will not normally require an offer to be made under this Rule in these circumstances unless either:

a) the shareholding in the second company constitutes a substantial part of the assets of the first company; or

b) one of the main purposes of acquiring control of the first company was to secure control of the second company".

The "second company" both under the 'chain principle' referred to in the Bhagwati Committee Report as well as in the City Code on Takeovers and Mergers is the target company and the first company is the medium or vessel or vehicle for attaining control on the target company. In the present case Coflexip would be the 'first company' and SEAMEC the actual target and the liability to make an exit offer to the shareholders of SEAMEC would arise only if either one of the two conditions prescribed is fulfilled. It would therefore have to be proved by the shareholders of SEAMEC that Coflexip was taken over (if at all) in April 2000 by Technip with the assistance of ISIS so that control of SEAMEC could be obtained or that Coflexip's shareholding of SEAMEC constituted a substantial part of Coflexip's assets.

The standard of proof required to establish such concert is one of probability and may be established "if having regard to their relation etc., their conduct, and their common interest, that it may be inferred that they must be acting together: evidence of actual concerted acting is normally difficult to obtain, and is not insisted upon" . While deciding whether a company was one in which the public were substantially interested within the meaning of Section 23A of the Income Tax Act, 1922 this Court said:-

"The test is not whether they have actually acted in concert but whether the circumstances are such that human experience tells us that it can safely be taken that they must be acting together. It is not necessary to state the kind of evidence that will prove such concerted actings. Each case must necessarily be decided on its own facts ".

In Guinness PLC and Distillers Company PLC the question before the Takeover Panel was whether Guinness had acted in concert with Pipetec when Pipetec purchased shares in Distillers Company PLC. Various factors were taken into consideration to conclude that Guinness had acted in concert with Pipetec to get control over Distillers Company. The Panel said :-

"The nature of acting in concert requires that the definition be drawn in deliberately wide terms. It covers an understanding as well as an agreement, and an informal as well as a formal arrangement, which leads to co-operation to purchase shares to acquire control of a company. This is necessary, as such arrangements are often informal, and the understanding may arise from a hint. The understanding may be tacit, and the definition covers situations where the parties act on the basis of a "nod or a wink".. Unless persons declare this agreement or understanding, there is rarely direct evidence of action in concert, and the Panel must draw on its experience and commonsense to determine whether those involved in any dealings have some form of understanding and are acting in co-operation with each other ".

According to the Dictionaire Permanent du Droit des Affairs French law does not make proof of the concerted action dependant upon the existence of a written document. "However, given the serious consequences linked to the existence of a concerted action, only serious presumptions drawn from factual date can lead to a qualification of a concerted action. The mere observation of similarity of behaviours cannot constitute such a proof. Even the common position of certain shareholders is not necessarily indicative of the existence of a concerted action. Such shareholders may have adopted legitimately a similar position, independently, because of their own strategic interest". (Extract from the 1989 French Securities and Exchange Commission Report). In this background of the law we may consider briefly the relevant facts.

IFP had promoted Technip and Coflexip in 1958 and 1971 respectively. In 1975 IFP promoted ISIS as a wholly owned subsidiary to hold its investments. It is the admitted position that IFP retained majority control of ISIS until October,2001.

The main shareholders of Technip at all material times were ISIS, Gaz de France and Sogerap (which later came to be known as Fina Total Elf and is hereafter referred to as 'Elf'). They held 11.8%, 10.9% and 6.4% of the shareholding whereas 65.9% of the shareholding was held by the public. In 1994 ISIS, Gaz de France, Elf and Technip entered into an agreement inter alia granting a right of preemption to each other in respect of their respective shareholdings. The shareholders of Coflexip till April 2000 were ISIS, Elf and Stena (incorporated in the Netherlands), apart from American investors who held 50% of the shareholding. The first three shareholders had entered into a similar shareholders agreement with a right of preemption.

Coflexip through a chain of subsidiaries purchased 49.85% of the shareholding in SEAMEC on 25th October, 1999. In December, 1999, the Chairman CEO of Coflexip made a proposal to the Chairman/CEO of Technip to examine the merits of a merger between Coflexip and Technip. In January, 2000 Stena intimated that it would not support a merger of Coflexip and Technip as it was not part of Stena's strategy to hold an equity stake in an engineering and construction company.

On 31st March, 2000, Stena offered to sell its shares in Coflexip held by it and its associates J.P. Morgan, being 29.7% of the shareholding of Coflexip, to Technip. ISIS had three representatives on Coflexip's Board of 11 Directors, who also had two Directors in Technip. On 7th April, 2000, the Board of Technip approved the deal with Stena to purchase its 29.68% shares in Coflexip. ISIS and Elf abstained from voting as they were shareholders in both Coflexip and Technip.

On 11th April, 2000, several events took place. ISIS wrote a letter to Stena renouncing its preemptive rights under the shareholders agreement in favour of Technip. There is no binding that it would have been financially possible for ISIS to have exercised its preemptive rights given the financial implications particularly the necessity to make a further public offer to purchase the balance shares of Coflexip as it would have crossed the threshold as prescribed under French Law. On the same date Elf also renounced its preemptive rights under the shareholders agreement in favour of Technip. An agreement was then entered into between Technip and Stena for the acquisition of Stena's 29.68% shares in Coflexip at the rate of Euros 119 per share. Statements of intent were filed by Technip with Stock Exchange Authorities and with Coflexip. Coflexip in turn wrote a letter to Technip on the same date agreeing not to acquire equity shares in a competing company without prior written consent of Technip. The declaration required by French law was made to the CMF by Technip on 28th April, 2000 that Technip.

a) did not directly or indirectly hold any other shares in Coflexip;

b) it was not acting in concert with any other and had no plans for any such action;

c) it had no intention to increase its equity stake within 12 months after acquisition;

d) undertaking not to acquire new equity shares in other companies involved in Coflexip's scope of activities except with the prior written approval of Coflexip;

e) agreeing that violation of any of the aforesaid stipulation would entitle Coflexip to claim damages.

This was published by CMF on 4th May, 2000. A similar declaration or statement of intent was given to COB. Both the authorities accepted the declaration and there was no protest to the publication by any member of Coflexip or anyone else for that matter. There is thus no dispute that Technip agreed to acquire 29.68% shares in Coflexip on 11.4.2000. Nor is it disputed that it complied with the requirements of Art 356-1.

Clearly a purchase of 29.68% shares in a company would not by itself give the purchase de jure control of the company under French Law. The acceptance of the statement of intent filed by Technip before the Stock Exchange Authorities would not however be conclusive of the matter. It may be that the Market Authorities agree to the publication of a statement or a notice or a financial publication. It may also be that those professional independent bodies have professionally verified the contents of such communications and have been satisfied with their accuracy. However, there is no adjudicatory process and there was no judicial decision of any authority which we could recognize as a foreign judgment on any principle of judicial comity or conflict of laws. To return to the narration of facts:-

On the same date i.e. 11th April 2000 three appointees of Technip were co-opted on the Board of Coflexip. According to Technip there was in fact no change in the daily management of Coflexip. Coflexip's Board of Directors consisted of eleven Directors, of which Technip's Directors were only three. The President of the Board and the Managing Director continued to be the same. The respondents have argued that there was in fact an effective change in the management. Of the 11 Directors of Coflexip, three belonged to ISIS. Therefore, ISIS and Technip together had a total of six out of the eleven Directors on Coflexip's Board. Additionally, Technip's Directors were appointed to the Strategic Committee as well as the Audit Committee of the Board. The respondents point out that all these appointments were made even before payment of the purchase price of the shares by Technip to Stena. The purchase of shares between Stena and Technip was completed on 19th April, 2000, on which date and Stena's 29.68% shares in Coflexip was registered in favour of Technip. Technip has argued that the effect of the purchase of the Stena's shares was merely a strategic alliance between Coflexip and Technip and Technip did not control Coflexip. On the other hand there was evidence of a possible acquisition of Technip by Coflexip. This position continued till January, 2001 when IFP agreed to sell its entire interest in ISIS to Technip. According to Technip and IFP this was the first time IFP had come into the picture.

In February, 2001 the Chairman of Coflexip expressed his reservation about the proposed sale of ISIS's shares in Coflexip to Technip. Coflexip continued to act independently of Technip with regard to various policy decisions. Technip offered to purchase the balance shares of Coflexip at a premium of 25% on 3rd July, 2001. The price offered by Technip was not immediately acceptable to the Board of Coflexip. A Special Committee was set up to consider whether the price was adequate. ISIS voted in favour of setting up of the committee. As it happened, the Special Committee recommended a higher price, so that the Technip had to improve its offer to purchase Coflexip's share. These facts according to Technip showed that ISIS was not acting in concert with Technip. Technip has said that the purchase of 100% shareholding was duly approved by Regulatory Authorities of USA, Finland and Netherlands and on 11th October, 2001 Technip acquired control of 99.04% of the share capital of ISIS and 98.36% of the share capital of Coflexip. Coflexip's shares were registered in the name of Technip on 19th October, 2001.

We are of the opinion that having regard to the balance of probabilities there was no evidence that Technip obtained de facto control of Coflexip in April 2000. The evidence would rather suggest that it was nothing more than a strategic alliance. The mere fact that in two Annual General Meetings of Coflexip Technip was in the majority cannot by itself establish its control over Coflexip. It may be that in a company with a large and dispersed membership, a comparatively small proportion of the total shares, if held in one hand, may enable actual control to be exercised. But the obtaining of a majority in a shareholders‘ meeting may have been the outcome of absenteeism or some other factor. It is not as if Technip exerted its influence over any policy matters of Coflexip. Besides this was not the case in the Show Cause Notice. The allegation was that ISIS and Technip acted in concert in the matter of purchase of Stena's shares in Coflexip by Technip. That has not been established.

Technip's explanation for ISIS not exercising its preemptive right under the shareholders agreement is plausible. The explanation was that ISIS was a subsidiary of IFP and it is not the policy of IFP to manage companies in which it invests. ISIS therefore was not interested in acquiring further shares in Coflexip nor did it have the financial means to do so. ISIS was a

Government controlled company and was holding shares on behalf of IFP, a Government body, and its failure to exercise its rights of preemption could be a Government decision should IFP have caused ISIS to proceed with such a huge investment, it could have been in breach of the relevant EU regulations as intervention of the State in Private Industry.

In any event there is no evidence that Technip acquired Coflexip if it at all did so in April 2000, so as to gain control of SEAMEC. Yet that is the aspect with which we are concerned. SEBI said that on the material before it, it was difficult to hold that IFP along with ISIS was acting in concert with Technip for the purpose of acquiring shares/voting rights/control of Coflexip so as to indirectly acquire control over SEAMEC in April 2000. But in view of the admitted takeover of Coflexip by Technip in July 2001 directed the publication of an offer to SEAMEC's taking that as the effective date.

In reversing this judgment, SAT held that ISIS and Technip had acted in concert to gain control over Coflexip in April, 2000. We are of the opinion that the approach of the SAT was entirely wrong. For the purposes of determining Technip's obligations under the Regulation it should have addressed itself as SEBI had done to the question whether ISIS and Technip were acting in concert to obtain control over the target company, namely, SEAMEC. In other words, did the shareholding of Coflexip in SEAMEC constitute a substantial part of the assets of Coflexip, or was the main purpose of acquiring control of Coflexip the acquisition of control over SEAMEC?

According to the SAT, the reasons which established that ISIS and Technip were acting in concert in April 2000 were as follows:

(i) " there was shareholders agreement dated 2.11.1994 between Stena group on one side and ISIS and others on the other to control Coflexip.It is also noted that ISIS group had not exercised its preemptive right to block Technip's entry."

(ii)"(it was clear)from the shareholding pattern of Technip, Coflexip and ISIS that IFP was having common interest."

(iii)"Whether these companies belonged to one "group" or that they were companies under the same management" may be in dispute. But no one can dispute that they belonged to one family in the real sense..ISIS and IFP had one lineage

- the common parenthood in IFP.

.Gaz de France and Total Fina Elf-both associated with IFP family."

(iv)" Coflexip and Technip are having interest in the Petroleum sector, IPF could be interested in these 2 entities joining together and forming a combine and that having regard to their common interest, it may be inferred that they must be acting together."

(v)"Technip Chairman's letter that they were ultimately planning to take over Coflexip and they "were on this merger, passing through a number of necessary stages: which included "the acquisition of 30% of Coflexip in April 2000"

(vi) "ISIS has its nominees on the Board of Technip. ISIS has its nominees of Coflexip. ..Thus in a 11 member Board of Coflexip Technip ISIS combine had a majority."

(vii)"From the material available on record there is every justification to infer that the plan was to combine Technip and Coflexip and form a strong combined entity to be a business leader in the petroleum sector and that it was with this end in view Technip in which ISIS had interest acquired Coflexip in which also ISIS had interest."

(viii)" total holding of these two companies were around 47% sufficient enough to control Coflexip in view of its 48% shares widely held by public. It is also noted that in fact in the annual general meeting of Coflexip held in May 2000 and May 2001(before the merger effected on 3.7.2001) Technip had exercised 54% and 57% of the voting rights, that this itself is indicative of the fact that Technip had more than 50% voting rights at its command, even though on record it was holding only 29%."

(ix)"ISIS objecting to the setting up of a committee to revise the offer price, is but natural as an increase in offer price was to its advantage and by doing so it was not in any way acting against its objective of helping Technip to acquire control over Coflexip. Adding a little more financial burden on Technip by asking for higher offer price can not be viewed as a hostile action from ISIS or as evidence of non co- operation."

(x)"Technip possibly wanted to strengthen its position dejure as well with 99% and they acquired shares to that level through the public offer in July, 2001. In my view the acquisition raising the shareholding to 99% in Coflexip was the final act whereas the process started on 12.4.2000."

(xi)" in my view Technip had decided to take over control of Coflexip and to achieve the said objective, acquired 29.68% shares of Coflexip on 12.4.2000. the evidence before me leads to the conclusion that ISIS had acted in concert for the said purpose."

We need not go into the reasons separately although we must say that we disapprove of the introduction of the concept of a joint family into corporate law when the statutory provisions, particularly Regulation 2(e) exhaustively defines what would amount to 'acting in concert'. More particularly when Regulation 3(1)(e)(i) provides that:- (1) "Nothing contained in Regulations 10,11 and 12 of Regulations 10,11 and 12 these Regulations shall apply to;

(e) Interse transfer of shares amongst:-

(i) group companies, coming within the definition of group as defined in the Monopolies and Restrictive Trade Practices Act, 1969 (25 of 1969)".

The 'IFP family' if any would be nothing more than such a group. Furthermore, it is abundantly clear that even the name of SEAMEC does not feature in any of the several reasons put forward by SAT whereas that, as we must emphasise, should have been the primary point of focus. The respondents have sought to adduce further evidence before us to the effect that SEAMEC was in the contemplation of Technip when it purchased Stena's shares in Coflexip. There is no question of allowing any fresh evidence to be adduced at this stage. Besides we do not think that any evidence of mere contemplation of SEAMEC's assets would do. That should have been the principal objective in order to trigger the Regulations as it was not the respondent's case before SAT that the shareholding of Coflexip in SEAMEC constituted a substantial part of the assets of Coflexip nor has SAT so found. SEBI had noted that the takeover of SEAMEC was only an incidental fall out of the control of Coflexip and that SEAMEC formed a 'small and insignificant portion of the total business of Coflexip' contributing merely 2% of the total asset base of Coflexip as on December, 2000. The finding was not reversed by SAT.

We are thus of the opinion that SEBI's order must prevail and the order of SAT must be set aside. The other issues as to the rate of interest, the adjustment of dividend and the identification of the shareholders of SEAMEC would arise only if SAT's order had been upheld. As we are allowing the appeals of both Technip and IFP it is unnecessary to determine them. Consequent upon our decision to allow the appeals the bank guarantees furnished by Technip to secure the difference in amounts between the share prices which would be payable by Technip had SAT's view prevailed must be and are hereby discharged.

The appeals are for these reasons allowed without costs.

CHAPTER TWENTY-ONE

S.B.P. and Co. v. M/S Patel Engineering Ltd. and Anr. [2005]4 Suppl. SCR 688 : (2005) 8 SCC 618

(The power exercised by the Chief Justice of High Court or the Chief Justice of India under Section 11(6) of the Act is not an administrative power. It is Judicial power.)

QUESTION OF LAW BEFORE THE COURT:

Whether the Chief Justice of the Supreme Court and the Chief Justices of the High Court function as Courts or persona designata under Arbitration and Conciliation Act, 1996 ?

LEGAL BACKGROUND OF THE CASE:

Section 11 of the Arbitration and Conciliation Act, 1996, inter alia, provides that persons of any nationality, unless otherwise agreed by parties, may be arbitrator but under the procedure for appointment of Arbitrator, agreed upon the parties if any party fails to appoint the arbitrator or the parties or the two appointed arbitrators fail to reach an agreement expected of them or the person, including the institution appointed as arbitrator or fails to perform any function entrusted to him or it.

Under that procedure agreed upon by the parties, then any party may request the Chief Justice or any person or institution designated by him to take necessary measure for securing appointments of Arbitrator. This decision on appointment shall be final.

But the Chief Justice or his designated person/institution shall have due regards to any qualifications required of the Arbitrator as agreed by parties in their agreement and all other considerations as are likely to secure the appointment of an independent and impartial Arbitrator.

In the case of Konkan Rly. Construction vs. Mehul Construction case, question for decision on the nature of aforesaid power of Chief Justice or his designated person under Section of the Arbitration and Conciliation Act, arose,

1. What is the nature of the order that is passed by the Chief Justice or his nominee in exercise of Power under sub-section 6 of Section 11 of the Act.
2. Even if the said order is held to be the administrative in nature, what is the remedy open to the person concerned if his request for appointment of Arbitrator is turned down by Chief Justice or his nominee for some reason or the other.

Three Judge held that Order was of administrative nature and not judicial nature. The same ratio was reiterated by the Constitution Bench in Konkan Rly. Construction vs. Rani Constructions, (2002) 2 SCC 388.

JUDGEMENT:

While deciding the case, the majority found that the power exercised by the Chief Justice under Section 11(6) of the Act, is judicial power and not administrative power for the following reasons:

When any party request under Section 11(6) of the Act, the Chief Justice has necessarily to decide:

(i) Whether there is a valid arbitration agreement

(ii) Whether the subject matter of the claim is covered by that agreement

(iii) Whether the person requesting for relief disputes the other ingredients of the Section regarding the qualifications of the persons agreed to be appointed by the agreement etc.

It is difficult to contemplate that the Judicial Authority of Chief Justice of India or Chief Justices of High Courts would only act mechanically or would merely see the original agreement produced by the parties and mechanically refer the parties to an Arbitrator. Thus, the Order under Section 11 of the Act, made by the Chief Justice of India or Chief Justices of High Courts is Judicial Order.

On the above analysis the Seven-Judges Bench of the Supreme Court held as under:

(i). The power exercised by the Chief Justice of High Court or the Chief Justice of India under Section 11(6) of the Act is not an administrative power. It is Judicial power.

(ii). The power under Section 11(6) of the Act in its entirety, could be delegated by the Chief Justice of High Court only to another Judge of that Court and by the Chief Justice of India to another Judge of the Supreme Court.

(iii). In case of designation of a Judge of the High Court or the Supreme Court, the power that is exercised by the designated Judge would be that of the Chief Justice as conferred by the Statute.

(iv). The Chief Justice or the designated Judge will have the right to decide the preliminary aspects as said above. These will be his own jurisdiction to entertain the request, the existence of a valid arbitration agreement, the existence or otherwise of a live claim, the existence of the condition for the exercise of his power and on the qualifications of the arbitrator or arbitrators. The Chief Justice or the designated Judge would be entitled to seek the opinion institution in the matter of nominating an arbitrator qualified in terms of Section 11(8) of the Act, if the need arises but the order appointing the arbitrator could only be that of the Chief Justice or the designated Judge.

(v). Designation of a Distt. Judge as the authority under Section 11(6) of the Act, by the Chief Justice of the High Court is not warranted on the scheme of the Act.

(vi). Once the matter reaches the Arbitral Tribunal or the sole arbitrator, the High Court would not interfere with the orders passed by the Arbitrator or the Arbitral Tribunal during the course of arbitration proceedings and the parties could approach the Court only in terms of Section 37 of the Act.

(vii). Since an order passed by the Chief Justice of High Court or by the designated Judge of that Court is a judicial order, an appeal will lie against that order only under Article 136 of the Constitution to the Supreme Court.

(viii). There can be no appeal against an order of the Chief Justice of India or a Judge of the Supreme Court designated by him while entertaining an application under Section 11(1) of the Act.

(ix). In a case where an Arbitral Tribunal has been constituted by the parties without having recourse to Section 11(6) of the Act. Arbitral Tribunal will have the jurisdiction to decide all matters as contemplated by Section 11(6) of the Act.

(x). Since all were guided by the decision of this Court in Konkan Rly Corpn. Ltd. Vs. Rani Constitution. (P) Ltd. and orders under Section 11(6) of the Act, have been made based on the position adopted in that decision, we clarify that appointments of Arbitrators or Arbitral Tribunals thus far made, are to be treated as valid. All objections being left to be decided under Section 16 of the Act. As and from this date, the position as adopted in this judgment will govern even pending applications under Section 11(6) of the Act.

(xi). Where District Judge had been designated by the Chief Justice of the High Court under Section 11(6) of the Act, the appointment orders thus far made by then will be treated as valid; but applications if any pending before them as on this date will stand transferred, to be dealt with by the Chief Justice of High Court concerned or a Judge of that Court designated by the Chief Justice.

(xii). The decision in Konkan Rly Corpn. Ltd. vs. Rani Constitution. (P) Ltd. is overruled.

What do you mean by 'persona designata' ?

When the Chief Justice of India or Chief Justice of High Courts or their nominees act to appoint under Section 11(6) of the Arbitration and Conciliation Act, 1996, act as 'personal designata'.

CHAPTER TWENTY-TWO

Rameshwar Prasad and Ors. Vs. Union of India and Anr. [2006] 1SCR 562 : (2006) 2 SCC 1

(Court passed an interim order which virtually created a constitutional anomaly by allowing the second election to go on. Indeed, this interim order itself rendered the petition infructuous because when the judgment was delivered in this case already the second government was in power and that is the reason why President's order was declared unconstitutional, but revival of the status quo cabinet was not ordered.

CONSTITUTION

Constitution of India, 1950

Articles 356, 174 – General election – No party or coalition of parties secured clear majority – Governor making a report to President of India – Dissolution of Bihar Assembly by Presidential order. Held Proclamation dissolving the legislative assembly of State of Bihar is unconstitutional. No order to restore the status-quo- ante.)

(Under Article 32 of the Constitution of India)

(With W.P. (C) No.255 of 2005, W.P. (C) No.258 of 2005 and W.P. (C) No.353 of 2005)

CORAM : Y.K. SABHARWAL, K.G. BALAKRISHNAN, B.N. AGRAWAL, ASHOK BHAN AND ARIJIT PASAYAT, JJ.

Date of Judgment: Oct 07, 2005

FACTS OF THE CASE :

1. The general elections to the Legislative Assembly of Bihar were held in the month of February 2005. The Election Commission of India, in pursuance of Section 73 of the Representation of the People Act, 1951 in terms of Notification dated 4th March, 2005 notified the names of the elected members.

2. As no party or coalition of the parties was in a position to secure 122 seats so as to have majority in the Assembly, the Governor of Bihar made a report dated 6th March, 2005 to the President of India, whereupon in terms of Notification G.S.R.162(E) dated 7th March, 2005, issued in exercise of powers under Article 356 of the Constitution of India, the State was brought under President's Rule and the Assembly was kept in suspended animation.

3. By another Notification G.S.R.163(E) of the same date, 7th March, 2005, it was notified that all powers which have been assumed by the President of India, shall, subject to the superintendence direction and control of the President, be exercisable also by the Governor of the State. The Home Minister in a speech made on 21st March, 2005 when the Bihar Appropriation (Vote on Account) Bill, 2005 was being discussed in the Rajya Sabha said that the Government was not happy to impose President's Rule in Bihar and would have been happy if Government would have been formed by the elected representatives after the election.

4. That was, however, not possible and, therefore, President's Rule was imposed. It was also said that the Government would not like to see that President's Rule is continued for a long time but it is for elected representatives to take steps in this respect; the Governor can ask them and request them and he would also request that the elected representatives should talk to each other and create a situation in which it becomes possible for them to form a Government.

5. The Presidential Proclamation dated 7th March, 2005 was approved by the Lok Sabha at its sitting held on 19th March, 2005 and Rajya Sabha at its sitting held on 21st March, 2005.

6. The Governor of Bihar made two reports to the President of India, one dated 27th April, 2005 and the other dated 21st May, 2005. On consideration of these reports, Notification dated 23rd May, 2005 was issued in exercise of the powers conferred by sub-clause (b) of Clause (2) of Article 174 of the Constitution, read with clause (a) of the Notification G.S.R.162(E) dated 7th March, 2005 issued under Article 356 of the Constitution and the Legislative Assembly of the State of Bihar was dissolved with immediate

effect.

7. These writ petitions have been filed challenging constitutional validity of the aforesaid Proclamation dated 23rd May, 2005.

8. Fresh elections in State of Bihar have been notified. As per press note dated 3rd September, 2005 issued by Election Commission of India, the schedule for general elections to the Legislative Assembly of Bihar has been announced. According to it, the polling is to take place in four phases commencing from 18th October, 2005 and ending with the fourth phase voting on 19th November, 2005.

9. As per the said press note, the date of Notification for first and second phase of poll was 23rd September and 28th September, 2005, date of poll being 18th October, 2005 and 26th October, 2005 respectively. Notifications for third and fourth phases of poll are to be issued on 19th and 26th October, 2005 respectively.

JUDGEMENT:

MINORITY OPINION:

1. Approved the validity of the President's Order. Firstly, non-applicability of the Bommai's case since there was no assembly in existence in Bihar as in the case of Karnataka and Nagaland assemblies which were dissolved. But it is submitted that the different fact situation can neither deviate or detract or dilute the principles laid down in Bommai case nor displace its essential reasoning.

2. It said, there was no material to show that the Governor actually prevented the staking of claim by the Janata Dal (U); the latter took no preliminary step to stake its claim that was prevented by the Governor. With due respect to the Court, it is submitted that the minority completely overlooked that the whole object and aim of recommending the dissolution of the Assembly with indecent haste was to prevent Nitish Kumar even from staking the claim to form the government.

3. As Justice Pasayat noted, if the governor felt that what was being done was morally wrong, it couldn't be treated as politically right. This is his perception. It may be erroneous. It may not be specifically spelt out by the Constitution so far as his powers are concerned. But it ultimately is a perception.

MAJORITY OPINION:

1. The President allowed himself to be hurried into signing the order of dissolution. He could have asked the Council of Ministers headed by the Prime Minister to wait; he could have taken his own time, could have

made necessary consultations before signing the impugned order dissolving the Bihar Assembly, and should have taken a decision only after careful consideration. Moreover, he could have sent the matter back to the Cabinet for reconsideration.

2. All these rights and powers of the President are well within our constitutional framework. Inasmuch as what was declared unconstitutional by the Court in the present case was the Presidential notification, one cannot absolve the President's office of discharging its constitutional responsibility

Keeping in view the questions involved, the pronouncement of judgment with detailed reasons is likely to take some time and, therefore, at this stage, we are pronouncing this brief order as the order of the Court to be followed by detailed reasons later.

Accordingly, as per majority opinion, this Court orders as under:

1. The Proclamation dated 23rd May, 2005 dissolving the Legislative Assembly of the State of Bihar is unconstitutional.

2. Despite unconstitutionality of the impugned Proclamation, but having regard to the facts and circumstances of the case, the present is not a case where in exercise of discretionary jurisdiction the status quo ante deserves to be ordered to restore the Legislative Assembly as it stood on the date of Proclamation dated 7th March, 2005 whereunder it was kept under suspended animation

CHAPTER TWENTY-THREE

I.R.Coelho V. State of Tamil Nadu [2007] 1SCR 706 : (2007) 2 SCC 1: AIR 2007, SC 861

(I.R Coelho case, is the latest of the land mark judgments on the interpretation of the doctrine of basic structure of the constitution as laid down in ***Kesavananda Bharti case***. The court in the present case went a step further and articulated a distinction between what is termed as the **"essence of the rights test"** and the "**rights test**" corresponding to the distinction between the foundational value behind an express right and the express right provided for in the constitutional text in this context. The judgment in ***I.R. Coelho*** vigorously reaffirms the doctrine of basic structure. Indeed it has gone further and held that a constitutional amendment which entails violation of any fundamental rights which the Court regards as forming part of the basic structure of the Constitution then the same can be struck down depending upon its impact and consequences. The basic structure doctrine the judiciary cannot be deprived of the power of judicial review nor can the rule of law be abrogated)

FACTS OF THE CASE:

1. The case arose out of an order of reference made by a five judge constitution bench in 1999. The GudalurJanmam Estates (Abolition and Conversion into Ryotwari) Act, 1969, that vested forest lands in the Janmam estates in the State of Tamil Nadu, was struck down by the Supreme Court in ***Balmadies Plantations Ltd. &Anr.*** v. ***State of Tamil Nadu,*** as it was found to be outside the scope of protection provided to agrarian reforms

under article 31-A of the Constitution.

2. By the Constitution (Thirty-fourth Amendment) Act, the Janmam Act was inserted in the ninth schedule, which was challenged. In its referral order, the constitution bench noted that, according to ***Waman Rao &Ors. v. Union of India &Ors,*** amendments to the Constitution made on or after 24.4.1973 (the date of the ***KesavanandaBharati*** judgment) inserting various laws in the ninth schedule were open to challenge on the ground that such amendments are beyond the constituent power of Parliament since they damage the basic structure of the Constitution.

3. The referral order further stated that the judgment in ***Waman Rao*** needs to be reconsidered by a larger bench so that it is made clear "whether an Act or regulation which, or a part of which, is or has been found by the courts to be violative of one or more of the fundamental rights conferred by articles 14, 19 or 31 can be included in the ninth schedule or whether it is only a constitutional amendment amending the ninth schedule which damages or destroys the basic structure of the Constitution that can be struck down".

ISSUE BEFORE THE COURT :

1. Whether on and after 24.4.1923(Date of the judgment in ***kesavananda Bharti V. State of Kerala*** when the basic structure doctrine was propounded, is it permissible for the parliament under **Article 31**-B to immunise legislations by inserting them into the ninth schedule and thus outside the purview of the courts?

2. if so, what was its effect on the power of judicial review of the court?

Historical Background of the Ninth Schedule:

1. After the Constitution was enacted, several agrarian and land reforms legislations were passed. These were challenged in State High Courts on the ground of violation of fundamental rights.

2, The Patna High Court struck down certain land reform legislation as being violative of fundamental rights. Similar legislation was upheld by the Allahabad and Nagpur High Courts and appeals from these judgments were pending in the Supreme Court.

3. The Union Government, with a view to put an end to all this litigation, passed in Parliament the Constitution [First Amendment] Act, 1951. By this amendment Article 31-B and Ninth Schedule were enacted in the Constitution. The intent and effect was that any legislation placed in the Ninth Schedule could not be challenged on the ground that it was violative of any fundamental right.

4. It is interesting to note that only thirteen Acts, all dealing with agrarian reforms, were initially placed in the Ninth Schedule. In course of time that number swelled to 284. Many of the Acts, which had no relation with agrarian or socio-economic reforms, were indiscriminately placed in the Ninth Schedule.

DEVELOPMENT OF LAW :

Pre Kesavananda Bharti case

1. The dispute arose right after the first amendment Act, inserting Article 31-B & ninth schedule. Its constitutional validity was upheld in ***Sri Sankari Prasad Singh Deo vs. Union of India and State of Bihar,*** it was held that Article 13(2) does not affect amendments to the Constitution made under **Article 368** because such amendments are made in the exercise of constituent power.

2. In ***Golak Nath&ors. Vs. State of Punjab &Anr,*** a bench of 11 judges considered the correctness of the view that had been taken in Sankari Prasad and Sajjan Singh case. By majority of six to five, these decisions were overruled. It was held that the constitutional amendment is 'law' within the meaning of Article 13 of the Constitution and, therefore, if it takes away or abridges the rights conferred by Part III thereof, it is void. It was declared that the Parliament will have no power from the date of the decision (27th February, 1967) to amend any of the provisions of Part III of the Constitution so as to take away or abridge the fundamental rights enshrined therein.

3. Soon after Golak Nath Case, the Constitution (24th Amendment), Act 1971, the Constitution (25th Amendment) Act, Act. 1971, the constitution (26th Amendment) Act, 1971 and the Constitution (29th Amendment) Act, 1972 were passed.

4. These amendments were challenged in **Kesavananda Bharti case**. In this case, the constitutionality of the 29th Amendment was challenged which amended the Ninth Schedule to the Constitution inserting therein two Kerala Amendment Acts in furtherance of land reforms. By a majority of seven to six, Golak Nath's case was overruled. The majority opinion held that though the amending power of the Parliament extends to all the Articles, Article 368 did not enable the Parliament to alter the basic structure or framework of the Constitution. There are implied or inherent limitations on the power of amendment under Article 368.Within these limits, every article can be amended.

Post Kesavananda Bharti Case

1. In the case of ***Indira Nehru Gandhi v. Raj Narain***, Sub clause (4) and (5) of Article 329A, that tried to keep the election matters outside the purview of the courts, were struck down by the court as they were found to be violative of the basic structure of the constitution. It was assumed that even after a statue is included in the 9th Schedule, its provision would be open to challenge on the ground that they took away or abrogated all or any of the fundamental rights and therefore damaged or destroyed a Basic Structure.

2. The view that the legislation included in the Schedule is subject to the test of basic structure, expressed by Justice Mathew in *Indira Gandhi* case, found the support of a unanimous court in ***Waman Rao v. Union of India***. The court identified article 32 as part of the basic structure.

3. Then citing ***Minerva Mills* case** where the court by a majority of 4 to 1 struck down clauses (4) and (5) of Article 368 which provided for exclusion of judicial review and unlimited amendment power to the Parliament respectively. Judicial review held to be a basic feature of the constitution.

4. Similar views were reiterated in ***L. Chandra Kumar V. Union of India &Ors***. In ***S.R Bommai&Ors. V. Union of India &Ors***, it was again reiterated that the judicial review is a basic feature of the Constitution and that the power of judicial review is a constituent power that cannot be abrogated by judicial process of interpretation.

JUDGMENT:

1. Citing all the aforementioned cases and recognizing the judicial mandate on doctrine of basic structure and the power of judicial review, it concluded that after 24th April 1973 (the date of the decision in KesavanandaBharati), laws placed in the Ninth Schedule would not enjoy blanket immunity but the court will examine the nature and extent of infraction of a fundamental right by a statute, sought to be constitutionally protected, and on the touchstone of the basic structure doctrine as reflected in Article 21 read with Article 14 and Article 19 by application of **the rights test** and **the essence of the right test**. Applying the above mentioned tests to the ninth schedule laws, if the infraction affects the basic structure, then such a law(s) will not get the protection of the ninth schedule.

2. With regard to a law judicially pronounced to be violative of fundamental rights and which is subsequently inserted in the Ninth Schedule after the 24th April 1973, the Court ruled that such a violation/ infraction shall be open to challenge on the ground that it destroys or

damages the basic structure as indicated in Article 21 read with Article 14, Article 19 and the principles underlying thereunder..

3. The court held that the constitutional validity of the ninth schedule laws could be adjudged by applying the **direct impact and effect test, *i.e.*, rights test**, which requires that it is not the form of a law, but its effect, that would be the determinative factor. It is the court that is to decide if this interference is justified and if does or does not amount to violation of the basic structure.

4. **The role of the court is "determination by court whether invasion was necessary and if so to what extent"**. This position then serves to shift the determination of the need for the law from the Parliament to the courts for decision. It also allows the courts the flexibility of both the rights test and the essence of rights test in dealing with the validity of such cases.

5. The determination of the effect of the infringement in either case would be for the courts to determine. This ultimately may be the key point in the judgment. It could be said to be a modified version of Golaknath judgement, because in ***Golak Nath*** any abridgement of part III would be invalid, but here the degree of invasion would be examined by the courts in the light of tests subsequently developed to test the infringement of fundamental rights

Thus Coelho case is one of the landmark judgments on the interpretation of the doctrine of basic structure of the constitution as laid down in Kesavananda Bharti case.

- In this case, a nine-member bench of Supreme Court held that ninth schedule items are not immune to judicial review as it is part of the constitution.
- Further, nothing in the Ninth schedule can abrogate fundamental rights as they form basic features of the constitution.
- The objective behind Article 31B of the Constitution is to remove difficulties and not to wipe out judicial review per se.
- Therefore every amendment to the constitution including amendment to the Ninth schedule has to be in accordance with the basic structure doctrine.

OTHER EXAMPLE OF USE OF JUDICIAL REVIEW BY THE COURT :

- Striking down of NJAC (99th constitutional amendment) terming it to be unconstitutional.
- Establishing the upper limit of reservation to 50% in Indira Sawney case

Therefore, judicial review is a crucial aspect and cornerstone to our constitutional setup. However necessary care should be taken to ensure that judicial review doesn't lead to judicial overreach which is harmful to a democratic set up like India.

CHAPTER TWENTY-FOUR

Common Cause (A Regd. Society) vs. Union of India (2008) 6 SCR 262: (2008) 5 SCC 511

Writ Petition (Civil) No.580 of 2003), Dated: April 11, 2008.

(Directives of a legislative nature cannot be given by the Court, since legislation is the task of the legislature and not of the Court. Petitioner is a registered society raised a various issues through writ petition related to road safety and also giving direction making enactment of a Road Traffic Safety Act in this regard. Seven-Judge Bench of this Court has clearly held that directives of a legislative nature cannot be given by the Court, since legislation is the task of the legislature and not of the Court. If it is given, will amount to impermissible legislation by the judiciary. Court held that "Not only should the Court not give such directives because that would violate the principle of separation of powers, but also because these are highly technical to be left to be dealt with by administrative and technical authorities who have experience and expertise in the matter." And thus petition was dismissed.)

FACTS OF THE CASE:

1. The Petitioner is a Society registered under the Societies Registration Act which claims to be engaged in espousing problems of general public importance. In the present case, the petitioner has referred to the rising number of road accidents in the country which are taking place in cities, towns and on National Highways causing deaths, injuries etc. The

Petitioner has referred to the defects in the licensing procedure, the training of drivers, and the need for suspending licenses in case of negligent driving, and driving under the influence of alcohol, which causes accidents etc. He has also referred to the inadequate infrastructure relating to roads and inadequate provisions of traffic control devices including traffic signals, traffic signs, road devices and other safety measures.

2. It has been stated in the Petition that there should be proper and continuous coordination between various authorities which are connected with roads and control of traffic, and for this purpose the only appropriate remedy is to establish Road Safety Committees. The Petitioner has also emphasised the need for having readily available ambulances for shifting the injured persons in road accidents to hospitals for immediate treatment.
3. The Petitioner has also stated that there should be road safety education for the users of roads, pedestrians, traffic participants including cyclists, handcarts men, bullock- cart drivers etc., who generally have low socio-economic and educational background and do not know traffic rules and regulations.
4. The Petitioner has alleged that pedestrians and non-motorised traffic face enormous risks as they account for 60% to 80% of road traffic fatalities in the country. All non-motorised traffic need to be given thorough and repeated orientation in observance of road traffic rules and avoidance of any situations which can cause accidents. These road safety education programmes can include written material for those who are literate and also illustrations, slides, specially prepared films, and also publicity through the medium of TV and Radio.
5. The Petitioner has also alleged that there is a paramount need for enactment of a Road Traffic Safety Act to lay down regulations dealing with specific responsibilities of drivers, proper maintenance of roads and traffic-connecting signs and signals etc., and all rules and regulations for observance by all concerned including pedestrians and non-motorized traffic. The Road Safety Act should contain all the regulations and the requirements relating to avoidance of accidents, responsibilities of respective Departments of State Governments, Municipal bodies, police authorities, and the penalty for non-observance of prescribed regulations. The Act should specify the duties, responsibilities, rights, directives and punishments in case of failures by anyone e.g. driver,

vehicle, road user etc.

6. The Petitioner has alleged that the number of accidents has increased greatly over the years in India and hence he has filed this Writ Petition with the following prayers:

(i) to issue a writ, direction or order in the nature of Mandamus and/or any other Writ, direction or order directing Respondent 1 (the Union of India) in consultation with representatives of Respondents 2, 3, 4, 5 and 6 (the Government of NCT of Delhi, and the State Governments of Maharashtra, Tamil Nadu, West Bengal and Karnataka) and also representatives of other States/UTs:

(a) to set up fully satisfactory procedures of licensing of vehicles and licensing of drivers, for ensuring that the vehicles are fully equipped with all the safety travel requirements, and also ensure that drivers of private vehicles as well as drivers of public vehicles including buses and trucks, are fully trained and are competent to drive the respective types of vehicles, and also to organise high-level training arrangements for the drivers of respective types of vehicles; appropriate procedures for suspension/cancellation of driving licences in the event of any default or for involvement in any accident;

(b) to ensure provision of all infrastructural requirements of roads, including signs, signals, footpaths, repairs of roads, and all such other requirements which will help to minimise risks of accidents on the roads;

(c) to set up methodology and requirements for undertaking scientific analysis of every accident, for ensuring that similar causes do not recur which can lead to accidents, thereby minimising the possibilities of accidents;

(d) to establish suitable organisations for providing education to all types of users of roads, through experts as well as use of suitably devised visual and audio media;

(e) to ensure the availability of ambulances for immediate removal of injured persons to hospitals;

(f) to set up committees of Experts in each State/UT and in the bigger cities for dealing with these various requirements for minimisation of accidents on the roads;

(ii) to direct Respondent 1 to formulate a suitable Road Traffic Safety Act to meet effectively the various requirements for minimisation of road accidents; and

(iii) to pass such other and further orders as may be deemed necessary to deal effectively with the various matters relating to traffic safety on the roads and minimisation of road accidents, on the facts and in the circumstances of the case.

JUDGMENT :

1. The Court held that in our opinion the prayers made by the petitioner in this petition require us to give directions of a legislative or executive nature which can only be given by the legislature or executive. The seven Judge-Bench decision of this Court in P. Ramachandra Rao case has clearly observed (in paras 22-27) that giving directions of a legislative nature is not a legitimate judicial function. A Seven-Judge Bench will clearly prevail over smaller Bench decisions.
2. In P. Ramachandra Rao case the question considered by the Seven-Judge Bench was whether the bar of limitation for criminal trials fixed by smaller Benches of this Court in Common Cause, A Registered Society vs. Union of India (1996) 4 SCC 33, Raj Deo Sharma vs. State of Bihar (1998) 7 SCC 507 and Raj Deo Sharma (II) vs. State of Bihar (1999) 7 SCC 604 was valid. The Seven-Judge Bench of this Court was of the view that the directions given by the smaller Bench decisions mentioned above were invalid as they amounted to directions of a legislative nature which only the legislative could give.
3. The correctness of the Three-Judge Bench decision in case of Raj Deo Sharma (II) vs. State of Bihar of this Court was considered by the Seven-Judge Bench in P. Ramachandra Rao case and the Seven-Judge Bench held that these decisions were incorrect as they amounted to impermissible legislation by the judiciary (vide para-23).
4. The Seven-Judge Bench was of the view that in its zeal to protect the right to speedy trial of an accused the Court cannot devise and enact bars of limitation when the legislature and statute have chosen not to do so. In paras 26 & 27 of the judgment in P.Ramachandra Rao case the Seven-Judge Bench of this Court has clearly held that directives of a legislative nature cannot be given by the Court, since legislation is the task of the legislature and not of the Court.
5. The Court held that the Motor Vehicles Act is a comprehensive enactment on the subject. If there is a lacuna or defect in the Act, it is for the legislature to correct it by a suitable amendment and not by the Court. What the petitioner really prays for in this petition is for various

directions which would be legislative in nature, as they would amount to amending the Act.

6. The Court in Union of India vs. Deoki Nandan Aggarwal (1992) Supp. 1 SCC 323 & AIR 1992 SC 96, a Three-Judge Bench of this Court observed (vide para 14): (SCC p. 332)

"14.....it is not the duty of the Court either to enlarge the scope of the legislation or the intention of the legislature when the language of the provision is plain and unambiguous. The Court cannot rewrite, recast or reframe the legislation for the very good reason that it has no power to legislate. The power to legislate has not been conferred on the courts. The Court cannot add words to a statue or read words into it which are not there. Courts shall decide what the law is and not what it should be. The court of course adopts a construction which will carry out the obvious intention of the legislature but could not legislate itself."

The Court cannot direct legislation vide Union of India vs. Prakash P. Hinduja (2003) 6 SCC 195 (vide SCC para 30: AIR para 29) and it cannot legislate vide Union of India vs. Deoki Nandan Aggarwal.

1. In Union of India vs. Assn. for Democratic Reforms (2002) 5 SCC 294 (vide AIR para 21) this Court observed: (SCC p. 309, para 19)

"19. At the outset, we would say that it is not possible for this Court to give directions for amending the Act or the statutory rules. It is for Parliament to amend the Act and the Rules. It is also established law that no direction can be given, which would be contrary to the Act and the Rules."

8. In Union of India vs. Prakash P. Hinduja (vide AIR para 29) this Court observed: (SCC pp. 216-217, para 30)

"30. Under our Constitutional scheme Parliament exercises sovereign power to enact laws and no outside power or authority can issue a direction to enact a particular piece of legislation. In Supreme Court Employees' Welfare Assn. Vs. Union of India (SCC para 51) it has been held that no court can direct a legislature to enact a particular law.

9. A perusal of the prayers made in this Writ Petition (which have been quoted above) clearly shows that what the petitioner wants us to do

is legislation by amending the law. In our opinion, this will not be a legitimate judicial function. The petitioner has prayed that we direct the Union of India to formulate a suitable Road Traffic Safety Act, but it is well settled that the Court cannot direct legislation.

10. In Bal Ram Bali vs. Union of India, JT (2007) 10 SC 509, this Court observed that Courts cannot issue any direction to Parliament or to the State Legislature to enact a particular kind of law.

11. The directives sought for in this petition require the expertise of administration and technical officials, apart from financial resources. Not only should the Court not give such directives because that would violate the principle of separation of powers, but also because these are highly technical to be left to be dealt with by administrative and technical authorities who have experience and expertise in the matter. For instance, what should be the maximum permissible speed for vehicles in a city, where should speed breakers be fixed, when should heavy vehicles be allowed on roads, and other matters for ensuring road safety are all matters to be dealt with by the authorities concerned under the Motor Vehicles Act and other enactments, and it would be wholly inappropriate for the judiciary to meddle in such matters.

12. Chapter VII of the Motor Vehicles Act, 1988 has provisions for control of traffic. These include fixing limits of speed (section 112), restriction on use of certain vehicles (section 115), power to erect traffic signs (Section 116), fixing parking places (Section 117), making driving regulations (Section 118), duty to obey traffic signs (Section 119), requirement for drivers to make such signals as are prescribed (Section 121), safety measures for drivers and pillion riders on two-wheelers (Section 128), wearing of protective headgear (Section 129), etc. These provisions are obviously meant for road safety, and if further provisions are required for this purpose the petitioner may approach the legislature or authority concerned for this purpose, but this Court can certainly not amend the law.

13. The people must know that courts are not the remedy for all ills in society. The problems confronting the nation are so huge that it will be creating an illusion in the minds of the people that the judiciary can solve all the problems. No doubt, the judiciary can make some suggestions/recommendations to the legislature or the executive, but these suggestions/recommendations cannot be binding on the legislature or the executive, otherwise there will be violation of the

Seven-Judge Bench decision of this Court in P. Ramachandra Rao case and violation of the principle of separation of powers.

14. The Court further held that " Before concluding, we would like to refer to the decision of this Court in Dattaraj Nathuji Thaware vs. State of Maharashtra, AIR 2005 SC 540 in which it is stated that public interest litigation has nowadays largely become "publicity interest litigation", "private interest litigation", or "politics interest litigation" or the latest trend "paise income litigation". Much of PIL is really blackmail.
15. Thus, PIL which was initially created as a useful judicial tool to help the poor and weaker section of society who could not afford to come to courts, has, in course of time, largely developed into an uncontrollable Frankenstein and a nuisance which is threatening to choke the dockets of the superior courts obstructing the hearing of the genuine and regular cases which have been waiting to be taken up for years together.

With the observations, the writ petition is dismissed.

CHAPTER TWENTY-FIVE

STATE OF WEST BENGAL & Ors. V. COMMITTEE FOR PROTECTION OF DEMOCRATIC RIGHTS WEST BENGAL & Ors. [2010] 2 SCR 979, (2010) 3 SCC 571

(Investigations in the incident was handed over to the CBI, an independent agency as per hon'ble High Court had directed investigation from the CBI without states approval. Aggrieved by this order, state of West Bengal move to Supreme Court and hon'ble court affirmed the order of high court and concluded that a direction by the High Court under Article 226 of the Constitution to the CBI to investigate an offence committed within the territory of a State without the consent of that State will neither impinge upon the federal structure of the Constitution nor violate the doctrine of separation of powers and shall be valid in law.)

FACTS OF THE CASE:

1. One Abdul Rahaman Mondal (hereinafter referred to as, "the complainant") along with a large number of workers of a political party had been staying in several camps of that party at Garbeta, District Midnapore, in the State of West Bengal. On 4th January, 2001, the complainant and few others decided to return to their homes from one

such camp.

2. When they reached the complainant's house, some miscreants, numbering 50-60, attacked them with firearms and other explosives, which resulted in a number of casualties. The complainant managed to escape from the place of occurrence, hid himself and witnessed the carnage.
3. He lodged a written complaint with the Garbeta Police Station on 4th January, 2001 itself but the First Information Report ("the FIR" for short) for offences under section 148/149/448/436/364/302/201 of the Indian Penal Code, 1860 (for short "the IPC") read with sections 25/27 of the Arms Act, 1959 and Section 9 (B) of the Explosives Act, 1884 was registered only on 5th January, 2001. On 8th January, 2001, Director General of Police, West Bengal directed the C.I.D. to take over the investigations in the case.
4. A writ petition under Article 226 of the Constitution was filed in the High Court of Judicature at Calcutta by the Committee for Protection of Democratic Rights, West Bengal, in public interest, inter alia, alleging that although in the said incident 11 persons had died on 4th January, 2001 and more than three months had elapsed since the incident had taken place yet except two persons, no other person named in the FIR, had been arrested; no serious attempt had been made to get the victims identified and so far the police had not been able to come to a definite conclusion whether missing persons were dead or alive.
5. It was alleged that since the police administration in the State was under the influence of the ruling party which was trying to hide the incident to save its image, the investigations in the incident may be handed over to the CBI, an independent agency. And the hon'ble High Court had directed investigation from the CBI. Aggrieved by this order of High Court state of West Bengal move to Supreme Court.

ISSUE BEFORE THE COURT:

The issue which has been referred for the opinion of the Constitution Bench is whether the High Court, in exercise of its jurisdiction under Article 226 of the Constitution of India, can direct the Central Bureau of Investigation (for short "the CBI"), established under the Delhi Special Police Establishment Act, 1946 (for short "the Special Police Act"), to investigate a cognizable offence, which is alleged to have taken place within the territorial jurisdiction of a State, without the consent of the State

Government.

PETITIONER`S ARGUMENT:

1. The petitioner put forth an argument based on two basic features of the Indian Constitution - federal setup and separation of powers.
2. As per Constitutional and statutory provisions, the State Legislature has jurisdiction over police matters and the Parliament cannot encroach upon it without the consent of the concerned State government.
3. It was argued that these restrictions over the powers of the Parliament, reflective of our federal setup, extend also to the judiciary, barring the courts from directing the police of one state to investigate an offence in another state without its consent, as such a direction would be in breach of the federal setup envisaged by the Constitution.
4. It was further argued that the separation of powers doctrine prevents the courts from exercising the executive power of directing the police force of one State to carry out investigations in another without the latter's consent.
5. Even in situations where the investigations are not carried out impartially, the judiciary should leave the matter to the wisdom of the Parliament to enact an appropriate legislation.
6. In short, the petitioner argued that the impugned direction of the High Court is violative of the federal structure and separation of powers doctrine, both of which are basic features of the Constitution.

ARGUMENT OF RESPONDENT, UNION OF INDIA:

1. It is the duty of the courts to uphold the Constitutional values and to enforce the Constitutional limitations as an ultimate interpreter of the Constitution.

2. learned counsel submitted that the judicial review being itself the basic feature of the Constitution, no restriction can be placed even by inference and by principle of legislative competence on the powers of the Supreme Court and the High Courts with regard to the enforcement of fundamental rights and protection of the citizens of India.

3. Learned counsel asserted that in exercise of powers either under Article 32 or 226 of the Constitution, the courts are merely discharging their duty of judicial review and are neither usurping any jurisdiction, nor overriding the doctrine of separation of powers.

JUDGMENT :

1. The Supreme Court rejected the petitioner's arguments and concluded that a direction by the High Court under Article 226 of the Constitution to the CBI to investigate an offence committed within the territory of a State without the consent of that State will neither impinge upon the federal structure of the Constitution nor violate the doctrine of separation of powers and shall be valid in law.
2. The Court held that judicial review itself being a basic feature, while exercising powers under Articles 32 and 226, the courts are merely discharging their duties and not violating the federal setup or the separation of powers doctrine.
3. The court held that, it necessary to emphasise that despite wide powers conferred by Articles 32 and 226 of the Constitution, while passing any order, the Courts must bear in mind certain self-imposed limitations on the exercise of these Constitutional powers. The very plenitude of the power under the said Articles requires great caution in its exercise. In so far as the question of issuing a direction to the CBI to conduct investigation in a case is concerned, although no inflexible guidelines can be laid down to decide whether or not such power should be exercised but time and again it has been reiterated that such an order is not to be passed as a matter of routine or merely because a party has levelled some allegations against the local police. This extra-ordinary power must be exercised sparingly, cautiously and in exceptional situations where it becomes necessary to provide credibility and instil confidence in investigations or where the incident may have national and international ramifications or where such an order may be necessary for doing complete justice and enforcing the fundamental rights. Otherwise the CBI would be flooded with a large number of cases and with limited resources, may find it difficult to properly investigate even serious cases and in the process lose its credibility and purpose with unsatisfactory investigations.
4. Application of the Basic Structure Doctrine To justify the judiciary's power of directing the CBI to investigate offences in other States without its consent, the Court ended up pitting one basic feature of the Constitution (judicial review) against two others (federal structure and separation of powers) put forward by the petitioner.
5. However, the question of the violation of basic structure of the Constitution does not even come into the picture in this case as the basic structure doctrine is used only when a challenge has been made to a

Constitutional amendment.

6. This case does not deal with any Constitutional amendment, but with the action of the judiciary itself. Extending the basic structure doctrine to judicial actions is taking it far beyond the limits within which it was intended to apply.
7. To complicate matters further, the Court concluded that "any law that abrogates or abridges [fundamental] rights would be violative of the basic structure doctrine".

CHAPTER TWENTY-SIX

Smt. Selvi v. State of Karnataka [2010] 5 SCR 381: (2010) 3 SCC 263

(The right to remain silent.Technology has absolutely outpaced the developments in law and human mankind. Narco Analysis is one such scientific advancement that has become progressively, perhaps alarmingly, common term in India. Some constitutional questions that encompass the era of technology are crucial to answer, are the methods adopted by the investigative authorities are ultra vires to the fundamental's rights of an individual, Whether the techniques are a boon or a bane for the accused, whether human rights are at stake because of such practices.)

BENCH : K.G. Balakrishnan, R.V. Raveendran, J.M. Panchal

FACTS OF THE CASE :

One of the most important and significant development is the growth in technological advancements. Now since every coin has two sides, technological advancements too have its pros and cons. One such advancement in the technology that we are here concerned about is the use of scientific techniques such as Narcoanalysis (NARCO), polygraph examination (PE) and the Brain Electrical Activation Profile (BEAP) test. These days the impugned techniques are being used in various fields for various purposes. We here are concerned with the use of these techniques in the criminal justice system. The impugned techniques help the investigating authorities to get relevant information from the accused. But now the word consent comes into the picture. The accused are involuntarily administered to these tests and hence a whole lot of question regarding the violation of human rights and fundamental rights arises. The landmark judgment of Smt. Selvi and Ors v. state of Karnataka, raises the important legal issues with respect to the involuntary administration of the impugned techniques and also makes a clear stand so as to what all should be done and taken care of while using these techniques.

Smt. Selvi and Ors v. State of Karnataka, is a criminal appeal in the supreme court of India bearing Criminal Appeal No 1267 of 2004. The case talks about the legal questions related to the involuntary administration of certain scientific techniques, namely narcoanalysis, polygraph examination and the Brain Electrical Activation Profile (BEAP) test for the purpose of improving investigation efforts in criminal cases. The case gives emphasis on major legal issues including privacy or personal liberty, self-incrimination and substantive due process.

THE LEGAL ISSUES BEFORE THE COURT:

1. Whether the involuntary administration of the impugned techniques violates the 'right against self-incrimination' enumerated in Article 20(3) of the Constitution?
2. Whether the investigative use of the impugned techniques creates a likelihood of incrimination for the subject?
3. Whether the results derived from the impugned techniques amount to 'testimonial compulsion' thereby attracting the bar of Article 20(3)?
4. Whether the involuntary administration of the impugned techniques is a reasonable restriction on 'personal liberty' as understood in the context of Article 21 of the Constitution?

JUDGMENT:

A three-judge bench including the then chief justice of India, K.G. Balakrishnan, J. RV Raveendran and J. JM Panchal held that involuntary administration of the impugned techniques violates the 'right against self-incrimination'

"This Court has recognized that the protective scope of Article 20(3) extends to the investigative stage in criminal cases and when read with Section 161(2) of the Code of Criminal Procedure, 1973 it protects accused persons, suspects as well as witnesses who are examined during an investigation. The test results cannot be admitted in evidence if they have been obtained through the use of compulsion. Article 20(3) protects an individual's choice between speaking and remaining silent, irrespective of whether the subsequent testimony

proves to be inculpatory or exculpatory."

Also, the court held that it violates the basic human right of an individual as the forcible administration of these techniques amounts to cruelty and is an intrusion of mental privacy. The bench ruled that involuntary administration of the impugned techniques violates the standard of substantive due process as given under article 21(3).

"we hold that no individual should be forcibly subjected to any of the techniques in question, whether in the context of investigation in criminal cases or otherwise. Doing so would amount to an unwarranted intrusion into personal liberty. However, we do leave room for the voluntary administration of the impugned techniques in the context of criminal justice, provided that certain safeguards are in place. Even when the subject has given consent to undergo any of these tests, the test results by themselves cannot be admitted as evidence because the subject does not exercise conscious control over the responses during the administration of the test"

The court also highlighted the guidelines that are laid down by the National Human Rights Commission for the administration of the polygraph test on the accused. The court held that these guidelines should be strictly adhered to for all kinds of such techniques.

In our considered opinion, the compulsory administration of the impugned techniques violates the `right against self- incrimination‘. This is because the underlying rationale of the said right is to ensure the reliability as well as voluntariness of statements that are admitted as evidence. This Court has recognised that the protective scope of Article 20(3) extends to the investigative stage in criminal cases and when read with Section 161 (2) of the Code of Criminal Procedure, 1973 it protects accused persons, suspects as well as witnesses who are examined during an investigation. The test results cannot be admitted in evidence if they have been obtained through the use of compulsion. Article 20(3) protects an individual's choice between speaking and remaining silent, irrespective of whether the subsequent testimony proves to be inculpatory or exculpatory. Article 20(3) aims to prevent the forcible `conveyance of personal knowledge that is relevant to the facts in issue'. The results obtained from each of the impugned tests bear a `testimonial‘ character and they cannot be categorised as material evidence.

We are also of the view that forcing an individual to undergo any of the impugned techniques violates the standard of `substantive due process' which is required for restraining personal liberty. Such a violation will occur irrespective of whether these techniques are forcibly administered during the course of an investigation or for any other purpose since the test results could also expose a person to adverse consequences of a non-penal nature. The impugned techniques cannot be read into the statutory provisions which enable medical examination during investigation in criminal cases, i.e. the Explanation to Sections 53, 53-A and 54 of the Code of Criminal Procedure, 1973. Such an expansive interpretation is not feasible in light of the rule of `ejusdem generis‘ and the considerations which govern the interpretation of statutes in relation to scientific advancements. We have also elaborated how the compulsory administration of any of these techniques is an unjustified intrusion into the mental privacy of an individual. It would also amount to `cruel, inhuman or degrading treatment' with regard to the language of evolving international human rights norms. Furthermore, placing reliance on the results gathered from these techniques comes into conflict with the `right to fair trial‘. Invocations of a compelling public interest cannot justify the dilution of constitutional rights such as the `right against self-incrimination'.

In light of these conclusions, we hold that no individual should be forcibly subjected to any of the techniques in question, whether in the context of investigation in criminal cases or otherwise. Doing so would amount to an unwarranted intrusion into personal liberty. However, we do leave room for the voluntary administration of the impugned techniques in the context of criminal justice, provided that certain safeguards are in place. Even when the subject has given consent to undergo any of these tests, the test results by themselves cannot be admitted as evidence because the subject does not exercise conscious control over the responses during the administration of the test. However, any information or material that is subsequently discovered with the help of voluntary administered test results can be admitted, in accordance with Section 27 of the Evidence Act, 1872. The National Human Rights Commission had published `Guidelines for the Administration of Polygraph Test (Lie Detector Test) on an Accused‘ in 2000. These guidelines should be strictly adhered to and similar safeguards should be adopted for conducting the `Narcoanalysis technique' and the `Brain Electrical Activation Profile‘ test. The text of these guidelines has been reproduced below:

(i) No Lie Detector Tests should be administered except on the basis of consent of the accused. An option should be given to the accused whether he wishes to avail such test.

(ii) If the accused volunteers for a Lie Detector Test, he should be given access to a lawyer and the physical, emotional and legal implication of such a test should be explained to him by the police and his lawyer.

(iii) The consent should be recorded before a Judicial Magistrate.

(iv) During the hearing before the Magistrate, the person alleged to have agreed should be duly represented by a lawyer.

(v) At the hearing, the person in question should also be told in clear terms that the statement that is made shall not be a `confessional' statement to the Magistrate but will have the status of a statement made to the police.

(vi) The Magistrate shall consider all factors relating to the detention including the length of detention and the nature of the interrogation.

(vii) The actual recording of the Lie Detector Test shall be done by an independent agency (such as a hospital) and conducted in the presence of a lawyer.

(viii) A full medical and factual narration of the manner of the information received must be taken on record.

In this way present batch of appeals was disposed of accordingly by the court. Thus we see that

1. **The involuntary administration of the impugned techniques violates article 20(3) of the Indian Constitution.**
2. **The involuntary administration of the impugned techniques violates the right to privacy and personal liberty as given under article 21 of the Indian.**
3. **The involuntary administration of the impugned techniques is against basic human rights..**

"Judgments such as D.K. Basu v. State of West Bengal, have stressed upon the importance of preventing the 'cruel, inhuman or degrading treatment' of any person who is taken into custody."

We all are aware that an accused is innocent unless proven guilty and subjecting an accused to such treatments would, therefore is injustice on his part and humanity and constitutional morality should be kept above all. It create an interrelation between article 20(3) and article 21 of the Indian Constitution i.e. right against self-incrimination should be read as a part of the right to personal liberty.

A number of provisions from CRPC including sec 161(2) talk about an accused's right to remain silent and that he/she should not be forced to give any testimony which might result into penal provisions against himself.

"The protective scope of Article 20(3) read with Section 161(2), CrPC guards against the compulsory extraction of oral testimony, even at the stage of an investigation."

CHAPTER TWENTY-SEVEN

Natural Resources Allocation In Re , Special Reference No. 1 of 2012 [2012] 9 SCR 311: (2012) 10 SCC 1

(This case revolves around the questions which was asked by the president to the supreme court about the allocation of natural resources. After the 2g spectrum case there was a mindset in each and every state auction is perhaps the best method for allocation of resources. The court in this case clarify various principles which shall be applied by the government at the time of allocation of resources. The court held that it is not the concern of the court that which policy is adopted by the government for allocation of resources but the important aspect is the in every method government should abide itself with Article 14 of Indian Constitution.

If the government is making classifications amongst the people, the classifications must also be rational an every step taken by government towards the allocation of resources must be profit oriented and should on maximization of profits which shall be used for common good. The case also clarify that government has no right to donate the resources to any individual because each and individual has equal right on the resources.)

BENCH : S.H. Kapadia, C.J. And D.K. Jain, J.S. Khehar, Dipak Misra and Ranjan Gogoi, JJ

FACTS OF THE CASE

The president of India has power to seek opinion from Supreme court whenever any question of law arises. It is not necessary that the question of law which has arisen must be regarding to the present scenario, the president can also ask questions which are concerned with future of some events which are likely to arise.

The supreme court has also some powers when it comes to answering the questions which are raised by the president, the supreme court can deny to answer the question if it thinks that answering of a specific question would have direct bearing on the previous judgment given by the court or any other reasonable reason.

In 2012, under a presidential reference, Supreme court was asked to give its opinion on the allocation of natural resources.

Reason for the presidential reference on this topic was *Centre for public interest litigation v. union of India* popularly known as 2g spectrum case. The judgment of that case did not answer a few questions which the president thought shall need to be answered for the common interest of the citizens.

Apart from allocation of radio and spectrums there are various kinds of natural resources like petroleum, minerals, gas etc. the law therefore should not be ambiguous at the time of allocation of the natural resources to the private players in the market.

The distribution of natural resources by the state cannot be arbitrary and discriminatory; a state has to abide itself by article 14 of the constitution at the time of allocation of natural resources. Because there exist a fiduciary relationship between citizens and the government for the safety of natural resources and government cannot just allocate resources in such a way that it only benefits a single person.

When it comes to the classification at the time of allocation of resources, it must also be non-discriminatory and there must be reasonable grounds for distinction, there are various examples given in the case which shows how reasonably a law should applied.

In this case also the president believes that there are still some unanswered questions about the allocation of natural resources which need a concrete answer so that there must not be any ambiguity at state's end when it comes to the allocation of natural resources.

This ambiguity although was always there in the mind of the government but it increased after the judgment in 2g spectrum case, after the judgment in 2g case which held that perhaps auction is the best possible way to allocate resources so the president raises some questions and uses the power which lies in article 143 of the Indian constitution.

Out of all the questions Supreme court decided to answer the first five questions and the denied to answer last three questions because it had direct bearing on 2g spectrum case. The president has asked following questions to supreme court.

ISSUES BEFORE THE COURT :

1. Whether the only permissible method for disposal of all natural resources across all sectors and in all circumstances is by the conduct of auctions?

2. Whether a broad proposition of law that only the route of auctions can be restored to for disposal of natural resources does not run contrary to several judgments of the supreme court including those of the large benches?

3. Whether the enunciation of a broad principle., even though expressed as a matter of constitutional law, does not really amount to formulation of a policy and has the effect of unsettling policy decisions formulate and approaches taken by various successive governments over the years for valid consideration, including lack of public resources and the need to resort to innovative and different approaches for the development of various sectors of the economy?

4. What is the permissible scope for interference by courts with policy-making by the Government including method of disposal of natural resources?

5. Whether, if the court holds, within the permissible scope of judicial review, that a policy is flawed, is the court not obliged to take into account investments under the said policy, including investments made by foreign investors under multilateral/ bilateral agreements?[2]

Application of laws by the judge

1. Although the case includes dealing with various statutes like MMDR and various articles of Indian constitution. But the main focus in this particular judgment is Article 14 and implementation of article 14 when it comes to the allocation of natural resources.

2. Article 14 which states that the state shall not deny to any person equality before the law.

3. Equality in each and every aspect is necessary because the essence of equality will diminish if it becomes subjective to the facts and circumstances. Whatever the facts and circumstances of the may be but the principle of equality should always exist and a person must not miss the opportunity just because of the unequal treatment by the state or any instrumentality of the state.

Application of laws with facts

In this case where the president is concerned for the allocation of natural resources amongst the citizens of the country. Allocation of natural resources must be fair, transparent and non discriminatory and a single person must not get the benefit at the cost of the other citizens. In this case it has been stated that distribution of any kind of resource must be tested with principle of equality.

Any kind of allocation which fails to adhere with principle of equality shall be void. In this case it was also held that if the state is making any kind of classification at the time of distribution of resources, that classification must be reasonable should not resist a group of peole to participate in the bidding just because they do not fall under a specific category set by the state.

The suggestions given by Bose, J. about whether the legislation has violated article 14 or not plays a very crucial role while determining at the time of allocation of natural resources to get the insight of discrimination that the state has done amongst the citizens. According to the principle given by Bose, J. a judge must look deeply into each case for considering here as matter of law and not just one fact that do these laws which have been called in question offend a still greater law before which they must even bow.

In this case, the judges of the Supreme Court while considering auction as only option for the allocation of natural resources stated that although auction would help in maximization of profits for the government but it would very inappropriate if we make auction as a constitution mandate because if we do so it would make all the other ways of allocating resources void and mandatory auction might be contrary to economy as well.

JUDGMENT :

In the judgment Justice Khehar has held that the state while making contracts with private players the state must not act arbitrarily and must act in a fair and reasonable man. The court held that while making contracts with regards to allocation of resources must act like a prudent businessman which focuses on maximization of profits and the generated profits must be used for the common good and by common good court means that the welfare of public should held utmost importance and benefitting only a single person must not be the target the government should achieve because the resources which lies with the sovereign are the property of each and every individual that live in the state.

In the judgment the court has also referred to the report by CAG which shows the loss incurred by the government because of bad allocation policies. The court held that it cannot decide the best way possible to decide the method of allocation because it depends upon facts and circumstances of each case, in this reference Justice Khehar stated that the court will judge the method when it appears in the court of law.

At the point of auction as best possible method to allocate resources the court held that making auction as a constitution mandate for allocation of resources will make other methods void which would harm the policy of various sates which prefers other ways to allocate resources.

While answering firs question which is related to decide whether auction is the best possible way to allocate resources the court held that president's reference is not based on concrete factual problem so deciding a method for all the resources would be unjust. The court also held that no part of natural resources cannot be disposed as charity or donation each and every single bit of resource must reciprocate and the consideration of the resources must be use for the public welfare.

ANALYSIS OF JUDGMENT :

1. There was the ambiguity in the judgment of *Centre for public interest litigation v. union of India* which gave rise to the first question. The first question which asks that whether auction is the only option for disposal of all natural resources and under all circumstances is the repercussion of the ambiguity in the 2g spectrum judgment.

2. Although there was no mention about auction being the only permissible and intra vires method of disposal of natural resources and that the findings are limited to the case of spectrum but considering a specific method as best among various methods gives impression that if the highest judiciary bench has considered something as best method for allocation of

resources, why would the state contradict with the best method at the time of allocation?

3. The reason that petitioner approached the court in 2g spectrum case by invoking article 32 is because the union had adopted "First come first serve" policy which can have dangerous repercussions and the government cannot be so careless to give away resources on first come first serve basis. But the problem in the judgment was the statement which defines auction as perhaps the best possible way to dispose the natural resources and because of this the state thought that it was duty bound to dispose resources by the way of auction.

4. In this judgment not only consider individual rights but also gave equal importance to plural rights and balancing of both. He impeccably linked the concept of plural rights with the case of allocation of natural resources. It was stated that the true effect of article 14 in Indian constitution is equal protection of laws not only with the reference to individual rights but by ensuring that the rights of the citizens on the other side shall not be deprived which clearly means that an individual cannot be beneficiary at the cost of all the other remaining citizens.

5. The one important case which shows that the discriminatory acts done by the state at the time of allocation of resources must be considered void.

6. In *Rashbihari Panda v. State of Orissa* the state government decide to invite the same old contractors for tender for Kendu leaves. The validity of the scheme in this case must be adjudged in the light of Article 19(1)(g) and article of Indian constitution. The traders who wanted to deal in Kendu leaves and those who wanted to start business in Kendu leaves were not allowed to even participate in the tender process which was violative to Article 19(1)(g).

The court held that the contracts made by the state government till now cannot be considered as void but the future contracts that the state will make shall include all the businessman who want to trade in kendu leaves and any kind of discrimination among old contractors and new contractors must be avoided.

7. This case dose not prescribes the "best" method for allocation of resources and totally leaves this authority to the government to chose the best method for allocation of resources like in the case of *Centre for public interest litigation v. union of India.* In this case supreme court held that auction is perhaps the best method for allocation of natural resources which somehow bound the state government to allocate the resources in that

particular manner.

8. Court leaves it to the government to to choose the best possible method to adopt for allocation of resources. The resources that lies in the state belongs to every citizen and even a small piece of resource cannot be given as charity to anyone which bans the policy which supports favoritism and nepotism which amazingly answers the questions which was raised by the president.

CHAPTER TWENTY-EIGHT

Republic of Italy and Ors. v. Union of India and Ors. [2013] 4 SCR 595 : (2013) 4 SCC 721

(Articles 32, 136 – Orders dated 18.01.2013 – Question of jurisdiction of Court to try two Italian marines for committing murder of two Indian fishermen – Supreme Court already held that State of Kerala has no jurisdiction and that jurisdiction was of Central Government, which was directed to take steps – Investigation taken over by NIA – Same opposed. Held that directions were to Central Government to take steps for constituting a Special Court for trial and to entrust investigation to a neutral agency. Supreme Court cannot be called upon to decide as to which agency should conduct investigation. It was for Central Government to take decision. Central Government left to take further steps. In case of any jurisdictional error by Central Government, it will be open for accused to question the same before appropriate forum.)

ON APRIL 26, 2013

Writ Petition (C) No. 135 of 2012

With

Massimilano Latorre & Ors. v. Union of India & Ors.

Special Leave Petition (C) No. 20370 of 2012

[Under Article 32 of the Constitution of India]

FACTS OF THE CASE:

1. In 2012, Indian police had detained two Italian marines posted on oil tanker Enrica Lexie who had shot at two Indian fishermen on an Indian

vessel, apparently mistaking them for pirates operating near the Kerala Coast.

2. After three years, Italy moved the International Tribunal for Law of the Sea (ITLOS) seeking for two italian marines to stay in their own country during the trial process and also to stop India from going ahead with its criminal prosecution.

3. At that time, India had set up a specially designated court, as ordered by Indian Supreme Court, to determine the applicability of jurisdiction.

4. India's National Investigation Agency had already slapped charges against the two Italians under sections of the Indian Penal Code, related to murder, attempt to murder, mischief and common intent.

JUDGEMENT:

We do not see why this Court should be called upon to decide as to the agency that is to conduct the investigation. The direction which we had given in our judgment dated 18th January, 2013, was in the context of whether the Kerala Courts or the Indian Courts or even the Italian Courts would have the jurisdiction to try the two Italian marines. It was not our desire that any particular Agency was to be entrusted with the investigation and to take further steps in connection therewith. Our intention in giving the direction for formation of a special Court was for the Central Government to first of all entrust the investigation to a neutral agency. (Para 6)

Since steps have been duly taken for the appointment of a Court of competent jurisdiction to try the case, the Central Government appears to have taken steps in terms of the directions given in our judgment dated 18th January, 2013. It is for the Central Government to take a decision in the matter. (Para 6)

We, therefore, take note of the steps taken by the Central Government pursuant to the directions given in our judgment dated 18th January, 2013, and leave it to the Central Government to take further steps in the matter. (Para 8)

ALTAMAS KABIR, CJI.

1. These proceedings are an offshoot of the judgment delivered by this Court on 18th January, 2013, disposing of Writ Petition (Civil) No.135 of 2012 filed by the Republic of Italy through its Ambassador in India and the two marines who had been arrested by the Kerala Police in connection with the killing of two Indian fishermen on board an Indian fishing vessel at a distance of 20.5 nautical miles from the Indian sea-coast off the coastline

of the State of Kerala. While the Special Leave Petition was filed by the two marines challenging the dismissal of their Writ Petition No.4542 of 2012 by the Kerala High Court rejecting their prayer for quashing of FIR No.2 of 2012 on the file of the Circle Inspector of Police, Neendakara, Kollam District, Kerala, as being without jurisdiction, the Writ Petition (Civil) No.135 of 2012 was also filed for much the same reliefs. Both the matters were, therefore, taken up together for hearing and were disposed of together on 18th January, 2013.

2. While disposing of the two matters, this Court held that the State of Kerala had no jurisdiction to investigate into the incident and that till such time it is proved that the provisions of Article 100 of UNCLOS, 1982, applied to the facts of this case, it is the Union of India which alone has the jurisdiction to proceed with the investigation and trial of the Petitioner Nos.2 and 3 in the Writ Petition. We, accordingly, directed the Union of India, in consultation with the Chief Justice of India, to set-up a special Court to try this case and to dispose of the same in accordance with the provisions of the Maritime Zones Act, 1976, the Indian Penal Code, the Code of Criminal Procedure and the provisions of UNCLOS 1982. It was further directed that the proceedings before the Chief Judicial Magistrate, Kollam, would stand transferred to the Special Court to be constituted in terms of the judgment, upon the expectation that the trial would be conducted expeditiously. Liberty was given to the Petitioners to re-agitate the question of jurisdiction once the evidence was adduced on behalf of the parties.

3. On 14th March, 2013, the matter was mentioned by the learned Attorney General, on basis of Note Verbale No.89/635 dated 11th March, 2013, received by the Ministry of External Affairs, Government of India, from the Embassy of Italy in New Delhi, whereby it was indicated that the Government of Italy had decided not to return the accused marines to India to stand trial for the offences alleged to have been committed by them. Pursuant to the directions given on that date, the matter was again listed on 2nd April, 2013, and the learned Attorney General was requested by the Court to indicate what steps had been taken for constitution of a separate Court to try the two Italian marines separately on a fast track basis, in order to dispose of the matter as quickly as possible. The matter was then listed again on 22nd April, 2013, when the learned Attorney General informed the Court that pursuant to the directions of this Court in its judgment dated 18th January, 2013, the Government of India, in the Ministry of Home Affairs,

had appointed the National Investigation Agency created under the National Investigation Agency Act, 2008, to take over the investigation on the basis of FIR No.2 of 2012 dated 29th August, 2012, Coastal PS Neendakara, Kollam. The case was re-registered at PS NIA, New Delhi as Case No.RC-04/2013/NIA/DLI under Sections 302, 307, 427 read with Section 34 of the Indian Penal Code and Section 3 of The Suppression of Unlawful Acts Against Safety of Maritime Navigation and Fixed Platforms on Continental Shelf Act, 2002. The learned Attorney General submitted that the case is under investigation by the National Investigation Agency, and such investigation would be completed shortly.

4. The submissions made by the learned Attorney General were vehemently opposed by Shri Mukul Rohatgi, learned Senior Advocate, on behalf of the accused mainly on the ground that by handing over the investigation to the National Investigation Agency, the Government was also altering the forum before which the matter could be heard. Furthermore, by entrusting the investigation to the National Investigation Agency, the investigating authorities were being permitted to invoke the provisions of the Suppression of Unlawful Acts Against Safety of Maritime Navigation and Fixed Platforms on Continental Shelf Act, 2002, which provides for death penalty in regard to cognizance being taken on any of the scheduled offences. Mr. Mukul Rohtagi, learned Senior Advocate, who appeared for the Petitioners, urged that since the provisions of the aforesaid Act had not been included in the original charge-sheet, the investigating authorities could not be permitted to take recourse to the same, especially when directions had been given by this Court in the judgment dated 18th January, 2013, that the case was to be tried under the provisions of the Maritime Zones Act, 1976, the Indian Penal Code, the Code of Criminal Procedure and the provisions of UNCLOS 1982.

5. Mr. Rohtagi submitted that since the National Investigation Agency could only try the Scheduled Offences, referred to in the Act, the investigation could not, in any event, be taken up under the National Investigation Agency Act, 2008.

6. Having heard the learned Attorney General for India and Mr. Mukul Rohtagi for the Petitioners, we do not see why this Court should be called upon to decide as to the agency that is to conduct the investigation. The direction which we had given in our judgment dated 18th January, 2013, was in the context of whether the Kerala Courts or the Indian Courts or even the Italian Courts would have the jurisdiction to try the two Italian marines.

It was not our desire that any particular Agency was to be entrusted with the investigation and to take further steps in connection therewith. Our intention in giving the direction for formation of a special Court was for the Central Government to first of all entrust the investigation to a neutral agency, and, thereafter, to have a dedicated Court having jurisdiction to conduct the trial. Since steps have been duly taken for the appointment of a Court of competent jurisdiction to try the case, the Central Government appears to have taken steps in terms of the directions given in our judgment dated 18th January, 2013. It is for the Central Government to take a decision in the matter.

7. If there is any jurisdictional error on the part of the Central Government in this regard, it will always be open to the accused to question the same before the appropriate forum.

8. We, therefore, take note of the steps taken by the Central Government pursuant to the directions given in our judgment dated 18th January, 2013, and leave it to the Central Government to take further steps in the matter.

9. In addition to the above, we sincerely hope that the investigation will be completed at an early date and the trial will also be conducted on a day-to-day basis and be completed expeditiously as well.

10. The terms and conditions regarding bail, as were indicated in our Order dated 18th January, 2013, will continue to remain operative in the meantime.

Permanent Court of Arbitration

The ITLOS judgement of 2015 called on Italy and India to suspend all domestic prosecutions arising from the Enrica Lexie Case. It had also ordered not to initiate any steps that might jeopardize or prejudice the carrying out of any decision which the arbitral tribunal may provide.

The matter led to a long freeze in diplomatic relations between India and Italy, which were reset only in 2016.

Judgements in Favour of India:

The tribunal held that the actions of the Italian military officers breached India's freedom of navigation under UNCLOS Article 87(1)(a) and 90.

The tribunal also held that India is entitled for payment of compensation in connection with loss of life, physical harm, material damage to property and moral harm suffered by captain and crew of 'St Antony', the Indian vessel.

Judgements in Favour of Italy:

India had called on the Permanent Court of Arbitration (PCA) UNCLOS tribunal to adjudge and declare that PCA has no jurisdiction with respect to the case submitted to it by Italy. However, a majority of the court's five-member bench ruled 4-1 that it had jurisdiction in the matter.

Italian position that the marines, being members of the Italian armed forces in the official exercise cannot be tried by Indian courts, was held and immunity was granted to Italian marine officials.

Basis of the Judgement:

The tribunal observed that India and Italy had concurrent jurisdiction over the incident and a valid legal basis to institute criminal proceedings against the marines.

However, it also observed that the immunities enjoyed by the marines as State officials operate as an exception to the jurisdiction of the Indian courts and, hence, preclude them to judge the marines.

Permanent Court of Arbitration :

The Permanent Court of Arbitration (PCA) was established in 1899 and headquartered at the Hague in Netherlands.

It is an intergovernmental organization dedicated to serve the international community in the field of dispute resolution and to facilitate arbitration and other forms of dispute resolution between States.

It has a Financial Assistance Fund which aims at helping developing countries meet part of the costs involved in international arbitration or other means of dispute settlement offered by the PCA.

CHAPTER TWENTY-NINE

Novartis AG v. Union of India & others [2013] 13 SCR 148 : (2013) 4 SCC 721

(In this case Novartis challenged the rejection of its patent application by IPAB for Beta crystalline form of "Imatinib mesylate" wherein such challenge was rejected by the Supreme Court of India on the ground that the said drug did not produce an enhanced or superior therapeutic efficacy as compared to the known substance i.e., "Imatinib mesylate" means that the said drug did not involve an *inventive step and* considered ever-greening of already patented products by introducing minor changes *and not patentable as per* section-3(d) of Patent Act, 1970. Supreme Court in its judgement made clear that India is a developing country and the availability of medicines at a cheaper rate is necessary for the lives of 1 billion people.)

FACTS OF THE CASE:

1. In 1997, Novartis, a Swiss based pharmaceutical giant filed an application to grant patent to an anticancer drug *Glivec* which is used to treat Chronic Myeloid Leukemia (CML) and Gastrointestinal Stromal Tumours (GIST) on the basis that it invented the beta crystalline salt form (imatinib mesylate) of the free base, imatinib.. It is a critical drug which is patented in about 35 countries of the world.

2. However during those days, India did not grant patent to pharmaceutical products and agrochemical products. It was in the year 2005 in India; the drug products became the subject of patent in compliance with the TRIPS agreement. India thereon revised its patent law and started granting patents on pharmaceutical drugs.

3. Subsequently in 2006, the Madras Patent Office refused the patent application of Novartis for its drug Glivec stating that the said drug did not exhibit any major changes in therapeutic effectiveness over its pre-existing form, which was already patented outside India.

4. The said decision was based on Section 3(d) of the Indian Patents (Amendment) Act, 2005 which provides a known substance can only be patented if its new forms exhibit “enhanced efficacy”. The Patent Office did not find any enhanced efficacy in the drug Glivec and, therefore, considered it incapable of patentable under Section 3(d) of 2005 Act.

5. In May 2006, Novartis filed two writ petitions under Article 226 of the Indian Constitution before the High Court of Madras – one appealing against the order of Madras Patent Office rejecting its patent request and the other contesting that Section 3(d) of the Indian Patents Act is not in compliance with TRIPS and is vague, arbitrary and violative of Article 14 of the Constitution.

6. The Madras High Court refused the Writ Petitions of Novartis holding that it did not have jurisdiction to determine whether a domestic law is in contrary to international treaty, so it cannot decide whether Section 3(d) is in compliance with TRIPS. As far as Section 3(d) is considered, the objective of the Amending Act was to prevent evergreening and to make easy the access to life-saving drugs to the citizens. Therefore, it cannot be considered to be vague and arbitrary.

7. The new phase of litigation started in Intellectual Property Appellate Board, which is an appellate body of patent controller. IPAB considered the beta-crystalline form of imatinib mesylate as new and an inventive step but refused to grant a patent to the drug of Novartis since it was hit by Section 3(d) of the Act. Novartis challenged the said order by filing Special Leave Petition before the Supreme Court.

ISSUES BEFORE THE COURT:

1. According to the provision of section-3(d) of Patent Act, 1970 what is a known substance?

2. According to section-3(d) of Patent Act, 1970 what is the meaning of Efficacy?

3. According to section-3(d) of Patent Act, 1970 whether increase in bioavailability qualify as increase in therapeutic efficacy?

4. Whether the invention "Beta crystalline form of imatinib mesylate" claimed by Novartis is more efficacious than the substance that it was derived from i.e. "Imatinib mesylate”?

JUDGMENT:

The Supreme Court adopted the following approach-

1. Court observed that the product was one of the new forms of the substance and not the whole substance. It has always existed in the original amorphous form. The product thus has to qualify the test laid down in Section 3(d) of the Patent Act.
2. The Section clearly specifies that a new form of the substance in not patentable under Indian law unless it enhances its "known efficacy".
3. Novartis contended that the physico-chemical properties of the polymorph form of the imatinib molecule, i.e. better flow properties, better thermodynamic stability and lower hygroscopicity, resulted in improved efficacy and hence is patentable under Indian law.

The Apex Court rejected this contention stating that in the case of medicines, efficacy means "therapeutic efficacy" and these properties while they may be beneficial to some patients do not meet this standard. The Supreme Court also held that patent applicants must prove the increase in therapeutic efficacy based on research data in vivo in animals.

The Supreme Court held that the true intention to enact section 3(d) was to prevent the concept of evergreening and thus if the invention does not fulfil the test of Section 3(d), it cannot be granted a patent. The court further specified that this case should not be interpreted to mean that Section 3(d) bars all incremental inventions. It is with regard to the field of medicine especially in cases of life-saving drugs, a great acre and caution needs to be taken so as to protect the right to life of the masses.

CHAPTER THIRTY

Dr. balram Prasad v Dr. Kunal Saha and ors [2013] 12 SCR 30 : (2014) 1 SCC 384

(Hon'ble Apex court hold the three doctors and the hospital culpable to civil liability for medical negligence which had led to the death of Anuradha, a child psychologist and wife of claimant Dr. Kunal Saha, who had come to her home town Kolkata in March 1998 on a summer vacation. Deceased complained of skin rashes on April 25 and consulted Dr Sukumar Mukherjee, who, advised her only to take rest without prescribing any medicine. However, skin rashes resurfaced again with greater passion in early May. Dr Mukherjee prescribed Depomedrol injection 80 mg twice daily to be taken on daily basis, however this prescription of Dr. Mukherjee was not approved by experts. Administration of injection led to deterioration of Anuradha's condition, following which she had to be admitted at AMRI on 11 May under Dr Mukherjee's supervision and subsequently she was shifted to Mumbai's Breach Candy Hospital, and her diagnosis stated that she was diagnosed to be suffering from life threatening disease called toxic epidermal necrolysis (TEN). Anuradha succumbed to her ailment on May 28, 1998.)

FACTS OF THE CASE:

The claimant (Dr Balram Prasad) filed Original Petition No. 240 of 1999 on 09.03.1999 before the National Commission claiming compensation for Rs.77,07,45,000/- and later the same was amended by claiming another sum of Rs.20,00,00,000/-. After the case of Malay Kumar Ganguly Vs. Dr. Sukumar Mukherjee [1] was remanded by this Court to the National Commission to award just and reasonable compensation to the claimant by answering the points framed in the said case, the National Commission held the doctors and the AMRI Hospital negligent in treating the wife of the claimant on account of which she died. Therefore, this Court directed the National Commission to determine just and reasonable compensation payable to the claimant.

However, the claimant, the appellant-Hospital and the doctors were aggrieved by the amount of compensation awarded by the National Commission and also the manner in which liability was apportioned amongst each of them. While the claimant was aggrieved by the inadequate amount of compensation, the appellant-doctors and the Hospital found the amount to be excessive and too harsh. They further claimed that the proportion of liability ascertained on each of them is unreasonable. Since, the appellant-Hospital and the doctors raised similar issues before the Court.

ISSUES BEFORE THe COURT:-

1) Whether the claim of the claimant for enhancement of compensation in his appeal is justified. If it is so, for what compensation he is entitled to?

2) While making additional claim by way of affidavit before the National Commission when amending the claim petition, whether the claimant is entitled for compensation on the enhanced claim preferred before the National Commission?

3(a) Whether the claimant seeking to amend the claim of compensation under certain heads in the original claim petition has forfeited his right of claim under Order II Rule 2 of CPC as pleaded by the AMRI Hospital?

3(b) Whether the claimant is justified in claiming additional amount for compensation under different heads without following the procedure contemplated under the provisions of the Consumer Protection Act and the Rules?

4. Whether the National Commission is justified in adopting the multiplier method to determine the compensation and to award the compensation in favour of the claimant?

5. Whether the claimant is entitled to pecuniary damages under the heads of loss of employment, loss of his property and his traveling expenses from U.S.A. to India to conduct the proceedings in his claim petition?

6. Whether the claimant is entitled to the interest on the compensation that would be awarded?

7. Whether the compensation awarded in the impugned judgment and the apportionment of the compensation amount fastened upon the doctors

and the hospital requires interference and whether the claimant is liable for contributory negligence and deduction of compensation under this head?

8. To what Order and Award the claimant is entitled to in these appeals?

ARGUMENT OF APPELLANT:

1. Though, the appellant-Dr. Balram Prasad was accused in the criminal complaint lodged by the claimant he was neither proceeded against as an accused in the criminal complaint nor before the West Bengal Medical Council but was named as a witness.

2. Further, it is stated by the claimant that he urged before the National Commission as well as before this Court in unequivocal terms that the bulk of the compensation awarded would have to be in the proportion of 80% on the AMRI Hospital, 15% on Dr. Sukumar Mukherjee and balance between the rest The appellant-Dr. Balram Prasad in Civil Appeal No.2867/2012 contends that he was the junior most attending physician attached to the Hospital,

3. He was not called upon to prescribe medicines but was only required to continue and/or monitor the medicines prescribed by the specialist in the discipline. But realizing the seriousness of the patient, the appellant had himself referred the patient to the three specialists and also suggested for undertaking a skin biopsy.

4. The duty of care ordinarily expected of a junior doctor had been discharged with diligence by the appellant.

5. It is further contended that in his cross-examination before the National Commission in the enquiry proceeding, the claimant himself has admitted that the basic fallacy was committed by three physicians, namely, Dr. Mukherjee, Dr. Haldar and Dr. Roy Chowdhury. The above facts would clearly show that the role played by the appellant-Doctors in the treatment of the deceased was only secondary and the same had been discharged with reasonable and due care expected of an attending physician in the given facts and circumstances of the instant case.

6. In the light of the above facts and circumstances, the contention of the claimant that the death of the claimant's wife was neither directly nor contributorily relatable to the alleged negligent act of the appellant-Dr. Balram Prasad, it is most respectfully submitted that the National Commission was not justified in apportioning the damages in the manner as has been done by the National Commission to place the appellant on the same footing as that of Dr. Baidyanath Haldar, who was a senior doctor in-charge of the management/treatment of the deceased.

7. The learned senior counsel for the appellant-Dr. Balram Prasad further urged that the National Commission has also erred in not taking into account the submissions of the claimant that 80% of the damages ought to have been levied on the Hospital, 15% on Dr. Sukumar Mukherjee and the balance between the rest. It is urged that the proportion of the compensation amount awarded on the appellant is excessive and unreasonable which is beyond the case of the claimant himself.

8. The appellant Dr. Balram Prasad on the other hand relied upon the decision in United India Insurance Co. Ltd. Vs. Patricia Jean Mahajan (supra) and contended that multiplier method is a standard method of determining the quantum of compensation in India.

ARGUMENT OF RESPONDENTS / AMRI :

1. The learned senior counsel for the AMRI Hospital Mr. Vijay Hansaria argued that the submission made by the claimant Dr. Kunal Saha is not sustainable both on facts and in law since he himself had claimed special damages against the appellant-doctors, Dr. Sukumar Mukherjee, Dr. Baidyanath Haldar and Dr. Abani Roy Choudhury in his appeal and therefore, he cannot now in these proceedings claim to the contrary. On the other hand, the claimant Dr. Kunal Saha argues that though the National Commission claims that this Court did not make any observation on apportionment of liability while remanding the matter back to it for determining the quantum of compensation, this Court had implicitly directed the bulk of compensation to be paid by the Hospital.

2. It is further urged by the learned senior counsel Mr. Vijay Hansaria for the appellant-AMRI Hospital relying on Sarla Verma's case (supra) that the multiplier method has enabled the courts to bring about consistency in determining the 'loss of dependency' more particularly in the death of victims of negligence.

AMRI states that the drugs had been administered and nursing care had been given as per the directions of the doctors.

It is the case of the appellant-AMRI Hospital that the National Commission should have taken note of the fact that the deceased was initially examined by Dr. Sukumar Mukherjee and the alleged medical negligence resulting in the death of the deceased was due to his wrong medication (overdose of steroid). Therefore, the Hospital has little or minimal responsibility in this regard, particularly, when after admission of the deceased in the Hospital there was correct diagnosis and she was given best possible treatment. The National Commission erred in apportioning the liability on the Hospital to the extent of 25% of the total award. This Court in the earlier round of litigation held that there is no medical negligence by Dr. Kaushik Nandy, the original respondent No.6 in the complaint, who was also a doctor in the appellant-Hospital.

38. Further, the learned senior counsel for the AMRI Hospital submitted that the arguments advanced on behalf of the appellants- doctors Dr. Balram Prasad in C.A. No.2867/2012, Dr. Sukumar Mukherjee in C.A. No.858/2012 and Dr. Baidyanath Haldar in C.A. 731/2012 with regard to percentage, on the basis of costs imposed in paragraph 196 of the judgment in the earlier round of litigation is without any basis and further submitted that under the heading – 'Individual Liability of Doctors' findings as to what was the negligence of the doctors and the appellant AMRI Hospital is not stated. If the said findings of the National Commission are considered, then it cannot be argued that the appellant AMRI Hospital should pay the highest compensation. Further, the learned senior counsel rebutted the submission of the claimant contending that since he had himself claimed special damages against the appellant-doctors, the Hospital and Dr. Abani Roy Choudhary in the complaint before the National Commission, therefore, he cannot now contend contrary to the same in the appeal before this Court.

When Dr. Mukherjee examined Anuradha, she had rashes all over her body and this being the case of dermatology, he should have referred her to a dermatologist. Instead, he prescribed "depomedrol" for the next 3 days on his assumption that it was a case of "vasculitis". The dosage of 120 mg depomedrol per day is certainly a higher dose in case of a TEN patient or for that matter any patient suffering from any other bypass or skin disease and the maximum recommended usage by the drug manufacturer has also been exceeded by Dr. Mukherjee. On 11-5- 1998, the further prescription of depomedrol without diagnosing the nature of the disease is a wrongful act on his part.

160. According to general practice, long-acting steroids are not advisable in any clinical condition, as noticed hereinbefore. However, instead of prescribing a quick-acting steroid, the prescription of a long-acting steroid without foreseeing its implications is certainly an act of negligence on Dr. Mukherjee's part without exercising any care or caution. As it has been already stated by the experts who were cross-examined and the authorities that have been submitted that the usage of 80-120 mg is not permissible in TEN. Furthermore, after prescribing a steroid, the effect of

immunosuppression caused due to it, ought to have been foreseen. The effect of immunosuppression caused due to the use of steroids has affected the immunity of the patient and Dr. Mukherjee has failed to take note of the said consequences."

JUDGMENT :

1. The Supreme Court vide its Judgment enhanced the compensation amount of Rs 1.73 crore, which was awarded by the National Consumer Dispute Redressal Commission (NCDRC) in 2011 to the tune of Rs 5.96 crore and asked the Kolkata- based Advanced Medicare and Research Institute (AMRI) and the doctors to pay the amount and also asked to pay interest at the rate of 6 per cent from the date of filing of the complaint in 1999 till the actual date of payment to Kunal Saha, a US-based Indian- origin doctor for medical negligence, which led to the death of his wife in 1998.

2. The Supreme Court in 2009 had held AMRI and the doctors guilty of negligence and the case was referred to the NCDRC for the sole purpose of determining quantum of compensation. The National Consumer Dispute Redressal Commission (NCDRC) earlier in 2011 had awarded Rs.1.73 crore. Cross appeals were also filed by AMRI and three doctors against the Commission's award. The Apex Court in its Judgment has partly allowed the appeals of claimant.

3. Hon'ble Apex court hold the three doctors and the hospital culpable to civil liability for medical negligence which had led to the death of Anuradha, a child psychologist and wife of claimant Dr. Kunal Saha, who had come to her home town Kolkata in March 1998 on a summer vacation. Deceased complained of skin rashes on April 25 and consulted Dr Sukumar Mukherjee, who, advised her only to take rest without prescribing any medicine. However, skin rashes resurfaced again with greater passion in early May. Dr Mukherjee prescribed Depomedrol injection 80 mg twice daily to be taken on daily basis, however this prescription of Dr. Mukherjee was not approved by experts. Administration of injection led to deterioration of Anuradha's condition, following which she had to be admitted at AMRI on 11 May under Dr Mukherjee's supervision and subsequently she was shifted to Mumbai's Breach Candy Hospital, and her diagnosis stated that she was diagnosed to be suffering from life threatening disease called toxic epidermal necrolysis (TEN). Anuradha succumbed to her ailment on May 28, 1998.

4. Dr. Saha had filed both criminal as well as civil case against the doctors and hospitals on the basis of gross negligence on their part during the

treatment, which led the death of her wife.

5. Hon'ble Supreme Court in 2009 absolved the doctors and the hospitals of criminal liability for medical negligence, however held them culpable of civil liabilities.

6. The Apex Court held that the deceased was earning $ 30,000 per annum at the time of her death. The appellant-doctors and the Hospital could not produce any evidence to rebut the claims of the claimant regarding the qualification of her wife. Further $30,000 per annum earned by the deceased during the time of her death was not from a regular source of income and she would have earned lot more had it been a regular source of income, having regard to her qualification and the job for which she was entitled to. Therefore, while determining the income of the deceased, Apex Court relied on the evidence on record for the purpose of determining the just, fair and reasonable compensation and her earning was determined at $40,000 per annum on a regular job. The multiplier method was applied for loss of income of deceased and estimating the life expectancy of a healthy person in the present age as 70 years, the Apex Court was inclined to award compensation accordingly by multiplying the total loss of income by 30. Keeping in view the value of Indian currency, the current value of Indian Rupee was taken at a stable rate of Rs.55/- per 1$ and accordingly under the head of 'loss of income of the deceased' the claimant was held entitled to an amount of Rs.5,72,00,550/- which is calculated as [$40,000+(30/100x40,000$)-(1/3 x 52,000$) x 30 x Rs.55/-] = Rs.5,72,00,550/-.

7. In respect to claim of medical treatment of deceased at Kolkata and Mumbai, the compensation was enhanced to the tune of Rs. 7,00,000/-. The claimant was also awarded an amount of Rs.1,50,000/- as compensation towards Travel and Hotel expenses at Bombay.

8. Hon'ble Apex Court while calculating *Non-pecuniary damages* has considered various facts and precedents e.g. *Arun Kumar Agarwal Vs. National Insurance Company*[2], wherein it has been held that in India the courts have recognized that the contribution made by the wife to the house is invaluable and cannot be computed in terms of money. The gratuitous services rendered by the wife with true love and affection to the children and her husband and managing the household affairs cannot be equated with the services rendered by others. A wife/mother does not work by the clock. She is in the constant attendance of the family throughout the day and night unless she is employed and is required to attend the employer's work for particular hours. She takes care of all the requirements of the

husband and children including cooking of food, washing of clothes, etc. She teaches small children and provides invaluable guidance to them for their future life. A housekeeper or maidservant can do the household work, such as cooking food, washing clothes and utensils, keeping the house clean, etc., but she can never be a substitute for a wife/mother who renders selfless service to her husband and children. It was also observed that it is not possible to quantify any amount in lieu of the services rendered by the wife/mother to the family i.e. the husband and children. However, for the purpose of award of compensation to the dependants, some pecuniary estimate has to be made of the services of the housewife/mother. In that context, the term "services" is required to be given a broad meaning and must be construed by taking into account the loss of personal care and attention given by the deceased to her children as a mother and to her husband as a wife. They are entitled to adequate compensation in lieu of the loss of gratuitous services rendered by the deceased. The amount payable to the dependants cannot be diminished on the ground that some close relation like a grandmother may volunteer to render some of the services to the family which the deceased was giving earlier.

9. Accordingly, the Civil Appeal No. 2867/2012 filed by Dr. Balram Prasad, Civil Appeal No. 858/2012 filed by Dr. Sukumar Mukherjee and Civil Appeal No. 731/2012 filed by Dr. Baidyanath Haldar are partly allowed by modifying the judgment and order of the National Commission in so far as the amount fastened upon them to be paid to the claimant as mentioned below. Dr. Sukumar Mukherjee and Dr. Baidyanath Haldar are liable to pay compensation to the tune of Rs.10 lakhs each and Dr. Balram Prasad is held liable to pay compensation of Rs.5 lakhs to the claimant. Since, the appellant-doctors have paid compensation in excess of what they have been made liable to by this judgment, they are entitled for reimbursement from the appellant-AMRI Hospital and it is directed to reimburse the same to the above doctors within eight weeks.

10. The Civil Appeal No. 692/2012 filed by the appellant-AMRI Hospital is dismissed and it is liable to pay compensation as awarded in this judgment in favour of the claimant after deducting the amount fastened upon the doctors in this judgment with interest @ 6% per annum.

11. The Civil Appeal No. 2866/2012 filed by the claimant-Dr.Kunal Saha is also partly allowed and the finding on contributory negligence by the National Commission on the part of the claimant is set aside. The direction of the National Commission to deduct 10% of the awarded amount

of compensation on account of contributory negligence is also set aside by enhancing the compensation from Rs.1,34,66,000/- to Rs.6,08,00,550/- with 6% interest per annum from the date of the complaint to the date of the payment to the claimant.

12. The AMRI Hospital is directed to comply with this judgment by sending demand draft of the compensation awarded in this appeal to the extent of liability imposed on it after deducting the amount, if any, already paid to the claimant, within eight weeks and submit the compliance report

CHAPTER THIRTY-ONE

Lalita Kumari v. Govt. of U.P. and Ors. [2013] 14 SCR 713 : (2014) 2 SCC 1

(Lalita Kumari was missing as she was kidnapped by someone but police did not register an FIR and under the direction of S.P. only FIR was registered but police did not do anything. Constitution Bench of the Supreme Court in Lalita Kumari v. Govt. of U.P [W.P.(Crl) No; 68/2008] held that registration of First Information Report is mandatory under Section 154 of the Code of Criminal Procedure , if the information discloses commission of a cognizable offence and no preliminary inquiry is permissible in such a situation. If the information received does not disclose a cognizable offence but indicates the necessity for an inquiry, a preliminary inquiry may be conducted only to ascertain whether cognizable offence is disclosed or not. Court also passed guideline regarding registration of FIR.

The Five Judge bench held that once a cognizable offense is made out under Section 154 of CRPC the police have to mandatorily register the FIR with some eceptions.)

FACTS OF THE CASE:-

1. The petition has been filed before this Court under Article 32 of the Constitution of India in the nature of habeas corpus to produce Lalita Kumari, the minor daughter of Bhola Kamat.
2. On 5.5.2008, Lalita Kumari, aged about six years, went out of her house at 9 p.m. When she did not return for half an hour and Bhola Kamat

was not successful in tracing her, he filed a missing report at the police station Loni, Ghaziabad, U.P.

3. On 11.5.2008, respondent no.5 met Bhola Kamat and informed him that his daughter has been kidnapped and kept under unlawful confinement by the respondent nos.6 to 13. The respondent-police did not take any action on his complaint. Aggrieved by the inaction of the local police, Bhola Kamat made a representation on 3.6.2008 to the Senior Superintendent of Police, Ghaziabad. On the directions of the Superintendent of Police, Ghaziabad, the police station Loni, Ghaziabad registered a First Information Report (F.I.R.) No.484 dated 6.6.2008 under Sections 363/366/506/120B IPC against the private respondents.
4. Even after registration of the FIR against the private respondents, the police did not take any action to trace Lalita Kumari. According to the allegation of Bhola Kamat, he was asked to pay money for initiating investigation and to arrest the accused persons
5. Ultimately, the petitioner filed this petition under Article 32 of the Constitution before this Court.
6. This Court on 14.7.2008 passed a comprehensive order expressing its grave anguish on non-registration of the FIR even in a case of cognizable offence. The Court also issued notices to all Chief Secretaries of the States and Administrators of the Union Territories. In response to the directions of the Court, various States and the Union Territories have filed comprehensive affidavits.
7. The short, but extremely important issue which arises in this petition is whether under Section 154 of the Code of Criminal Procedure Code, a police officer is bound to register an FIR when a cognizable offence is made out or he has some latitude of conducting some kind of preliminary enquiry before registering the FIR.

ISSUES BEFORE THE COURT:-

1. Whether the police officer should compulsorily register an FIR under Section 154 of Code of Criminal Procedure, 1973 relating to Cognizable offence

2. Or the police officer to check the authenticity of the complaint can conduct a preliminary inquiry before registering an FIR?

PETITIONER`S ARGUMENT :

1. The counsel for the petitioner stated to the court that when the officer-in- charge of the police station receives a complaint disclosing a cognizable offence, he has to mandatorily register an FIR under section 154 of the Code of Criminal Procedure.
2. Reliance was placed on the Judgments of The Supreme Court like *State of Haryana* v. *Bhajan Lal*, *Ramesh Kumari* v. *State (NCT of Delhi)* and *Parkash Singh Badal* v. *State of Punjab*.
3. The Counsel draws the attention of the court that under Section 154(1) of the Code the word "Shall" is used by the Legislation signifies the legislative intention and it is compulsory for the police officer to register the FIR.
4. He stated that under section 154 of the code there are no implicit provisions relating to Preliminary inquiry and there is no discretion left to the police officer.
5. In support of his arguments, he placed heavy reliance on the following judgments viz. *B. Premanand* v.*MohanKoikal*, *Hiralal Rattanlal* v. *State of U.P.* and *Govindlal Chhaganlal Patel* v. *Agricultural Produce Market Committee, Godhra*.

RESPONDENT`S ARGUMENT :

1. The counsel for the respondent submitted that the registration of an FIR cannot be subjected to a straitjacket formula as it is an administrative act requiring the application of mind, scrutiny, and verification of the facts.
2. No administrative act can ever be a mechanical one. He placed reliance on *Rajinder Singh Katoch*, *P. Sirajuddin* v. *State of Madras*, *State of U.P.* v. *Bhagwant Kishore Joshi*, and *Sevi* v. *State of T.N.*, which holds that before registering an FIR under Section 154 of the Code, it is open to the police officer to hold a preliminary inquiry to ascertain whether there is a prima facie case of commission of a cognizable offense or not.
3. The learned counsel submitted that a statute should not be interpreted in such manner where it leads to absence of any discretion to the police officer especially in Fake cases where registration of an FIR leads to an empty formality.
4. Also, for the receipt and recording of information, the report is not a condition precedent to the setting in motion of a criminal investigation.

The counsel explained that a provision for preliminary inquiry already exists in cases like Corruption, Medical Negligence and Matrimonial Offences.

5. The counsel submitted to the court that every statute should be interpreted while keeping in mind the provisions of Article 14, 19 and 21 of the Constitution which provides protection to an innocent person from baseless charges. In situations like these, a police officer needs to be equipped with the power of conducting a Preliminary inquiry.

JUDGMENT:-

A Constitution Bench of the Supreme Court in Lalita Kumari v. Govt. of U.P [W.P.(Crl) No; 68/2008] held that registration of First Information Report is mandatory under Section 154 of the Code of Criminal Procedure , if the information discloses commission of a cognizable offence and no preliminary inquiry is permissible in such a situation. If the information received does not disclose a cognizable offence but indicates the necessity for an inquiry, a preliminary inquiry may be conducted only to ascertain whether cognizable offence is disclosed or not.

The Supreme Court also issued the following Guidelines regarding the registration of FIR.

i. Registration of FIR is mandatory under Section 154 of the Code, if the information discloses commission of a cognizable offence and no preliminary inquiry is permissible in such a situation.
ii. If the information received does not disclose a cognizable offence but indicates the necessity for an inquiry, a preliminary inquiry may be conducted only to ascertain whether cognizable offence is disclosed or not.
iii. If the inquiry discloses the commission of a cognizable offence, the FIR must be registered. In cases where preliminary inquiry ends in closing the complaint, a copy of the entry of such closure must be supplied to the first informant forthwith and not later than one week. It must disclose reasons in brief for closing the complaint and not proceeding further.
iv. The police officer cannot avoid his duty of registering offence if cognizable offence is disclosed. Action must be taken against erring officers who do not register the FIR if information received by him

discloses a cognizable offence.

v. The scope of preliminary inquiry is not to verify the veracity or otherwise of the information received but only to ascertain whether the information reveals any cognizable offence.

vi. As to what type and in which cases preliminary inquiry is to be conducted will depend on the facts and circumstances of each case. The category of cases in which preliminary inquiry may be made are as under: (a) Matrimonial disputes/ family disputes (b)Commercial offences (c) Medical negligence cases (d)Corruption cases (e) Cases where there is abnormal delay/ laches in initiating criminal prosecution, for example, over 3 months delay in reporting the matter without satisfactorily explaining the reasons for delay. The aforesaid are only illustrations and not exhaustive of all conditions which may warrant preliminary inquiry.

vii. While ensuring and protecting the rights of the accused and the complainant, a preliminary inquiry should be made time bound and in any case it should not exceed 7 days. The fact of such delay and the causes of it must be reflected in the General Diary entry.

viii. Since the General Diary/Station Diary/Daily Diary is the record of all information received in a police station, we direct that all information relating to cognizable offences, whether resulting in registration of FIR or leading to an inquiry, must be mandatorily and meticulously reflected in the said Diary and the decision to conduct a preliminary inquiry must also be reflected, as mentioned above.

CHAPTER THIRTY-TWO

National Legal Service Authority v. Union OF India [2014] 5 SCR 119 : (2014) 5 SCC 438

(A writ petition was filed by the National Legal Services Authority of India (NALSA) in Supreme Court to legally recognize persons who fall outside the male/female gender binary, including persons who identify as "third gender". **National Legal Services Authority v. Union of India is a landmark decision by the Supreme Court of India**, which declared transgender people to be a 'third gender', affirmed that the fundamental rights granted under the Constitution of India will be equally applicable to transgender people, and gave them the right to self-identification of their gender as male, female or third-gender. This judgement is a major step towards gender equality in India. Moreover, the court also held that because transgender people were treated as socially and economically backward classes, they will be granted reservation in admissions to educational institutions and jobs.)

DECIDED ON : 15 April 2014

CORAM: K S RADHAKRISHNAN & A K SIKRI

FACTS OF THE CASE:

A writ petition was filed by the National Legal Services Authority of India (NALSA) in Supreme Court to legally recognize persons who fall outside the male/female gender binary, including persons who identify as "third gender".

QUESTION OF LAW:

The Court had to decide whether persons who fall outside the male/ female gender binary can be legally recognised as "third gender" persons.

It deliberated on whether disregarding non-binary gender identities is a breach of fundamental rights guaranteed by the Constitution of India.

PETITIONER`S ARGUMENT :

1. Shri Raju Ramachandran, learned senior counsel appearing for the petitioner – the National Legal Services Authority, highlighted the traumatic experiences faced by the members of the TG community and submitted that every person of that community has a legal right to decide their sex orientation and to espouse and determine their identity.

2. Learned senior counsel has submitted that since the TGs are neither treated as male or female, nor given the status of a third gender, they are being deprived of many of the rights and privileges which other persons enjoy as citizens of this country. TGs are deprived of social and cultural participation and hence restricted access to education, health care and public places which deprives them of the Constitutional guarantee of equality before law and equal protection of laws.

3. Further, it was also pointed out that the community also faces discrimination to contest election, right to vote, employment, to get licences etc. and, in effect, treated as an outcast and untouchable. Learned senior counsel also submitted that the State cannot discriminate them on the ground of gender, violating Articles 14 to 16 and 21 of the Constitution of India.

4. Shri Anand Grover, learned senior counsel appearing for the Intervener, traced the historical background of the third gender identity in India and the position accorded to them in the Hindu Mythology, Vedic and Puranic literatures, and the prominent role played by them in the royal courts of the Islamic world etc.

5. Reference was also made to the repealed Criminal Tribes Act, 1871 and explained the inhuman manner by which they were treated at the time of the British Colonial rule.

6. Learned senior counsel also submitted that various International Forums and U.N. Bodies have recognized their gender identity and referred to the Yogyakarta Principles and pointed out that those principles have been recognized by various countries around the world. Reference was also made to few legislations giving recognition to the trans-sexual persons in other countries.

7. Learned senior counsel also submitted that non-recognition of gender identity of the transgender community violates the fundamental rights guaranteed to them, who are citizens of this country.

8. Shri T. Srinivasa Murthy, learned counsel appearing in I.A. No. 2 of 2013, submitted that transgender persons have to be declared as a socially and educationally backward classes of citizens and must be accorded all benefits available to that class of persons, which are being extended to male and female genders.

9. Learned counsel also submitted that the right to choose one's gender identity is integral to the right to lead a life with dignity, which is undoubtedly guaranteed by Article 21 of the Constitution of India.

10. Learned counsel, therefore, submitted that, subject to such rules/ regulations/protocols, transgender persons may be afforded the right of choice to determine whether to opt for male, female or transgender classification.

11. Shri Sanjeev Bhatnagar, learned counsel appearing for the petitioner in Writ Petition No.604 of 2013, highlighted the cause of the Kinnar community and submitted that they are the most deprived group of transgenders and calls for constitutional as well as legal protection for their identity and for other socio-economic benefits, which are otherwise extended to the members of the male and female genders in the community.

RESPONDENT`S ARGUMENT :

1. Shri Rakesh K. Khanna, learned Additional Solicitor General, appearing for the Union of India, submitted that the problems highlighted by the transgender community is a sensitive human issue, which calls for serious attention.

2. Learned ASG pointed out that, under the aegis of the Ministry of Social Justice and Empowerment (for short "MOSJE"), a Committee, called "Expert Committee on Issues relating to Transgender", has been constituted to conduct an in-depth study of the problems relating to transgender persons to make appropriate recommendations to MOSJE.

3. Shri Khanna also submitted that due representation would also be given to the applicants, appeared before this Court in the Committee, so that their views also could be heard.

JUDJMENT:

<u>Defining "Third Gender"</u>

1. The Court upheld the right of all persons to self-identify their gender. Further, it declared that hijras and eunuchs can legally identify as "third

gender".

2. The Court clarified that gender identity did not refer to biological characteristics but rather referred to it as "an innate perception of one's gender". Thus, it held that no third gender persons should be subjected to any medical examination or biological test which would invade their right to privacy.

Fundamental Rights

1. The Court interpreted 'dignity' under Article 21 of the Constitution to include diversity in self-expression, which allowed a person to lead a dignified life. It placed one's gender identity within the framework of the fundamental right to dignity under Article 21.

2. Further, it noted that the right to equality (Article 14 of the Constitution) and freedom of expression (Article 19(1)(a)) was framed in gender-neutral terms ("all persons"). Consequently, the right to equality and freedom of expression would extend to transgender persons.

3. It drew attention to the fact that transgender persons were subject to "extreme discrimination in all spheres of society" which was a violation of their right to equality. Further, it included the right to express one's gender "through dress, words, action, or behaviour" under the ambit of freedom of expression.

4. Under Articles 15 and 16, discrimination on the ground of "sex" is explicitly prohibited. The Court held that "sex" here does not only refer to biological attributes (such as chromosomes, genitalia and secondary sexual characteristics) but also includes "gender" (based on one's self-perception). Thus, the Court held that discrimination on the ground of "sex" included discrimination on the basis of gender identity.

5. The Court held that transgender persons were entitled to fundamental rights under Articles 14, 15, 16, 19(1)(a) and 21 of the Constitution. Further, the Court also referred to core international human rights treaties and the Yogyakarta Principles to recognise transgender persons' human rights.

Further Directions

The Court held that public awareness programs were required to tackle stigma against the transgender community. It also directed the Central and State Governments to take several steps for the advancement of the transgender community, including:

1. Making provisions for legal recognition of “third gender” in all documents
2. Recognising third gender persons as a “socially and educationally backward class of citizens”, entitled to reservations in educational institutions and public employment.
3. Taking steps to frame social welfare schemes for the community

Legal Recognition:

The Court has directed Centre and State Governments to grant legal recognition of gender identity whether it be male, female or third-gender:

- Legal Recognition for Third Gender: In recognizing the third gender category, the Court recognized that fundamental rights are available to the third gender in the same manner as they are to males and females. Further, non-recognition of third gender in both criminal and civil statutes such as those relating to marriage, adoption, divorce, etc. is discriminatory to transgender individuals.
- Legal Recognition for Persons transitioning within male/female binary: As for how the actual procedure of recognition will happen, the Court merely states that they prefer to follow the psyche of the person and use the "Psychological Test’ as opposed to the ‘Biological Test.’ They also declare that insisting on Sex Reeassignment Surgery (SRS) as a condition for changing one’s gender is illegal.
- Public Health and Sanitation: Center and State Goverments have been directed to take proper measures to provide medical care to transgenders in hospitals and provide them separate public toilets and other facilities. Further, they have been directed to operate separate HIV/ Sero-surveillance measures for transgender people.
- Socio-Economic Rights: Centre and State Governments have been asked to provide the community various social welfare schemes and to treat the community as socially and economically backward classes. They have also been asked to extend reservation in educational institutions and for public appointments.
- Stigma and Public Awareness: These are the broadest directions - Center and State Goverments were asked to take steps to create public awareness to better help incorporate transgender individuals into society and end treatment as untouchables; take measures to regain their respect and place in society; and seriously address the problems such

as fear, shame, gender dysphoria, social pressure, depression, suicidal tendencies and social stigma.

The Court notes that these declarations are to be read in light of the Ministry of Social Justice and Empowerment Expert Committee Report on issues relating to transgender individuals.[

Court therefore, declared:

(1) Hijras, Eunuchs, apart from binary gender, be treated as "third gender" for the purpose of safeguarding their rights under Part III of our Constitution and the laws made by the Parliament and the State Legislature.

(2) Transgender persons' right to decide their self-identified gender is also upheld and the Centre and State Governments are directed to grant legal recognition of their gender identity such as male, female or as third gender.

(3) We direct the Centre and the State Governments to take steps to treat them as socially and educationally backward classes of citizens and extend all kinds of reservation in cases of admission in educational institutions and for public appointments. (4) Centre and State Governments are directed to operate separate HIV Sero-survellance Centres since Hijras/ Transgenders face several sexual health issues.

(5) Centre and State Governments should seriously address the problems being faced by Hijras/Transgenders such as fear, shame, gender dysphoria, social pressure, depression, suicidal tendencies, social stigma, etc. and any insistence for SRS for declaring one's gender is immoral and illegal.

(6) Centre and State Governments should take proper measures to provide medical care to TGs in the hospitals and also provide them separate public toilets and other facilities.

(7) Centre and State Governments should also take steps for framing various social welfare schemes for their betterment.

(8) Centre and State Governments should take steps to create public awareness so that TGs will feel that they are also part and parcel of the social life and be not treated as untouchables.

(9) Centre and the State Governments should also take measures to regain their respect and place in the society which once they enjoyed in our cultural and social life.

The hon'ble court also stated "We are informed an Expert Committee has already been constituted to make an in-depth study of the problems faced by the Transgender community and suggest measures that can be taken by the Government to ameliorate their problems and to submit its report with recommendations within three months of its constitution. Let the recommendations be examined based on the legal declaration made in this Judgment and implemented within six months."

www.ingramcontent.com/pod-product-compliance
Ingram Content Group UK Ltd.
Pitfield, Milton Keynes, MK11 3LW, UK
UKHW021907190726
13853UKWH00002B/552

9 798888 834305